UNIFIED THOUGHT ON MANAGEMENT

UNIFIED THOUGHT ON MANAGEMENT

DR. SAMAR DEB

Publications

KALPAZ PUBLICATIONS

DELHI-110052

UNIFIED THOUGHT ON MANAGEMENT
(Management)

Rs. 690

ISBN: 81-7835-281-8

Published in 2004 in India by
Kalpaz Publications
C-30, Satyawati Nagar
Delhi-110052
E-mail: kalpaz@hotmail.com

Laser Typesetting at: Varsha Graphics, Delhi
Printed at: Mehra Offset Press, Delhi

Dedicated

to

Managers and Social Architect

Contents

Preface

Management is a universal subject. Its application is widespread all through human social life. The creative potentials of human resource can be developed to integrate the base of social foundation for the purpose of sustainable growth which scientifically unifies the process of artistic play of things for better understanding of the principles and fundamental problems of the human society. Hence, the volume covers five important Chapters that go to furnish a dynamic and unified viewpoint on perspective development of human resources in relativistic manner to philosophizing the socio-economic parameters on the plane of human development through realities of management, in the changing order of the phase of social infrastructure as well as technological innovation; and thus, it is expected that the "Unified Thought on Management" will go to solve all types of human problems in scientific as well as sparkling manner. Keeping in mind this notion, "Introduction to Management Thought" is analysed in Chapter 1 that gives ample scope to understand actually what is meant by management. However, in Chapter 2, we have assessed the foundational conceptualities of organisational understanding. Hence, "Organisational Thought" in this Chapter covers a wide range of the oretical postulates about human behaviour based on human morale-building exquisitely required for the changing scenario of business and social activities, and it is dealt in a synthetical thought, so that development in real perspective could be enhanced to attain social and human growth. It is further strengthened through this study to human motivational goal without the help of which causing a social change for universal development would not be optimally attained to cope up with the changing need of the societal goal of human life in the twenty-first century. It is therefore, human transaction important in any organisation for managing things in objective manner to confine the subjective notion to the realities of human development with growth potentials. "Transactional Thought" is the another milestone of work dealt in Chapter 3. It is human resource, the development of which depends on correct organisational development. Hence, a practical exposition is the prerequisite conditionality for bringing managerial effectiveness to dynamically as well as philosophically synthesize human transactions. This, further requires an indepth study of the ego states of human beings - a scientific understanding leading to organisational development (OD) through change management in adaptive nature. All these are relative to the process of conflict resolution and solution of human social problems. It is thus, suggested in this Chapter through objective analysis of these postulates of human resource management with the fundamental principles and practices of human resource development (HRD) as a goal of organisational life and managerial re-engineering process (MRP) in the effective development of human organisations in sociological foundations. Another important aspect of managerial effectiveness in making human organisation relative to human growth through sustainable development is the devotional aspect that needs professional ethics as well as institutional dedication. Both these areas are covered in Chapter 4 under "Meditational Thought" whereby, we come across psychological foundations of managerial unision based on organisational mission, its right vision and an objective analysis as to how meditation can be made practical in managing human resources for unifying the principles of management strategy to cope with changing need of the society.This is dealt in yoga psychological principles which are fundamentally obtained for scientific order of human socio-economic development to the universal phase of the Cosmic view on human life -a 'philosophic order' needed in course of dealing with the meditational practices for social undertaking. Hence, this type of business psychology stressed on potential development of the human resources is related to the creative process of human performance for creative leadership through managerial approach. This fact is dealt in Chapter 5, on an understanding of "Creativity Thought" to illuminate the picture of the Relative Approach of the management to human societal order of life in unified nature.

The overall study of the five Chapters taken together gives a fundamental view on the notion of management process that go to solve present problems of the world. Therefore, a relative assessment of the facts and figures of the theoretical expositions is synthesized in a "Unified Thought" - not only scientific in nature, at the same time, the institutional suggestion as prescribed in the volume will make the issue of social development a permanent one in all spheres of human business and social activities to solve all types of socio-economic as well as human problems of life related concept. In a nutshell, the entire book is the answer to the twenty-first century order as to how the world-order should be guided for Cosmic nature of human development through business principles, and its real philosophy of management on scientific temper.

In the changing phase of the twenty-first century, the volume is the first and new one as an innovative technique of social re-engineering process for managerial re-engineering in effective development of human resources as well as leadership goal of organisational life style.

This book is expected to guide all students of management, professional people, social architect, and all those who are dedicating to the social cause of humanization, in order to attain scientific solution of human problems from sociological foundations.

Dr. Samar Deb

1
Introduction to Management Thought

Management is a universal discipline. It is the art of getting things done through and with others by effective utilization of limited resources, time and environment. However, while going to get things done through people, a manager of the twenty-first century is expected to applying his own skill with proper systematisation, and knowing exactly the philosophy about the mind of his people leading towards the attainment of the end-result of his tasks at hand. Thus, it seems that there is tri-polar processes and shape hidden within the horizon over the spectrum of the tasks, and in the thought of management – (i) application of the artistic skills of managers; (ii) dealing exactly with the cause-effect relationship inside particular issue of the subject; and lastly, (iii) knowing the philosophy of mind of the people dealt in by leading towards such an end-use (result). It is, therefore, the duty of every manager to have a clean understanding about the art, science and philosophy of management for getting the effective results.

As such an understanding over the issues of the art, science and philosophy of management will lead us objectively to grasp in positive manner as to the subject-matter; for this is very much essential, without the help of which applicability of the discipline becomes quite problematic in today's nature of complexity to the organizational structure and system employed for purposive use of resources. Here, it is therefore, expected that an analysis over the issues will lead us all to the idea of path-goal relational approach in exactly knowing – what management is.

Art of Management

By one school of thought, management is, by and large, considered "as the art" because of the 'specific gravity'[1] of the subject in doing specific things. An art refers to the way of doing specific things and also indicates how an objective is to be attained. Art of management means here, the knowing-how, and it is, therefore, the applicational side of doing particular things or job in the manner expected for getting it effectively. For example, a doctor not merely knows the science of medicine, but at the same time, he also practises it as an art on patients. Similar is the case with an engineer, a physicist, or a chemist.

From this idea, it is certainly enough to say that neither experience, nor education alone is a necessary condition or an indicator of a cause of managerial success at work. As J. Paul Getty[2] remarks that management "cannot be systematized, learned by rote nor practised according to formula. It is an art—even a creative art". To understand further, it is worthwhile to note that the art of management can be defined as skill[3] acquired by experience, study, and observation together which successful manager practises in his doing the day-to-day job. Thus, for managing through skills an outstanding manager takes every opportunity to the process of learning[4] from common experience, study, and observation while applying his mind towards the job. It is, therefore, undoubtedly observed from practical situations that good managers are probably good learners. Because, good managers may even make mistakes, but they will learn from those mistakes as they polish their managing art.

The art of management of those good managers is further concerned with their own active involvement for the activities of their organization; and thus, critically analysing and studying their situations[5] to formulate their own theories for explaining important events they are facing, and also knowing themselves further, to apply the theories as formulated, to their actual decision-making processes. It is clear now from the above understanding that those good managers are fundamentally observed at arriving at the capacity to manage well through a combination of experience, practice, judgment and intuition while dealing with the people and tasks they handle. These are the basic ideas we should all take into consideration as an advantage of, and to the extent of our capabilities. Therefore, it is predicted that there should be a challenging attitude to be formed [6] in our mind, particularly to the twenty-first century, when most of the organizations are going to be more and more complex; and in this sense, we should be willing to accept the challenge of mastering the 'art of management', for the managers of today have to face otherwise, lots of problems in the environment of their complex organisational structure.

Nevertheless, the art of management in the phase of challenge of change towards the organisational grounds has to be attained and adopted to the formulation of decision-making processes, in order to achieve managerial effectiveness with the systematic as well as efficient utilisation of the limited resources of the organisation. Hence, it requires a well-knit balance to the path-goal[7] relational aproach of the task of management.

Science of Management

There is another school of thought considers management as the science, as it deals with the systematized body of knowledge, having the approach of rationality in dealing with the tasks and the people, to which/whom it is concerned with. Thus, it can be said that the applicability of the art of management is supported by the concept of science of management that needs help of many of subjects like—mathematics, economics, psychology, anthropology, sociology, engineering and other fields of science. It is, therefore, apparent to note that management should be viewed from practical situations that solves problems of our day-to-day life also, while applying the subject-matter of the discipline towards such ends.

As economics is the study about the science of human behaviour as a relationship between limited means of human being with that of man's unlimited ends, also in management there is the scope of the study of such human behaviour; but that behaviour is guided by different fields of knowledge about science for coming across with the decision-making processes[8] of managers at enterprising level. Hence, in management science, at least, there is the necessity of taking care about the principles and concepts that have their own value and judgement, in regarding to the particular aspects of work in a given environment, which is further transferable, and can be integrated much towards the attainment of the goal of human enterprising capacities, capabilities and cognitive knowledge. Therefore, management science requires not only cause-effect relationship between ends and means of work; but also an impending qualification of human behavioural science as well as psychology of human mind as Sigmund Freud[9] observed long back, which managers can not ignore in modern times.

From the above, it can be well said that in considering management as the science, there is the objective analysis of each problem of organizing behaviour of men at work along with its subjective base, the foundation of which leads to the satisfaction of human goal towards such an end-means rational approach – the rationality of that very basis of human behaviour is guided by 'human psychology'[10] which has a scientific base, and the 'work philosophy'[11] that has to apply the laws of particular nature in generalization of the conceptual postulates of the behaviour of science. In a nutshell, the entire gamut of the subject-matter of management science deals with the techniques of business policy[12] analysis, strategic application of ideas, norms and values of human behaviour to solve various problems of life related to the organization of people at work towards attainment of goal.

Thus, in management practices, there is observation, introspection, reasoning, experience, testing of laws and concepts besides, the use of the operation of general laws where a manager has to systematize with all these principles and techniques of the body of knowledge, to help people in his (manager's) organizational decision-making processes for attaining with the results to live better lives. Therefore, the science of management in dealing with people must try to ensure that the people do not lose their freedom and their zest for living.[13] There is still now, researches being conducted by the experts and researchers over the world on such discipline, are also trying to bring it (management) at par with exact or natural sciences at this century. Even though, many works in the field of scientific findings of the empirical researches of the subjects mentioned aforesaid, are at the twentieth century onwards marked by a phenomenal build up of knowledge on management by both practitioners and philosophers, several schools of thought like – (i) the empirical school; (ii) management process school; (iii) behavioural school; (iv) decision-theory school; (v) quantitative school; and (vi) the systems school have proliferated with their own bodies of knowledge and bounds of discipline, and henceforth further trying to discover an all-embracing theory of management. It is, therefore, true that several concepts, principles and hypotheses are presented and related to each other, which have general applicability and transferability from culture to culture. On the basis of this standpoint, it is also claimed that such an exceptional work on the field of management has provided for the aura of fundamental truths, characteristics of natural and exact sciences.

Hence, in coming years, it is also expected that the subject-matter of management should not only be dealt with and confined to the process of human endeavour regarding task attainment for human satisfaction of goal, for leading a happy life. Besides, there should be all-including integrational idea for realization of the correct path and the truth about the life in realities of management[14]; so that the process of applying the principles of science in management subject to more fundamental as well as orientative nature, to the grounds of answering all problems of human life, and in a more systematic manner. We can thus, say that there are all justifications, at this stage, to consider upto this century-end that management is going to be absorbed within the limitless part of the cognitive approach[15] to accustom with the nature of rational judgement of human all creative endeavours towards the end of life[16].

Philosophy of Management

Management like any other discipline of natural and social sciences has been confined with the philosophy – it is that philosophy guided by the approach of life along with human work, for bringing life towards the unification with the great nature through practices of many works of life from cradle to grave, and is thus guided by the principles of social unification and values of life towards the process of making human life more and more perfect regarding human dealings, to understand the unified concept of the artistic skill of human nature on the one hand; and the scientific values of human practices on the other, to the assimilation process of human unification in the midst of its (management's) philosophical aspiration, for realization of the ultimate goal of human life in this great nature with more and more perfection – the perfection that leads to overcome the barrier of the great danger of human life cycle process bound with work philosophy and the cycle of work[17], here, on the Earth. All the happenings are mostly concerned with the philosophical aspirations for which understanding of human life is very essential to make the subject of management a unified process of dealing with the scientific aspects, artistic skills and philosophical mysteries of life.

As of now, management is said to have perplexed with the constraints of nature of human behaviour towards the integrative process of work element, by making human skills, in matters of aptitude, for the objective attainment of the goal of human life through different tasks habituated for the pose-dimensional order, in connection with the scientific element inherent with the relativeness of work attitude of man, and thus, brings in nature of man the social justice for ultimate goal of life – this is known as the freedom that acts behind human action without any prerogative nature[18] being contained for, and therefore, the scientific order of habitual action of man in society is so forth guided by the realization of human freedom, can only be managed through work culture. Thus, the philosophical explanation regarding the blue-colour thought of management on the human psychoanalytical[19] therapy of behaviour in work environment can be said to have been balanced by the concept of totality of the human condition. Thus, the knowledge of the self in work, which conjoins human life then becomes the art of the possible, and the said knowledge is there to teach us how to distinguish the possible from idle dreams. In short, as the process of unification to the nature of work with the great 'Nature' and the nature of man, science has established itself in our culture as the study of the limits of human freedom, pursued in order to enhance the exploitation of the remaining field of action.

In management of human action, to be free means to know one's potentiality; knowing potentiality is a negative knowledge, i.e., knowledge of what one is prevented from doing[20]. Therefore, it is apparent to note that 'there is a great uniformity among the actions of men, in all nations and ages'; 'human nature remains still the same, in its principles and operations'; and since science is knowledge of what nature is not, a science of man and his affairs is feasible and, indeed, necessary, if men wish to attain freedom—both negative and positive – in determining their own conditions. Thus, in considering management thought from philosophical standpoint, there is, of course, no particular reason why human uncompromising attitude could not be extended to embrace the totality of human deeds.

To consider Hume, a miracle would have been violation of the laws of nature, and such a violation is by definition impossible. If at all, in managing human actions, miracle seems to occur, it must be treated either as a mendacious report or as a natural event for which at present, no scientific explanation is available. On the basis of this, the philosophic view on management thought can be abscribed to the concept of miracle, as Peter Gay[21] has pointed out, in the vehement passion with which the preachers, on behalf of the Scientific Age regard this concept of human action. And, finally, regarding the concept of management on the basis of the balancing wheel, it is to be asserted that the realization of human goal of life, by dint of work, relates to the aspects of life itself with a truly mystical self-abandonment: where the individual submits to the society and this submission is the condition of his liberation ...... By putting thus himself, to get the things done, in a given time to the spatial thought on management postulates, as to the cyclical work environment, as pointed out earlier, the individual, under the wing of society, makes himself also to a certain extent, dependent upon it. But this is a liberating experience[22]. Thus, the philosophy of management has been an attempt to human endeavour, from time immemorial, to reconcile the claims of moral responsibility of human development to achieve the goal of life towards the realization of the supreme Self through the individual self, by means of disinterested nature of human work—this relates to the highest sacrifice for the great cause of the effective upliftment of the mankind to the door of optimum level of growth, for bringing life in passive order in the nature of work; so that the activities entered into for matching the goal of life have been attained through the process of relativistic as well as positivistic approach, in the midst of the universal integrity, towards the social unification process. Hence, every action of man must be guided by disinterested nature of inaction, by being wholly and solely absorbed in day-to-day activities of men, for making life to get into involved in the nature of human perfection for ever.

Towards the Making of Unity

In finding an unity in management, it must be conceived that the ancient people started their life with the art of knowing how to live for long years of their establishment in society, wherefrom came the science of actualizing this art more and more in later years, while they were observed from the history of mankind – growing towards knowing the best way of living the art through their all ancient civilizations; and therefore, came a Renaissance of Industrial Society formed with a view to philosophical aspirations for making life towards the process of unity through the universal way of living[23]. Thus, Industrial Revolutionary phases are optimistically utilized for the betterment of human civilization, in the course of managing human art of circulated culture and civilizations, in the context of scientific observations and discoveries and inventions of the greatest scientists of the world. But still, human mind have been working to finding out how to manage each aspects of living for the peace and harmony that could be fostered in civil society that men have developed so far. In this regard, it must be said that the dynamism of life will be possible, here, on the Earth, only when man learns the 'Theory of Balance' that is applicable in human civilization forever, and that has been in the world history with the testimony of human findings in the broad-field of management of human civilizations till date. Therefore, for the twenty-first century onwards, it is of great expectation from the modern thinkers that they would come forward with their new journey of life towards making management a more and more living subject—it is the only possibility remaining at hand, otherwise, this civilizations of ours at present, which is endowed with gift of journey of men, after a great struggle from the micro-organism to the highest order of life – coined as 'MAN' has every possibility without any natural disaster, but with the disaster of man himself, to be vanquished for ever.

Keeping in mind the great danger due to mistakes in management of human resources, it is niggardless to well say that we must preserve ourselves and further more to know – how to live in more civilized way. It is suggested because, the most important limitation of making mankind's civilization a noble one, is that of the selfish nature of man. However, when man will know himself that the hidden treasure of management is concealed to the darkness, which requires a bit more enlightenment through spiritualization of the philosophy of lives of man[24], without torchering the nature, which has caused for his living, must have to establish an effective way of balancing his discoveries and inventions of such otherwise scientific civilizations. Hence, the making of unity between man and man, leaving all other thinking (irrationality of human mind), but to think for the mankind only (rationality of realistic thinking of human mind), should be an accepted and the most universal principle of human management. It requires the balance of artistic way of doing things for the scientific systems of peaceful living through cent per cent eradication of the great danger of human hunger and misery from the world, that must be philosophically applied with the like principle of surface tension geometry of the universe – that man is also the most important part of the tension, which is possibly the centre of gravity of thinking behind all the mysteries of discoveries and inventions of human civilization, if any principle of science has to be accepted for understanding the universal laws of making life more and more active towards the management of human civilization.[25] This is the most rationalistic principle, can be established through common code of spiritualization of life in dedicating for the great and noble cause of men – the entire destiny of hunger and poverty is mistakenly taken to the economics of art of competition without cultural flow of unity, while managing activities of modern men, and is therefore, the unitary principle of universal law of nature should be applied to human civilization in a rapid manner, and in scientific revolution of human mind towards making such unity for the great destiny of human management principle – 'Dynamism through Relativity in human activity'.

In making human activities towards the goal-oriented nature, it is believed that management should be dealt with the austerity of life that shakes the rejuvenating aspects of leading a peaceful life, and can be searched through peace and tranquility – it is such a typical job has yet to be searched for ever, that nobody has found, for the time immemorial period there has been downfall of the civilizations of man, so as it trips to the heavenly abode of the destiny of real-goal – that after reaching where, there is no need to find a new policy, as to how should our life be based on any other principles; but the only principle of humanity driving each and every needs of man for coming across with the ultimate goal of life. It is the brevity requires to be created in mind, for the gravitational aspects of our relativity of unity in management of human resources could only be at the heal of charismatic goal of leading life towards making a point – the point which embraces all elements of life through perfect goal of human management. It is the philosophy needed to be kept with the Self, where the lower self is having every relationship at each point of time while performing different activities for making a life more and more to the destiny towards goal-orientedness. Thus, management has to find that creativity which, if applied must have the sensitivity analysis, that the sense of selflessness by means of sacrifice to the optimum level is brought to the aspects of human culture – the culture that gives birth to oneness in the midst of infinite diversity. Then only, it is possible through human to be attained the goal of life, for the lower self has a relationship with the higher Self, which is said to be here, the 'Cosmic Self'. The unitary aspects of such Self is bound by the universal principle of natural law that humankind has yet to search from the hidden idea of their life. When each individual can be felt to realize this, the management of any activity in the world must be treated to be universally applied through epoch-making approach to lead oneself towards the highest destiny of life – the goal to reach the highest perfection of life, after which no more training is required only the betterment through activity for getting in everything much more requiring for the promotion of life of each individual.

In modern time, it is very essential that every individual should work for the perfection of the body along with the survival need. If the theory of action of human being can be made totally on selfless basis, that very nature of human action must lead to the management of all human problems to a unity – it is such a unity, which can be ascribed to the philosophical aspirations for being, within the reach of everything, by all possible means, to have the scientific rational approach towards going ahead and ahead, and ultimately to know the Self, at the point of infinite stage of life; which is causing thereby an effective way of looking at things to the more enlightened picture, that man has yet to search-out from the very darkness of the hidden qualities of the self. Thus, the making of unity, by means of management of the self in action, seems to more applicable, while taking our actions scientifically – this is, here, called as the theory of action, which is relative to the principles of the psychology of 'Karma Yoga', can be found in Indian Order of Hinduism and its scriptures. However, while applying our mind towards the great nature, there seems to a great infinity, in the midst of which, all human management is functioned, without ignoring any principles of the natural system. At this moment, it is better to realize that the science of human management is goal-oriented towards the unitary balance for philosophizing each aspects of better living in societal order of life. Thus, the Cosmic view on management, to be discussed at length, else where in this volume, should be curbed in mental stature to the postulates of factorial and fundamental modeling of each aspects of human sociological behaviour; otherwise, human action, with perfection and eradication of poverty from this world, remains a vanity for ever, where no cultural, but one culture –human culture, can be tipped to be noted for all time to come on the Earth. Therefore, unity in diversity, while matching the coping idea of managing concept should be in mind in a balancing order, towards making the life quite perfect through management.

Place of Work in Management

The principal idea of work is fundamental in all discipline as in regard to the management process of getting things done. As in modern concept of management we find that it is the 'getting things', to which, it is further observed that the principal idea of – to get things done means to know exactly as to how to get it be done. Therefore, it is imperative to say that there is the principle on which every manager works. Not only that, in primitive society also, before the application of management science, there is a trace of such work principle – as we can say that the Indian concept of Vedic Principle on Karma[26] (work) has a wide connotation, notwithstanding of the fact that, there is always theory which guides every action of man in society – by dint of which man's survival becomes an active part of effective living with the efficient management of resources.[27] So well, is the case of work found in the history of the science of politics, wherein eminent persons are observed to be with the philosophy of work – it has found a place so scientifically while, as for example, the sovereignty of the State is expressed in terms of the theory of work (action), philosophically guiding the principles of human action in society, contains therein, the base of human action and reaction in the equal phase of the journey of life, for which, for a longer period of time, in the history of political science in human civilization there was great debate on the ethics of work[28]. Thus, again, after the application of scientific principles on the 'law of motion' over the concept of Newtonian assumptions, it is found that every action of man has an equal, as well proportionate and opposite reaction.

Therefore, it is also true that there is philosophical justification that work has a pivotal role to play in the phase of management of all human actions—for which Peter F. Drucker has probably, rightly said : Every organization must have a vision in managing all human activities, which is based on the principles of 'Management By Objectives'(MBO)[29]. Likewise, Arnold J. Toynbee[30], a famous historian has said about the work of man to the historical perspective, which is indirectly corollary to the principles of work, can be judiciously applied to the administrative science of human endeavour towards the achievement of man's organized way of life in society. Thus, there is wide application of the principles of work that can be treated as the motive force behind any enterprising goal – the very effectiveness is called ultimately the organizational goal, can be integrated towards the goals of the individual and each group in the organization.

To be more specific, we have to search from the Indian vedantic thought – because, by means of work or karma, in India, there has always been due stress on its principles towards the life of individual in societal living, by dint of which every individual has wider scope to overcome the risk entertained with work – bondage, and search for – liberation; this is quite philosophic but scientific backgrounds are fundamentally searched by not only rishis and sages, also eminent personalities like Swami Vivekananda, Rishi Aurobindo, the Gita has said the similar statement by means, exchanges of views between Srikrishna and Arjuna regarding – 'Karma Yoga', among others, that which brings light to management in historical perspectives to propagate the same notion as to the place of work in any field of human management – it is the only universal order by which the realistic proactive view on the effectiveness of organization can also be attained for the achievement of result when things are got to be done by the laws of karma or work, as found in Indian order of life.

Management for Man-power Development

By this time, we have learnt about the broader perspective of management as we have gone through concepts - from art, science and philosophy, to the making of its unitary view; howsoever, the work has been undertaken by the organismic attitude, so to bring under the perview of management in scientific methodological affair – it is the philosophy behind every work – that philosophy being related to human development, therefore, management must have to consider that there should be optimum possible level of development that requires to be attained through man-power resources, which is the core of the subject-matter of any management job. Nevertheless, it is the human resource that needs at first in management, a very great care of, to attain the tasks, for without development of the man-power resources, there could be no other methodological approach – where all human activities are found to assimilate towards this goal of life[31]. Thus, man-power resource should be felt in oneness – it is that horizon of life related concept which should be bound with beyond management of human resources, that being the actual reality needs an underlying object towards making management in changing the order of life, so that actual behaviour of men are guided by the principle of 'law of effect'[32]. It is, therefore, possible that man-power resource development can bring an actual methodological approach of management, if any, which counts at the key elements managing other resources towards this aspect of managerial goal – the goal which brings in management a real change with the very change on the phase of man-power resource, where each individual being is to be counted for optimum level of perfection through work philosophy that needs realistic sense of development of human resources of the world. As it is never possible to manage ignoring the value system of the societal order of life. When each individual is developed through an undertaking of social responsibility by means of providing equal opportunity for extreme point of development, the economic activities are thus, guided by the principle of real ethics; otherwise, the ethical rules and standards are violated towards achieving the goal of management in time and space. Again, the applicational side of this norm should be measurable in terms of performance of the organization which provides such needs of men as Abraham Maslow has said – the needs in his ladder is discussed in five categories like – (1) physiological, (2) safety, (3) love, (4) esteem and (5) self-actualisation. Hence, development of human being is confirmed by the basic needs approach of the Maslow's theory of human motivation[33]. Once the physiological needs are satisfied, human motivation finds a new channel for its satisfaction. Because, human motivation runs through a hierarchy. It is therefore, expected that management must provide such elementary basic needs as are universally accepted as in planned favourable working conditions of men. It is worth-noting in the perspective of organizational behaviour and the emergence of the 21st century technological breakthrough in India, it is imperative to identify and to formulate a national man-power policy for man-power management and human resources development programmes at macro-level and then, to implement the policy framework at micro-level.

Management and Human Creativity

It is a well-conceived fact that management of any kind seeks to attain the goal of sociological upliftment through human creative process at an optimum level that requires a scientific base for the development of particular society. Therefore, it is essential that management must have to be balanced with human nature of development, so that each and every kind of management's goal is not constrained with the level of performance and is measurable in terms of real objective that the society could be enhanced towards the possible level of situation in an open environment, considering the aspects of universal balance, and thereby, it actualizes the human asset in creative nature of development. From time immemorial periods in the history of mankind, the evolutionary process of human development is found with possibilities of human growth potentialities that encompasses with the process of sociological aspirations of men. Hence, it is very much common to think that there is the necessity of human creativity, which brings in management scientific level of developmental notion, causing to create a universal atmosphere surrounding the managerial environment in time and space. Thus, it is worthwhile to note that human creativity at all ages is a matter of human personality development – the factors of personality development are relative towards human traits of divergent as well as convergent combinations of creativity as found in empirical research findings on human creativity like, in the works of Guildford and Merrifield (1957) – they have also reported a large number of correlations between non-aptitude traits[34] and the measures of originality and ideational fluency.

The fact that creativity is found in every living cell is realized fact now. Creativity is not a property of the elite only, it is found in every person, the only difference being that in some it manifests more than others. Neither it is sole prerogative of certain professionals like artists, poets, painters and scientists, nor it is confined to only certain conventional areas of human endeavour, it is existent in every living cell, and also in all the fields of human endeavour. Thus, it is forthcoming in every field of human management process. Considering the aspects of human development with growth, it is further to be noted that management must be careful to see that there is equating conditions for such development, necessitated by every journey to the system of management in regard to foster the growth of human creativity, and sparks with optimum zeal for managing human resource as the most important asset which is the pillar of success for the goal-path and vice-versa relational approach towards the balance – it is the balance as sought in relativity with the systematization of the concept of self-realisation along with repercussions of managerial goal for relativistic assumptions towards pyramidical shape that mingles in manifestations through whole-squares from the top to beneath the level of grass-root development of human potentialities. The human resource is thus, established for unitary basic aspects of living towards a common level of human perfection possible for all – it is focused in managing human asset that can be understood only when there is an understanding on the universal concept of development in terms of human resource management. Because, it is human resource management considers the organised behaviour of men and is observable through the prism of magnified process of human management that managers are no more than human creative development agent in society. Thus, the responsibility of management is dependent on their responsiveness as to how much they are tending and interested to balance in scientific manner for the growth and development of society towards creative human development in terms of managerial goal.[35]

Now, it is sufficiently clear that every man is to be treated in management as equal in the phase of development – it is the creative process – a process with human creativity requires the applicational ideal with full perfection of sensitivity analysis by the managerial styles working in the given situations, so that social inequality through management can be fully eradicated by preventing the causes of diverse elements of downfall of human destiny.

As found in the Bible which depicts, "Earn thy bread by the sweat of thy brow" and the Gita says that he who eats without labouring for it eats stolen bread. The same idea also holds good in bringing a feeling of equality among the members of society. It is not only enough to think, but it is also a universal condition as it is the supreme condition of morality itself. Because, our social life has to be a life based on love and willing co-operation, and so, the doctrine of 'Bread Labour'[36] can be socially beneficial only when individuals take to it voluntarily.

From the above point of view, it can be undoubtedly concluded that human creativity in management must be considered with the principles of human social developmental aspects that lead towards human perfection in a universal way of journey through the process of life-related behaviour, for which managerial effectiveness is a must that requires relativistic assumptions on the aspects of path-goal relational approach. Thus, creativeness is a factor of human perfection with growth and development in managing through a real change that could be brought forth to the universal process of manifestations as found in natural laws. This makes the subject-matter of human creativity and management principles and policies more systematic in diverse elements of chaos,[37] where the different business and economic activities are to be carried on for the sake of human development in societal orderliness that requires adoption of alternative business strategies to the plane of management boundaries. Hence, it is management of human asset that helps to the changing values of any one variable and is thus, traditionally have been displayed as a function of time in which human life proceeds towards a systematic growth as like as the evolutionary process of growth displayed in the principles of biological or natural science. In short, the system of management for human creativity conditioned with sensitivity analysis requires a unitary aspect of human development through universal application of the principles of modern management that match with the vedantic principles of human society, as found in the history of long five thousand years and back to the original scientific development of mankind.[38]

Integrative Thought and Strategic Management

Management is so vast and depth in conceptualizing to the overall subject-matter, the rolling of which is unfolded to the destiny of mankind, and therefore, it is essential that the boundaries are to be integrated onto the specificity of every historic process of social development, coping thereby in each phase of historical growth in societal order in time and space – this requires particular strategy for scientific development through management of human organised behaviour. As we see that from the period of Adam Smith to Lionel Robbins, in the Economic Science of world history the foundation stone is laid down by means of human wealth and welfare considerations, and so, when there is a crises found in society, there also arises debate on the social responsibility of men managing different business activities. All human activities are alternatively done towards the achievement of such goal of life that leads to human perfection. And, it is management by which human development process in society is entertained for effluence of light through human growth and development in terms of need satisfying capacity that requires men to progress in civilizing the orbital space upon the systematic behaviour of gravitative nature of human development projected towards an understanding leading to the goal of human perfection. Thus, strategic management calls for alternative approaches on the principles of each developmental needs of men, seeking thereby unitary level of human development which is parallel to the growth of human society.

Again, in the science of development, it is quite essential that management system should be further unfolded with the particular strategy that needs modification which is in conformity as per need with the relativistic process of development, causing thereby to eradicate the endangering elements of the millionth part of unsystematic nature of human role – this has been found in question of particular type of social development from time immemorial period in human history of the evolutionary process of social development of human beings. Nevertheless, while pondering towards the goal of achieving the result of societal upliftment, it is commonly observed that there is always an urge to feel human selfish nature of development, focusing to the individual need and ignoring the need of the society, which is a totality concept. This limitation is very much necessary to be alternatively found in development process bringing to harvest the corporal life of development in an area of individual satisfaction, and thus, the totality concept is imbalanced – the nature of strategy, here, requires that management must be found with the fascination of universal goal of social life, ignoring the concept of individual satisfaction. Hence, it brings light to a broader view on the overall system of human development, the manifestations of which are needed towards the particular journey of life for the overall success of the society in balancing phase of human developmental aspects.

Human welfare in society, right from the period of Charles Babbage to the Scientific Management of Frederick Winslaw Taylor, has been found with systematic development of human discipline at the work place; and thereafter, in the period of administrative thought of management, it is in a new dimension argued by Henry Fayol that administrative discipline must be sought to bring with environment in a more systematic way of human development, with the strategies for getting the work done in a more disciplined manner, so that every social mission gets involved itself with the endless process of development. That being the sociological concept of management goal, it requires that every social behaviour of men in organized nature of living must commensurate with the behavioural aspect that binds men in society with economic nature of people's well-being. Thus, behavioural school of thought came across with the notion of social development. As for example the works of Weberian concept and that of Marry Parker Follett, Gilbreths and others are found to be creating more systematic nature of development on the management of resources of human welfare with the kind of behaviour by integrating the process of development balanced with the strategicity of empirical findings. However, it is here. to be noted that later development in the field of management science approach was guided by the process of the underlying concept of the mathematical school of management thought for bringing a balance towards the aspect of human development further in society, which is based on the concept of totality. Hence, the relative nature of development of society through management process is systematized in integrating the process of different strategies called at hand for an unitary approach of alternatively made theories by bringing on the overall aspects of human development. At present, there are different modern theories of management, but not a single is found to cover any wholesome idea. It is the integrative school of management thought balanced with the strategic management view that has found its own way to the process of human development in society through various economic as well as business activities of men meant for the purposiveness of result-oriented goal of life – this brings a perfection, if any found, at least with the short-comings of other areas of developmental needs of men in society, and to the broader view in finding a solution thereto, with the help of such strategic appraisal of the view that requires a new phase of balance on the science of management. This is the best highlight can be felt in mind, as found on the historical approach of Pareto's methodological thoughts on economic behaviour. Pareto, the economist, was interested in the practical implications of economic theory. Schumpeter is one of the few economists to fully appreciate Pareto's special interest in sociology:"It is, therefore, quite understandable that he [Pareto] should have experienced a wish and, in fact, a need to erect, alongside his pure theory another building that would shelter facts and reasonings of a different kind, facts and reasonings that would do something toward answering the question how the element taken care of by his economic theory might be expected to work out in practical life."[39]

From the above discussion, it can be asserted that the

integrative thought on management from economic viewpoint is also guided by the concept of Marshallian demand analysis. In order to support the position of particular strategic notion on management science behaviour, it is well-said that he [Marshall] included non-economic elements in his economics. In connection with human demand, Marshall discussed three types of wants. Two of these were treated as given biological needs, and artificial wants such as "the wanton vagaries of fashion". The third was a particular type of want associated with human development: "each step upwards is to be regarded as the development of new activities giving rise to new wants."[40] In short, it is undoubtedly to be noted that every strategy in managing human activities must be integrated towards the nature of managerial relativity of the vision of work that persists on the human creativity bound with the universal journey of life for a greater perfection at each step towards real perfection – it is the highest absolute truth which leads the subjective view of managing various activities of men in society in regard to higher and greater stage of development by means of relative growth that always tends towards the universal order of life in a free flow of the entire work environment for the ultimate goal of life, i.e., management dynamicity in movie. This exists in enterprising mission of men to the foundation of a perfect societal order unending towards the absolute boundaries of the goal-path relational approach that we would try to prove in a unified theory of management to the chapters dealt in hereafter. Hence, the concomitant principles of managing human activities must have to be established towards such needs of men in society that have been sought for, with the basic elements of management thought in this chapter, and therefore, the integrative nature[41] of human developmental aspects are guided by the principles and policies of each strategy towards such fundamental ideologies, so that the shortcomings of management as found in the world can be eradicated for the perfection of human life on those principles to be analysed at length, in the next chapters ahead.

Endless Unity – A Methodological Approach

In the philosophy of human management history, it has been observed that every society had to be developed through such path as always, there was a tendency to assimilate the entire process of human development inherent with the goal of eternal life. This is being found concealed to the spiritual manifestations of work-oriented human behavioural considerations leading towards the endless way to the destiny of humankind for embracing with the unitary goal of life for perfection – liberating or trying to be liberated from the bondage of work, by means of self-sacrifice. If there is any methodological approach in managing different social activities of men in societal order, it is only the supreme unity which is common to any other disciplines like – natural science, biological or social sciences; and howsoever it is being contemplated for, with the plane of natural laws, are all found to be enshrined with human destiny. Hence, in the very process of human management, the organismic behavioural attitudes are strengthened towards the unending journey of life for the optimum perfection through work behaviour in disinterested way – it is the standard evidenced in Indian order of the Vedantic sociological aspects of life, by which management spirit of men is broadened to have the relational specificity of the path-goal understandings, as we have seen in earlier discussions already made in this chapter, and therefore, it is essential to quote some eminent Indian thinker, and as one of them is, in this line of thinking can be exemplified under the following observation.

It was administered by Com. Bani Deshpande of 'The Universe of Vedanta' fame and Com. S.A. Dange, who wrote a Forward to that thesis. Com. Deshpande had conclusively established that the theory of the relativity of Space and Time and the materiality of Time was not only known to the ancient Vedic philosophers but they had proved it as scientifically as Einstein proved in modern physics, and that in the realm of philosophy, the Vedic outlook was not only scientific, to the extent of understanding of historic achievements of modern scientific theories, but it was based on a highly perfected and scientific theory of dialectical materialism now known in the name of Karl Marx in the last century.[42] Sri Aurobindo explains : "Change in the society was brought about not artificially from above but automatically from within and principally by the freedom allowed to families or particular communities to develop or alter automatically their own rules of life "achara". However, an Indian author Nagendra (1970) in his work tries to show as to how to establish relationship in human beings in between an emotional experience and an aesthetic experience. This bears heavily on the subject-matter of Indian thought of human management process that gives birth to an understanding regarding the methodological aspects of human belief on unitary way of thinking that Vedantic concept conforms to this philosophical aspirations for undertaking workmanship ideologies of behavioural attitude towards the perfection of human life. Hence, this methodology also stands on the principles of ancient philosophical notions of mankind's journey towards the highest perfection. As to this, the point of liberation of human endless unity towards the art of work can be further shown through his work where he has written as, "consequently, they (ancient Indians) cease to be part of direct physical experience of the spectator, raise him above the petty mundane experience of the self, refine the sensibility and sublimate his consciousness" (p.17). Thus, the organismic behaviour of men in ancient thought of managing themselves were concerned mainly with the aspects of life in an endless way of inward developmental needs, by dint of which the search for the ultimate truth was confined to the soul-searching element of life inherent with the work-philosophy of their behavioural traits, and they were further tending towards the missionary goal of life in new dimensional order that had scientific relationship in each organismic behaviour for attaining the tasks quite in an approach guiding their optimum upliftment of the basic necessities of life. However, while it is observed from the works of the renowned author, Nagendra who further writes as: "The aesthetic experience is not the experience of a personal emotion, it is the experience of a universalized or liberated emotion; it is an experience of a liberated state of mind and is free from egoistic interests. As such, it can be easily felt that it is one of perfect way of managing through a pleasant experience of life. It is a feeling of self-realisation or self-fulfilment through sublimated human emotions embodied in the works of art" (p.119f).

It is now clear that every approach in ancient Indian Vedantic thought was concerned with different lines of human management process in sociological aspirations for liberated life but the destiny of the journey of life as though, found in endless manner to be more beautifully coined with the universal nature of human development, there was a great assimilatory tendency, by means of which a path-goal relational approach was maintained. This is the most important methodology followed from time to time. And still, this day there is the prevalence of this kind of life aspirations in all spheres of human managerial goal as many as paths are found to be different, that there is a common goal - this is the liberation through human disinterested nature of work and development of life for an order higher and higher as can be possibly attained in any and every activity related to human sociological upbringings for the optimum achievements regarding the perfection of life. It is called universal philosophy in Indian order of Vedantic concept of management view as visioned for the goal of perpetual success of human life, in order of each and every step of succession, that brings men in society in a more systematic way of development by finding with unity in its methodological approach of resourceful managerial goal.

As in natural law, it is observed that there is system with unity to the entire Universe of the cosmological beauty, instead of diverse elements of chaos revolving round different objects; similarly, there is also in management having different paths, each forms the basis of work, by going round which an objective can be attained through a scientific nature of human development, and thus; it is the supreme method of human biological behaviour finding always the route to the development of its own destiny, clinging therefore, in an optimum experience which man has to search for, in managing through the destiny of the self. If it can be perfectly focused upon the magnified goal of life for the fuller perfection in all through this journey of life, there can be possibility of heavenly abode of mankind. Hence, it is suggested the objective nature of each social developmental need must be guided by the principles of such mission[43] that has a relationship with its works of life related behaviour. Considering such aspects of human dealings in management of different resources of the society with the skilful employment of efficient human resources, there also needs an effective task development that has yet to be broadly taken into consideration by each social law to encounter problems, at each issue, of social objectives. Thus, it is the smooth operations of work-behaviour needed to be underlying with the principles of life as the different schools of management thought for long thinking towards balancing – when there is optimum assimilation with the mental development of human beings associated with the tasks, management can be visualized as the most fundamental as well as basic need of life; upon which each sociological methodology has to be strengthened on time and space relationship. As Peter F. Drucker has said once that time is the most valuable and scarcest resource, the identification of society is based on this reference to time element. Because, a methodology of managerial goal is guided by such time-frame aspects of relativity that brings actual development in society, when the time is properly utilized. Therefore, in management, the objective analysis of human behaviour is always guided by this principle on time management.[44]

In short, an analysis on the value judgement of time will relate to the aspects of various elements of managerial goal of life that will further help to strengthen the base of management of human resources which lack its proper utilization. It is, therefore, a basic approach that every management function has to be kindled with numerous aspects of developmental goal in work behaviour. Thus, there is the optimum necessity that management should be viewed from the organismic cultural shape leading towards human behavioural foundations – this is done with a view to shape the prescribed methodology by understanding the theory of human growth with development that has its own way to find it out from the darkness to the light of human management process. This unity is integrated towards the developmental aspects, because each factor of social development is the production of life related works which every management function must search for attaining the tasks of performed behaviour.[45] Guiding this, management also should try to underlie the basic philosophies of life, as seen from the foregoing explanations. To search it, we have so far made an extreme estimation on each aspect of human developmental process in society, by means of management's new order of methodological surroundings – that each science of human work behaviour has to be related to, for the objective analysis as well as attainment of the tasks, for the goal must be thus, relativistically conjoined with the path where managerial performance depends, to a more extent on such different aspects as aimed at length in this chapter.

References

1. As the specific gravity of a substance, in science is described as the ratio of the weight of certain volume of it to that of an equal volume of water; so also applying in the language of art of management, it can be defined as: "the proportionate amount of skill required to be applied for certain work to the attainment of certain objective of management (relates to goal/output/results) that must be equal to, at a given amount of potential energy applied so ratiotically and therefore, the given skill here, is taken into consideration on the artistic applicational ideas, i.e., on the basis of the different factors of the man-power efficiency, potentiality, capability, experience, knowledge, training (conceptual, technical, on the job, off the job, etc.), intellect and so on". It is, therefore, treated to be human skill employed forth with so, which is specific towards goal-

path relationship, and this fact in detail will be analysed elsewhere afterwards in the chapters ahead.

2. Getty, J.Paul. "The Fine Art of Being the Boss", Playboy (June 1972), p. 143.

3. Skill is the art of doing things which has many types like : (a) managerial skill, (b) conceptual skill, and (c) technical skill. Here, by the term 'skill', it is considered to be managerial skill; the development of which is a must for every modern manager in any field of activities (job) for effective management of getting things done through (goal), by efficient utilisation of the resources of an organisation (path). See also Deb, S. "Managerial Skill Development. Its Need to Public Sector Enterprises" *Abhigyan*, Journal of Foundation for Organisational Research and Education and FORE School of Management, New Delhi, Winter, 1995, pp. 17-21.

4. In this regard, learning can be defined as any relatively permanent change in behaviour that occurs as a result of practice or experience. It is a key process – some would say the key process – in human behaviour. It can also be viewed as the psychological processes as described by the eminent psychologists like Ivan P. Pavlov (1890), Rescorla (1967), Kamin (1969), and many others; of which Thorndike's method is said to be the major-method. Swami Vivekananda said long ago that education is the manifestation of the divinity already in man. Behavioural scientists may not extend their belief to that extent but they also proceed on the assumption that unlike animals, human beings are born with an enormous potential of mental and intellectual capacity. It is the learning process that the art of management deals with, which can bring-out and augment all this capacity. In practice, the process of learning must fulfil certain conditions as: (1) Drive,

(2) Stimuli, (3) Response, (4) Retention, (5) Self-study, (6) Micro-process, (7) Reinforcement, etc. However, Thorndike's classic law of effect states, "of several responses made to the situation, those which are accompanied or closely followed by satisfaction (reinforcement)......will be more likely to recur; those which are accompanied or closely followed by discomfort (punishment) will be less likely to occur." Thorndike, Edward L., *Animal Intelligence,* The Macmillan Company, New York, 1911, p. 244. In a nutshell, cognition is the key to organizational behaviour. Many things can be learnt at present, through observation and analysis with the development of the audio-visual methodology. Hence, skill can also be acquired in this way. So, decision-making and problem-solving are also human cognitive processes as found in learning. See also Pareek, Udai; Rao, T.V. and Pestonji, D.M., *Behavioural Processes in Organisations,* Oxford and IBM Publishing Co., New Delhi, 1981.

5. Situations relate to an environment in which managers work. It is thus, consisting of the culture, climate, atmosphere of the work of managers towards the fulfilment and attainment of the organisational goal, and so requires managerial talent, intellect, vigore, capabilities, experience and education for efficient management of the resources of their (managers') organization, and bringing thereby the maximum output through minimum input application. It short, situations are changing in nature and relate to many factors of management as per norms, goals, enterprising attitudes, etc. Hence, situations demand for looking into management's strength in terms of various resources of the organization, instead of having different situational models and theories as the empirical research findings consider. However, researchers on various leadership studies have found importance of some models like: (i) the

Tennenbaum – Continuum of Leader Behavior; (ii) Fiedler's Contingency model; (iii) the House – Mitchell Path-Goal Theory; (iv) the Stinson-Johnson model; (v) Vroom –Yetten Contingency model; and (vi) the Hersey-Blanchard Tridimensional Leader Effectiveness model. See also Hemphili, John K.: "Situational Factors in Leadership", Monograph No. 32, Columbus, Ohio: Bureau of Educational Research, Ohio State University, 1949.

6. Attitudes are the keys to both thought and action. Virtually speaking, perception, learning and even motives influence behaviour via attitudes. Many factors contribute to the formation of attitudes. Among them are: (i) learning, (ii) experience, and (iii) personality. It is a mental and neutral state of readiness, organized through experience, exerting a directive or dynamic influence upon the individual's response to all objects and situations with which it is related. Allport, Gordon W., "Attitudes" in C. Muriron (Ed.), *Handbook of Social Psychology,* Clark University, Worcester, Mass., 1935. It is an enduring organization of motivational, emotional, perceptual and cognitive processes with respect to some aspects of the individual's world. Krech, D. and Cruchfield, R.S., Theory and Practice of Social Psychology, McGraw-Hill, New York, 1948. It is a persistent tendency to feel and behave in a particular way towards some object. Luthans, F., Organizational Behaviour, McGraw-Hill, Singapore, 1989.

7. Path-goal relational approach regarding the art of management considers for managerial effectiveness while applying decisions of proper judgment on the basis of situational approach, depending on the experience, education and observation of manager's capabilities; and is therefore, an excellent example of the need to diagnose a situation before attempting with the process of particular intervention. The path-

goal model is an illuminating idea that builds upon two major concepts like – (i) the Ohio State Leadership studies, and (ii) the Expectancy Model. Here, it is expected that the relational approach should be balanced for understanding and applying the decision-making processes of the managers with the situational needs, according as to their environmental conditions and problems encountered thereto. See also Mark J. Knoll and Charles D. Pringle, "Path-Goal Theory and the Task Design Literature:A Tenuous Linkage", *Akron Business and Economic Review,* 17, No. 4 (Winter 1986), pp. 75-83; Richard L. Daft, *Management,* 3rd ed. (Fort Worth Tex.: Dryden Press, 1993), p.493; John E. Stinson and Thomas W. Johnson, "The Path-Goal Theory of Leadership : A Partial Test and Suggested Refinement", *Academy of Management Journal,* 18, No. 2 (June 1975), pp. 242-252.

8. Decision-making is the basic job of any manager. Attitude measurement, which is the basis of behavioural study, becomes the part of decision-making. Viewed in a vacuum, decision-making seems like a fairly straightforward process. However, it involves collection of data regarding the problem, organizing and analysing the data, and drawing necessary observations and calculations. To be more precise, any managerial decision to be effective must be backed by some sort of empirical study. In a nutshell, situational leadership serves as the framework of decision-making process, because it can indicate which style of decision-making is most apt to succeed in a given situation. See also Eden, C. and Harris, J., 'Management Decision and Decision Analysis', Wiley, New York, 1975. According to the management science group, managers are perceived as decision makers. Thus, managers must therefore be able to use in their decision making processes, mathematical models and computers to help them arrive at optimum decision......It

(decision) means, according to behavioural scientists, the leadership and motivational ability, interpersonal behaviour, and the value system of a person who takes up such a decision, where leadership skill is importantly required for successful executives, though such a manager having a mathematical background can use mathematical concepts and techniques as an aid to his decision making activity, because of involvement of human beings in decisions whose attitudes cannot be so easily quantified. It is because, in most of the decisions of operations research techniques observation has found place of the partial utilization of the intellectual potentialities of the average human beings, whose potentials are philosophically derived as though infinite, under the conditions and circumstances of modern industrial life. See also McGregor, D., *The Human Side of Enterprise,* McGraw-Hill Book Company, Inc., New York, 1960. Hence, the process of decision to be more and more scientific must have to be participative and flexible in nature, in the context of managerial effectiveness and organisational goal attainment in a given situation of organisational culture, dynamics and environment, etc. to cope up with the real needs of human problems and enterprising path-goal relationship. See also Hallmann, R. and Ulrich, M.F., *"Participative and Flexible Decision Making", Journal of Small Business Management,* 21, no.1 (Jan. 1983), pp.1-7; Mitchell, R., *"Managing by Values", Business Week,* August 1, 1994, pp. 46-47.

9. Freud, S., *New Introductory Lectures on Psycho-analysis,* New York, Norton, 1933, p.105. See also Young, J.Z., *Doubt and Certainty in Science,* Oxford University Press, London, 1951; Russell, B., Power, Allen & Unwin, London, 1938; Arber, A., *The Mind and the Eye,* Cambridge University Press, London, 1954.

10. Sinha, J., *Indian Psychology–Emotion and Will,* Vol. II,

Sinha Publishing House, Calcutta, 1961; Skinner, B. F., *Science and Human Behaviour,* Macmillan, New York, 1953; Herzberg, F., Work and the Nature of Man, World Publishing, Cleveland, 1966; Davis, K., *Human Behaviour at Work: Organization Behaviour,* Tata McGraw-Hill, New Delhi,1978; Hull, C.L., Principles of Behaviour, Appleton - Century Crofts, New York, 1943, Lawler; III, E.E., "What do Employees really Want ?" paper presented at the American Psychological Association convention held in Montreal, August,1973; and Mehta, M. L., *Jaina Psychology,* Sohanlal Jain Dharma Pracharak Samiti, Amritsar, 1955.

11. Vroom, V.H., *Work and Motivation,* Wiley, New York, 1964; Aurobindo, Sri: *Essays on the Gita*, Sri Aurobindo Ashram, Pondicherry, 1972; Muller, M.: *Six Systems of Indian Philosophy,* Longmans Green, London, 1903; Radha Krishnan, S., *Indian Philosophy,* Vol.I (Second Edition), Allen and Unwin, London, 1929; Desai, M., *The Gospel of Selfless Action,* Navajivan Publishing House, Ahmedabad, 1946; and Rohit, M., The Cell of Upanishads', Bharatiya Vidya Bhavan, Bombay, 1970.

12. As Glueck views the development in business policy as arising from the use of planning techniques by managers. Glueck, W.F. and Jauch, L.R., *Business Policy and Strategic Management,* (4th edn.), McGraw-Hill, New York, 1984, pp. 4-5. However, the origin of business policy can be traced back to 1911, when Harvard Business School (HBS) introduced an integrative course in management aimed at the creation of general management capability. In practice, the development of the genesis of business policy has been on different lines. See also Christensen, C.R.; Andrews, K.R.; Bower, J.L.; Hamermesh, R.G. and Porter, M.E.: *Business Policy – Text and Cases,* (5th edn.), (Homewood, Ill.: Richard D. Irwin, 1982); Ansoff, H.: *Implanting Strategic*

Management, (Englewood Cliffs, New Jersey: Prentice-Hall, 1984) and Toffler, A: *The Third Wave*, (New York: Bantam Books, 1980).

13. Elwin, Verrier: 'The Tribal World of Verrier Elwin', Oxford University Press, Bombay, 1964, pp. 302-303.

14. Assuming thus, we should judge results, not by statistics or the amount of money spent on work only, but by the quality of human character that is involved with the said work. Elwin, V.: "A Philosophy for NEFA", North East Frontier Agency, Shillong,. 1955.

15. Conant, J.B., *On Understanding Science*, Oxford University Press, London, 1947.

16. Cassirer, E., *Essay On Man*, Yale University Press, New Haven, 1945.

17. The great danger of human life cycle process related to the work environment is mainly, concerned with the true concept of death. If born, the man must die – is the philosophy, which can be overcome, if the system of work is well-known in advance; otherwise, the same work may be a suicidal death, for which man should have to dangle down to the Earth – for he is not concerned with the real philosophy behind managing the self. This self realization must be accompanied with the cycle of work, so that the suicidal death can be crossed through overcoming the danger of unknown mystery of work philosophy. The unknown can easily be known by happiness to work culture, in terms of good management. The system of management is said to be good, when it relates to the process of disinterested way of working by sacrificing the self, which is never searching anything more than perfection. It is the mystry concealed to the inherent behaviour of the self, which is not always known in general parlence of working environment. Therefore, good management

requires the concept of real happiness, where man can absorb the self in all surroundings, so to attain actual happiness; which is otherwise, through any other alternatives become quite absurd as well as obstacle to the barrier of the cyclical flow of work culture that never designs the structure of perfectness, that is a qualitative and cognitive aspect of human life. Hence, management philosophy requires the science of known behaviour of human life, which is generally said to be unknown, and is guided by the unknown skills of human work can be made known to the perfect utilization of unknown potentialities of human life towards the success of goal of life through management of the individual self for the greater cause of the Self of the universe, in the midst of pain and pleasure while achieving the goal of life through activities.

18. Nature is a cultural concept. From sociological view point, it stands for that irremovable component of human experience, which defies human will and sets unencroachable limits to human action. Nature is, therefore, a by-product of the thrust for freedom. Hence, neither the images nor models of nature prevalent at any given time can be considered necessary attributes of the concept. In regard to the philosophy of management, it can be undoubtedly said that the 'thematic content' of the concept, as Gerald Holton would put it, has changed in the last century almost beyond recognition. Holton, G.: *'The Thematic Origins of Scientific Thought,* Harvard University Press, 1973, pp. 35-6. The intrinsic order and harmony of the law-abiding cosmos has been replaced by the management at this century, and is on, by an impenetrable labyrinth which, only thanks to the scientist's chalk marks, becomes; discovery of the 'objective order' needs to the cause-effectiveness relativity of management approach calls upon the necessitating touching-stone, and has been replaced by the imposition of intelligible order

upon meaningless diversity. The one element which has survived, and, indeed, has emerged unscathed from all these ontological revolutions, is the experience of constraint effectively placed on human action and imagery. And this is, perhaps, the only 'essence' of nature – philosophically pared to bones of theoretically unprocessed pristine experience and, is regarded to the unified concept of human goal of life.

19. In Habermas's view, psychoanalytic therapy provides a typical pattern for the dialogue activated by emancipatory interest. It seeks not only to validate itself, but to authenticate. It involves, therefore, a different, wider notion of truth-testing. Habermas, J.: *Theory and Practice*, Heinemann, London, 1974. Translated by John Viertel.

20. Proper knowledge can assure that a man will never experience his constraints as oppression; it is the unknown, unsuspected necessity which is confronted as suffering, frustration, and humiliating defeat. However, an informed action, on the contrary, needs necessity as its positive foundation. A genuinely free action in management would not be possible were there no necessity : free action, on sociological perspectives, means reaching one's ends by a chain of appropriate acts; but it is the necessary laws of managing with the art of human skills, connecting acts with their effects, which make them 'appropriate' to the intended ends.

21. Gay, P.: *The Enlightenment – An Interpretation,* Vol.1. See also *The Rise of Modern Paganism,* Wildwood House, London, 1970, p.148.

22. Durkheim, Emile: *Sociology and Philosophy,* Cohen

and West, London, 1965, pp. 57, 72. Translated by D.F. Pocock.

23. Shri Bipin Chandra Pal, one of the exponents of Hindu Nationalism observed: "The peculiar value and distinction of our concept of Swadhinata (Self-dependence) and Swatantrya (Self-subjection) lies in the grandeur of the connotation of the word (Swa) or 'Self'. This Swa is both the individual self and the Universal Self; and the two are really one. And mana's range of real freedom or self-dependence as we would call, it expands in proportion as he is able to realize his unity with Universal Self." He further remarks on such concept of world order regarding the end of civilization as: "The ideal end of civilization is perfection of man, not merely in his physical and material, but equally also, in his moral and spiritual aspects. It is more, it is the perfection of a man as a social unit, as a limb and organ of the social whole". The social reformer speaks more about the mission like: "The great mission this ancient land and its composite people among the modern nations of Europe, Asia and America, is to replace existing international competitions by international co-operation, to substitute......the nations of the world shall be as One People, living at peace with one another, working together for the furtherance of the common good and the relevation of God in man." Adapted from Third Way, Thengadi, D. complied by Bhanu Pratap Shukla, Janaki Prakashan, New Delhi, 1995, pp. 41-46.

24. As per the Vedantic Truth, it can be said undoubtedly that few thinkers on social science have given at different places, and in different time in the history of mankind that 'All is One'. One such personality, called by the name of revered Sri Guruji in India by the masses, Sri M.S. Golwalkar once believed that the World unity and human welfare can be made real only to the extent mankind realizes this absolute

"Vedantic Truth Concept". However, what he implied was not elimination of all distinctive features of nations and rolling them all into one uniform pattern. He visualized various groups of people coming together in a spirit of familism realizing the innate oneness of mankind while preserving their individual nationalities. The different human groups are marching forward, all towards the same, each in its own way and in keeping with its own characteristic genius. The destruction of the special characteristics, whether of an individual or of a group, will not only destroy the natural beauty of harmony but its joy of self-expression. To seek harmony among the various and diverse characteristics has been our special contribution to the world thought.

25. In human sociological perspectives, "neither the images nor models of nature prevalent at any given time can be considered necessary attributes of the concept. The 'thematic content' of the concept (as Gerald Holton would put it, and is already referred to in foregoing explanations under the concept of 'philosophy of management') has changed in the last century almost beyond recognition. The intrinsic order and harmony of law-abiding cosmos has been replaced by an impenetrable labyrinth......and this is, perhaps, the only 'essence' of nature, pared to the bones of theoretically unprocessed pristine experience". Op. cit.

26. As to the postulates of Karma, the teachings of the Gita goes like –work keeps up the cycle of the universe, and it is duty of every individual to help. Thus, the ideal of the Gita is not based on negativism, asceticism or escapism. It is not negation of actions, but performance of actions in a detached spirit. Hence, it is not Naiskarma, but 'Niskama Karma'. In short, the giving up is not of action itself, but of interest, desire, fruit,

attachment regarding action. Because, desire binds a man; he should therefore act in such a way when action does not bind. The Gita synthesizes both 'Pravirtti' and 'Nivrtti'. As Professor M. Hiriyanna says: "The Gita teaching stands not for renunciation of action, but for renunciation in action". The explanations are all guided by the principle consisting of the three constituent Gunas of Prakrti – Sattva, Rajas and Tamas, necessarily give rise to actions. – *Bhagavadgita,* Gita Press, Gorakhpur.

27. This work principle can further be substituted by the opinion that there are various needs for which individual and groups work in society. Among others, survival and growth needs are essential, for whatever else reason there might be working principle – the resources are managed for these two basic fundamental needs of men. As Maslow (1970) has said once, the desire to know and understand is very useful, not for mere survival, but for the growth of the individual personality and the culture and civilization to which the individual belongs. Thus, it can be attributed that self-realisation on the basis of work through integration of the higher and the lower self becomes the vital point of work. The Gita expresses this view of self as: "For him who has conquered his (lower) self by the (higher) self his self is a friend but for him who has not possessed his (higher) self, his very (self) will act in enmity like an enemy" (VI. 5-6). Thus, the principle of possession inherent with law of karma (work) which has been depicted impressively at times in the Indian vedic literature, either historically or literally confines to the concept of work. See also Maslow, A.H. : *Motivation and Personality,* Harper, New York, 1954; and the various Chapters and slokas depicted on the principles of 'Karma Yoga' and 'Jyana Yoga' in the Gita. Professor Harold Koontz by his agreement with the concept of management as the notion of getting things done through and with people in organized

groups opines that the art of doing must be creating an environment in which people can perform as individuals and yet to co-operate towards attainment of groups' goals. The art further should be to remove blocks to such performance, a way of optimizing efficiency in reaching goals. The author therefore observes that the co-operative endeavour of men should be guided by the principle of the theory of Karma – that brings effectiveness in work in realistic manner towards the perfection of individual from all bondages of life. This kind of philosophic (visionary) goal enlightens the activities in order to set free the mission of the enterprising objective of human beings towards the subjective view of management process – planning, organizing, controlling all human activities in an unending nature.

28. The doctrine of sovereignty, even in its barely legal aspect, is a complete solvent of this theory...... The ultimate unity of sovereignty is distinguished by the very means which secure it; for these means do not appear at all on the legal face of our institutions. – Frederick Pollock, *History of the Science of Politics,* Akashdeep Publishing House, Delhi, 1990 (Reprinted), p.117. It seems, therefore, it is not possible to discuss continental theories of the State in a moderate compass without assuming a certain knowledge of the general history of philosophy. The separation of politics from ethics (including the ultimate metaphysical foundations of ethics),......as the theory of legislation is based on philosophy of ethics. – *Ibid.,* pp.119-20. He further explains – but the analytical branch of political science, including the pure science of positive laws, is altogether independent of ethical theories, though not of the fact that in every commonwealth these are received moral standards which the rules of law must in the long run follow. And this the definite scientific result which we in England say that the work of the past century has given us. The various discussions on

the concept of sovereignty of the State have placed it to our notional view point that the science of the history of politics as the author preferred to say on the overall subjective idealism was that with Huxley, who was no dealer in empty phrases, that government is the corporate reason of the community; with Burke, philosopher and statesman, that a State "is not a partnership in things subservient only to the gross animal existence of a temporary and perishable nature", but " a partnership in all science, a partnership in all art, a partnership in every virtue, and in all perfection"; in which our resemblance is found to the extent that the principle of work is the foundation stone above all misgivings of human society, as they established on the basis of human perfection regarding achievement of the result.

29. Peter F. Drucker regards management as the 'life giving, acting, dynamic organ of the institution'. – Drucker, Peter F. : *Management – Tasks, Responsibilities, Practices,* Heinemann, London, 1974, p.x. Thus, he emphasizes on translating the basic purpose and mission of business into objectives as otherwise they remain insight, good intentions and brilliant epigrams which never become achievement. On MBO, Drucker says, "Business enterprise must build team-efforts, must all pull in the same direction, contributions must fit together to produce a whole – without gaps, without friction, without unnecessary duplication of effort. Business performance, therefore, requires that each job be directed toward the objective of whole business". – Drucker, Peter F.: *The Practice of Management,* Harper & Bros., New York, 1954, p.121. This is said to be oneness in Indian vedic concept of work which is common irrespective of the nature of job man performs for ultimate perfection in the nature of managing activities with goal-path relational approach.

30. Toynbee, Arnold Joseph, *A Study of History,* this work is completed in ten volumes wherein it is observed that the author has tried to synthesize the historical material. Thus, he tried to invent fresh frameworks of classification and interpretation, on the basis of his subtle study of a large number of historical facts......and makes a comparative interpretation of history. – Adapted from Majumder, R.K. and Srivastav, A.N.: *Historiography* (*Method of History*), SBD Publishers' Distributors, Delhi, 1994, p. 384. While investigating the great cultures of the past, he tries to discover the general principles of historical process which could serve as an illustration and even a demonstration of human history in its period of growth, highest perfection and decay.

31. The ultimate goal of human life is liberation. The liberation is possible only when men are guided by the concept of salvation in managing through change in transcendent approach with a steady progression by means of actual work towards perfection. Thus, self-realisation can be said to be the optimum need that can be fulfilled through man-power resource development –it is the development of human potentiality by managing people to change with extreme perfection in work behaviour in organized way of living.

32. In psychology, the 'law of effect' is dealt with the learning theory. In this regard, Thorndike's classic law of effect is illustrative which depicts an illuminative viewpoint and already referred to the preceeding analysis of this chapter. However, it is further to be said that this law is not only an illustrative idea of learning in psychological perspective. In philosophy also, it is called that there is law of God. As Gandhi says that God's law and God are not different from each other. Thus, God is also, at times, described as Law. However, it is essential to note that Gandhi tries to gather the results of the

studies and searches of different sciences and comes to find that there is a Law governing every movement and every development in every part of the universe. Hence, this principle of law is like "all things in the universe including the sun and the moon and the stars obey certain laws. Without the restraining influence of these laws the world would not go on for a single moment". –*Young India,* 23.1.1930.

33. Maslow, A.H. – "A Theory of Human Motivation", *Psychological Review,* Vol.50, 1943. See also, *Motivation and Personality,* New York, 1954.

34. Non-aptitude traits include impulsiveness, self-confidence, ascendance inclination away from neuroticism, aesthetic expression, tolerance in ambiguity, and disorderliness.

35. In regard to managerial goal, it is very important to note that managers as leaders have their own choice and therefore, it might be expected, the more alike the situations, the more the composition of leadership remained the same. – Kolasa, Blair J. : *Introduction to Behavioural Science in Business,* Wiley Eastern, p. 520. As a matter of fact, it can be asserted that leadership role changes according to situations, the style of manager depends therefore on the environment in which and where a manager works. It is specific and relative to particular situation. However, an important determinant of managerial effectiveness is initiative. Thus, managerial goal is concerned with self-assurance or self-confidence on the part of each manager which is an important factor for managerial effectiveness.

36. Every one must take to Bread Labour voluntarily. There is no question of any compulsion. Compulsion gives rise to discontent and revolt. – Lal, B.K., *Contemporary Indian Philosophy,* Motilal Banarsidass, Delhi, 1995, p.142.

37. Chaos has wide connotations and a universal concept......in organizational structure. – Deb, S., *Contemporary Issues On Management,* Atlantic Publishers and Distributors, New Delhi, 2001, p. 4.

38. A reference to understand this broad view can further be enlightened at least, through and with the works of S. Sundara Srinivasan. – Srinivasan, S.S.: *Thirukural and Modern Management,* Minerva Press, New Delhi.

39. Schumpeter, J.: "Vilfredo Pareto (1848-1923)", *Quarterly Journal of Economics,* LXIII (May, 1949), p.167.

40. The main concern of myself in this chapter is basically to understand the "interdependency of social phenomena" concept and therefore, its implications relate to, for individual specialized disciplines which together constitute the social sciences that management is concerned. However, it is important in integrative process of human development in society through management of human work behaviour in organized life, and therefore, bears heavily on the concept of strategic view regarding the relativity aspects dealt in management science behaviour of human work interrelationships.

41. This integrative nature is the law of nature, and is therefore, universal which any management thought has to conform with the natural laws, because without obeying nature no life on the Earth can exist for long. Hence, every mission must be guided by the visionary zeal of the world view with a work culture culminating thereby the principles of management for the strengthening of the base of universal application of such policies and principles. It is the integration found to be conveyed on that respect, in so far as the strategicity of the concept of

management is concerned. Thus, it is vital towards fulfilling the fundamental needs of men in society.

42. In this regard, Com. Dange declared in unequivocal terms that the famous 'Nasadiya Sukta' of the Rig Veda heralds not only the beginning of philosophy but of dialectical materialism also, in the most ancient record of world history. Substantiating to this, the views of the western thinkers, it can be undoubtedly asserted that gradually the westerners came to realize that a good constitution does not always guarantee good citizens. Hence, in modern times, there is now in the west a growing awareness of the important role of socio-cultural and religious institution as a factor in economic growth. After 1979, this realization dawned upon China also. Their leaders then resolved to inaugurate an era of 'spiritual civilization' maintaining their drive for material progress but without materialistic philosophy. They came to experience that when people do not cherish and uphold spiritual values, they become incapable of possessing national character, integrity, self-discipline and dutifulness. – Thengadi, D.: *Third Way,* Janaki Prakashan, New Delhi, 1995, p.75.

43. It is guided by the illumined mind which does not work primarily by thought, but by vision. It can also be supplemented with the idea of Sri Aurobindo as he says: "the higher mind brings a greater consciousness into the being through the spiritual idea and its power of truth, so the illumined mind brings in a still greater consciousness through a truth-sight and truth-light and its seeing and seizing power. – Sri Aurobindo, *The Life Divine,* p. 839. He further states, "The overmind ......is the final consummating movement of the dynamic spiritual transformation......a more manifold delight of being." – *Ibid.,* p. 846. Thus, the mission of management behaviour has to follow this principle of life, among

others for the conceivability of the ultimate reality.

44. Deb S., *Contemporary Issues On Management,* Atlantic Publishers and Distributors, New Delhi, 2001 (Chapter 1).

45. The essential qualities and relationships necessary for successful management can be explained and understood in terms of commitment, a characteristic common to all individuals recognized for managerial excellence. Managers carryout their tasks in an interpersonal world. Other people continually view the manager's manner, bearing, and conduct. From their observations, they form impressions of the manager's values, beliefs, and attitudes. Excellent managers make a powerful and positive impression on others because they blend a set of positive beliefs with an equally appropriate set of positive behaviours. These beliefs and actions form "commitments". – Hersey, P.; Blanchard, H.K. and Johnson, E.D.: *Management of Organizational Behavior – Utilizing Human Resources*, Prentice Hall of India Private Limited, New Delhi, Seventh Edn., 1998, p. 446. Again, it is worth-noting that there are five fundamental commitments which the most effective managers are to share viz., (i) commitment to the consumer; (ii) commitment to the organization; (iii) commitment to self; (iv) commitment to people and (v) commitment to task. Each of these are further having their own attributes which a modern manager has to follow for the effectiveness of the tasks performed by himself or herself in a given set of environmental issues in getting his or her tasks to be performed for the attainment of organizational goal. Being action-oriented simple described as accomplishing. Excellent managers get things done. They execute. They maintain positive momentum. Realistic deadlines are set and met. In short, people are encouraged to take action, and a sense of positive direction and accomplishment results.

2
Organisational Thought

Genesis of Thought

Human race, in the history of human civilization has had to be evolved with the process of group effort, where, it has been observed from the world history that every civilization had got its tremendous goal to be achieved through diverse field of social activities, conforming thereby the optimum necessity of living for maintaining the social peace and tranquility. Thus, it is human organization gives birth to human civilization, be it either formal or informal, has come to be realized for the attainment of common goal through unified approach, though diverse or numerous paths are seemed to be adopted for the acculturation of human adaptive nature of living. It was therefore, found with the system of work, in whatsoever being it is fundamentally approached for the perfection of human lives in society. Every process of the systematic effort of men has always been contemplated for the unification with the inherent meaning of life that causes an effective behaviour to be optimized for the attainment of human accomplished nature of job towards the ultimate goal of life – it is called here, perfection, as we have seen in the First Chapter.

The organismic approach of behaviour has given birth to the process of organization in historical perspective that the books of management as dealt in about human civilization has penetrated for understanding this viewpoint, and thus, organizational concept bears heavily on human management in a quite systematic nature of the subjective correlation of human affairs, and to deal with the objective attainment of those tasks for the unification of life tending towards such goal of life that regards for the perfection. It is the organization helps men in society for better living and unites for the common plateform of an universal understanding. The passage of human life in civilized manner is encountered with the philosophical mission that all the thinkers on social science should agree; because of the nature of human hereditary aspects of genetically manifested form of authenticity, it is expected that management of human affairs in society should be approached through such an environment which gives rise to a universal common plateform – it is called here, organization.

It is, therefore, apparent to note that the structural view of organizational concept, though seems to be very recent origin in management literatures; it bears yet in mind to say that there were good attributes that gave birth to many civilizations in the ancient world, for which further, it had been possible on the part of our forefathers to attain their goal of social life, in terms of leading an organized way of living. As can be seen from the world history, it was the ancient India which had developed in times of Indus Valley civilization[1], the account of which can be traceable from the records of the reminiscences of the past activities, and hence, it had diverse elements of a full-growing civilization which, now, no civilized country can deny the fact. Thus, the organization which had developed in Indus Valley culture people, still, it is believed that our past cultural heritage on the Earth was quite a forward looking tendency of our forefathers who established good social relationships throughout the world, in so far as the trade and commerce of the ancient India is concerned. However, during the regime of different kings and queens in the long past of the history, it has been observed that human civilizations were growing with different types of organisations to which people modified their mode of living. This modification of human behaviour was guided by all aspects of universalization, and so, there was the necessity of new order of life for the reorientation as well as reconstruction of the social will of the people who provided their skills and knowledge in the built-up operations of the new socio-cultural order, henceforth concerned.[2] Gradually, in historical perspective, it has been followed that the present form of formal as well as informal organisations are structurally developed in new pattern, for the furtherance of the newer and newer social order in changing situation, to which the western concept of the present forms of organisations rather deals with the materialistic activities of human life in philosophical or spiritual order, as already dealt in the previous Chapter that after 1979 in China also, there was adaptive nature of the old cultural view of human social life, among others; which the Western part of the modern organisations in different countries adopted, as the common code of understanding through management of human resources.

It is, therefore, very important and significant role played by the organization in society from time immemorial period in the history of human civilizations, the record of which, even the modern as well as ancient history goes back to date to traceout the consequences of the said journey of life – a pioneering work is being done in this respect by Toynbee[3] in this line of thinking. Claiming thus the concept of organization as a historical phenomenon for the upliftment of the societal goal of life, it goes to say like this :

"...............Time is the changing phenomena, where the only constant is the time itself in which human civilization undergoes a complex change through cross-cultural multi-dimensional human activities, and this, order of life of human civilization is like complex chemical changes that orderly goes on, to enhance an equitably balanced state of affairs, wherein we see that human organization in society only remains with the adaptive nature of life beyond the screen. It is the great pleasure to accumulate knowledge and wisdom which find in place of organized living unifying thereto, the basic necessities for survival. Considering such aspects of the approach that calls for a structural relationship in the midst of informal way of free development of each culture of human civilizations, organisations are thus, placed at the central point of human resources development."

"If there is always an upward journey with forward looking for globalisation of the cultural heritage of human talents and skills with every nature of creativity to be utilized for the purposeful journey of life, there aims to be an understanding guided by such universal philosophy of the organizational culture as well as the key-note of the basic issues of its further and fuller development – this requires the concept of the organization, now, at the present problems to be further modified with the old versions of the holistic nature of development, giving therefore, to all in it a chance for fuller personality development. Keeping in mind the similar aspects of human life in societal order, an organizational cultural idea though, has been placed here, in terms of a neo-modern approach in historical perspective as well as philosophical order, spiritualizing thereby the life of all working with any organizations, at any time, and in any place of the world".

An observation of the above must further be guided by the issues like –(i) structural homogeneity; (ii) formal-informal conditionalities; (iii) discipline and orderliness; (iv) authority-responsibility-accountability relationships; (v) quality circles; (vi) changing elements for the survivality; (vii) growth with development originating towards human personality; (viii) universalisation of social order of human life; (ix) entrepreneurship abilities with cultural transformation from one generation to another generation; and besides, (x) transactional approach as a whole. Therefore, the entire aspects on the concept of the organizational thinking, must be guided by the 'Ideational Approach', where these commandments are horizontally, vertically, laterally and in circular flow require to be modified and implemented from time to time, and from place to place; according as to the nature of changing requirement of the society. Following both the pattern of ancient as well as modern management principles and postulates of life culture, each organization has to be conceived from the view point of universalisation for the highest orderliness of human social life culture, nurturing each element of the structural aspect of human organization for the perfection of human life – this is poignantly felt inherent with the art of management for the systematization, in terms of the strategicity of the concept of organizational goal that each manager has to survive with for the optimum level of development, in a structurally relative aspects of getting the works and every performances to be done and accomplished through a mutually conducive environment. Hence, the genesis of the organisation is a managerial concept that has its relationship with the path-goal concept of the organizational thought for managerial communication – it is communication purposefully activated towards the need of human perfection through generalizations of each activity of men, in regard to unifying freedom[4] of life.

Phases of Theoretical Development

We have seen that the concept of organization is not a new one. It is as old as the civilization. However, it is true that the theoretical framework of the development of the organization is a very recent one, which developed only after the development of science and technology and its application in the field of business activities more and more. After the 'Industrial Revolution' in the West, the western thinkers in the field of business had sought to produce more by means of applying of the concept of science in industrial activities. As for example, it is quite important to note Frederick Winslow Taylor, who is said to be the father of the 'Scientific Management'. For the first time, he thought of an applicability of the rules and principles of science in business and industrial activities, which produced more goods of particular kind in industry according to the needs of the society, in place of limited production as found previously before such new methods and techniques of production was employed – where it is observed that only the rules of thumb-and-impression, or trial-and-error method of production technique was employed by the employers to manage work and the workers at the work environment.

It is thus, observed that he (Taylor) had studied the motion by which machine operates and also the fatigueness of the workers worked with the machines in his new theory. By this, he came to know that a system could be employed through which not only the employer, but also the workers in industries would be benefitted. Again, at a later stage, it is further observed that Henri Fayol, another in the field of industry simplified more the production technique with the system of management by his 'Administrative Discipline' – the concept of organizing different human socio-economic activities in relation to human performance. Mention can also be made about Max Weber, who propounded the 'Bureaucratic Model', and therefore, it can be undoubtedly asserted here, that the Classical Organisation Theory developed only in the early years of the period of Industrial Revolution[5], when large scale production was undertaken which was necessitated by population growth and the development of science in the field of industries[6]. Thus, the production efficiency was the need of the hour of these periods. However, it is of prima facie important subject to note here, that Classical Organization Theory regards the organization as a formal structure which is created and run, for the first time by the Western part of the history, according to certain rules and principles in the field of management. Hence, this theory evolves from the three important streams which are: (1) Scientific Management formulated by F.W. Taylor; (2) Theory of General Administration propounded by Henri Fayol; and (3) Ideal Bureaucracy propagated by Max Weber.

With this development, the people were not satisfied, because there were many problems and limitations encountered with production efficiency and the management of workers; where workers were observed to be discontented and they created problems in the field of industries for the effectiveness as well as efficiency of the overall results to get things done through, with the systematization. Therefore, many social scientists as well as humanists came ahead with their helping hands by suggesting that the proper system in management is not only guided by the problems of the workers in work-place, but their due attention regarding social needs. As for example, again, the famous experiments conducted for over five years (1927-32) by Elton Mayo and his team at the Hawthorne plant of the Western Electric Company is quite illuminating in this regard, to which the conclusions to be drawn from this and other researches of Mayo were summed up in the context of the sociological implications of the work, the workers, and the different groups which consist of different workers employed in particular industry, by D.C. Miller and W.H. Form in their combined work[7]. It is worth-noting that the core philosophy on which the Human Relations Approach as the organization theory had developed, it mainly stood on the grounds that workers respond – (a) to clearly demonstrate interest by management in the work they are doing and their own opinions thereof, and (b) to the informal social structure prevailing at the work place. However, in the modern and contemporary organizational thought, behavioural approach has an important place. It is nicely observed that behavioural organization theories generally deal with balance, fusion, roles and groups. In this regard, we can say very undoubtedly that theory of organizational equilibrium or balance was developed at this time of later periods of the Industrial Revolution era, which made a long journey after the saturated span of the periods, where Chester I. Barnard (1938), a great sociologist had put forward due emphasis on the management techniques through a balance henceforth sought to manage human resources in the field of industrial and commercial activities. This is further refined by Herbert A. Simon (1957), another new thinker in this field, who believed that workers were not only workers; what is more true about themselves are that they were at least, human beings who require the overall recognization, after an application of the psychological phenomena on their work and the work place, where it is further true that all workers are not alike; and hence, they are to be treated in organization with full care though, in varied manner with balancing the overall approach of their variegated needs and with a functional relationship of the relevant work environment. Thus, the 'Balance Theory of Organisations' – also called by this name, is concerned with human behaviour in joining, participating, remaining, and withdrawing from organizations. As Simon has also depicted three levels in the structure of an organization under this theory, say - bottom, middle, and top levels, and it is asserted by him that human involvement can be entrusted at any of these levels. Similarly, there were many social thinkers who contributed much by their respective theories on the systematic approach of an organizational theory in this line of thinking – in terms of workers needs in social set-up, in which organization is said to be the instrument of management. Bakke's theory has been quite identical to this view. He has observed: "The organization is to some degree remakes the individual and the individual to some degree remakes the organization, or the vice-versa relationship".[8]

From the above, it has been followed that the extreme development of social order has been necessitated the growth of an organization theory, but it could no longer remain consistent with the static needs of men. The dynamics in organizational behaviour has been caused due to ongoing growth of population with the resultant discoveries and inventions in scientific advancements, and their relevant applications from time to time in business and socio-economic life in historical perspectives. Thereafter also, people were not satisfied with these all sorts of development and hence, at the later part of the nineteenth century periods, there were a new search for – how to develop a new theory to further human achievements through result-oriented activities in effective manner. It is therefore, true to say that ' Systems Theory of Organisation' developed at this stage, which portrays the interrelations and interdependency of the individuals and elements in the organization, that has unified the organization theorists to view the organization as a whole from the viewpoint of management concept. It is based on the 'synergistic effect', which shows that the whole organization is greater than the sum of its parts. It should not be wrong to say that though open and closed systems are concerned under this approach – the open system seems to be more useful in the context of modern age. Again, this approach is based on the assumption that the whole organization structure for the smooth management of operations, consists of interdependent sub-systems, each of which functions in itself independently. Thus, the whole system while functions in itself – transforming the inputs into outputs, the sub-systems function in themselves – making thereby contribution to the whole system. Hence, it is also naturally as well as relativistically true to say that for the proper integration and coordination of the sub-systems with the whole system, and each sub-system with the other sub-systems – an internal organizational structure becomes necessary. In this regard, Fred Luthans, another management thinker has, therefore, rightly pointed out, "At the heart of the open system are the processes, operations, or channels which transform the inputs into outputs."[9]

However, these are also not the holistic concept on the organizational theories. As time passed on, there developed new more theories on the pattern of human organizing activities, and so, newer and newer concepts developed on human management science and its behaviour. Similarly, another theory – called as the 'Contingency Organisation Theory' developed, where Joan Woodward has been considered to be the pioneer of this theory, and later on, Paul Lawrence and Jay Lorch have also refined this by substituting their own views in respective manner. Gradually, action research has been started on organizational performance on line with the empirical research, and the findings are suggested in different works of the eminent thinkers - McKinsey[10] is one of them. Some others like – J.L. McKenny and P.G.W. Keen (1974),

V.P. Michael (1976) besides, Ouchi and Jaeger (1978) – who studied Japanese and American management practices and classified them under three headings[11]. Thus, there is the latest development has taken place on organization theory in recent time, in which the Contemporary School of Management Thought provides a framework for studying the more recent trends in management practice, such as the impact of global business on global perspectives: the search for excellence, and concern for productivity and quality, etc.

From the above, it has been observed that the organisation theories which developed from the Industrial Revolution era uptil date have concerned with the techniques of work and the management of human resources. It is, therefore, felt that the need of a unified management behaviour could be achieved through an organizational choice, which to the very extent of work management finds the particular type of result by means of providing human perfection at the work-place. Hence, all these theoretical aspirations of modern scientific civilizations are bridged through encountering problems of human management with creativity in different dimensions and approaches, giving birth to their respective pursuits for the systematic development of particular work-behaviour in an environment. It is thus, the environmental product that personifies the goal of human undertaking to make its headway through an organizational effort, for which a theoretical framework is needfully aspired with human path-goal relationship in leading the principles of work philosophy. It is the organisational theory actualises the self-assertive behaviour of men who are, otherwise guided by the philosophy of work – this work is the primary concept behind searching for new theories, as to how to organize more effectively to attain the goal in balanced but unending manner through different paths adopted strategically, in the pursuits of achieving different human socio-economic results which are the door to the success of human endeavour, that human beings are ever, from the long past in history searching to their march in evolutionary processes of living, and attaining it through perfection. In short, it should not be out of place to mention here that time is the only constant that has resulted to the change of different organisational theories in changing situations of the work environment, to which again, Rosemary Stewart, Peter F. Drucker, and alike many other new thinkers have placed their own opinion, as to how an organisation as an instrument of managerial performance helps in the personality development of each manager, according as to the nature of developmental needs and their organisational setting. Thus, the organisational theory helps in moulding individual behaviour in work-place to which human resources are creatively employed for the purpose of optimum development, and it gives ample opportunity for moral development, so that moral and productivity goes in parallelism. Some important psychologists like Pavlov, Maslow, McGregor, Allport, Katz, Herzberg, among others can be said to be worth-noting in this connection which depict an illuminating picture.[12]

Organisation and Human Motivation

Organisation is the primary instrument which helps human beings to enhance motivation at the work place, and thereby, it enriches the pillar of success in managing human resources towards the satisfaction of human needs. It is thus, one of the most important element of work (economic productivity) that has gone with timeliness in spatial orbit of the organisational environment; for, it has been found in human history that men are guided by some sort of need for which they unite together for a common purpose – it is in management science known as the goal. This goal is the another name of need which motivates men to work in co-operative effort for the performance that encompasses with the zeal of work culture in unitary spirit towards those ends of life men are, for ever, found to be organizing with such common need. As Maslow[13] has postulated a structure of needs, which is also true to organizational activities, it can be said that self-actualisation needs of man being related to an open environment, for which an organization is the only effective tool to establishment of human goal that takes an individual in group effort to the fulfilment of desire to become more and more what one is, to become everything that one is capable of becoming. It is thus, organization motivates man to work in united way for managing the self to the optimum necessity of human perfection. So, human motivation is a mental process, where it is found that the deficiency in regard to perfection is bridged through organizational effectiveness, for which there is the tools and techniques used for the purposiveness of goal attainment through organizational communication. This is also known as managerial communication, as Peter F. Drucker has once said in his 'Communication Theory'. Thus, the 'Motivation Cycle' in operative behaviour of man can be energetically infused in mind through the mental process of organizational techniques employed by managerial decision-making processes. This decision being again, strategically taken into account, according to situational analysis, an organization comes up with different tools and techniques as envisaged for human motivation, with a view to attaining human perfection. Thus, a manager who is also said to be a leader in commercial or industrial sense has to motivate his people at work place in organizational set-up, because of some performance that leads the entire organization towards the achievement of common goal and objectives of the organization. Hence, it is essentially to be remarked here that leadership, according to Keith Davis, is the ability to persuade others in organization to seek defined objectives enthusiastically. Because, it is the human factor that binds a group in organization together and motivates it toward goals...... Thus, leadership transforms potential into reality. It is the ultimate act that brings to success all the potential that is in an organization and its people.[14]

From this, we are now clear that organizational motivation is very much essential to energise skills of workers and employees which produce goods at the most resultant manner and is in correlation to its leadership traits. About the trait approach of leadership role in industry, it is nicely highlighted by Kolasa[15], who has said in regard to physical, mental and verbal abilities, along with personality traits of leadership and self confidence. Hence, we can predict that situational leadership approach, though it is comparatively of recent origin, is one of the elements of human motivational factor where all the indices towards the dependent as well as independent variables of work in industries are, nevertheless, guided by the organization approach of managerial effectiveness in its communication processes, without which it finds itself a barrier towards the attainment of human goal, along with organizational means-ends relationship in economic behaviour of man. Thus, it has necessitated for the significant role of human personality constraints that envisages for the development of human potentials in regard to such functions, which man confines towards the process of planning in its overall organizational approach of behaviouristic goal-orientedness, so that the successful achievement of results through human perfection can be attained in terms of mental undertaking towards the need of the organization, along with individual as well as group goal satisfaction. In short, according as to the nature of human motivational process, it has to be permeably said that organization brings all those essential conditionalities of work behaviour which results in human perfection. Thus, keeping in mind the Human Resource Development (HRD) perspective in modern organization, it goes to say in realistic manner that human motivation helps all modern organizations, if properly aided through human work culture to augment Quality of Work Life (QOWL) – which means employees empowerment, effective communication and information system in an organization, besides other attributes of human performance. All these go to restructure the organization in new dimensional order with a comprehensive human base and core human values in different systems as well as sub-systems of the organization as a whole, and thereby, it rationalizes human creativity and talent, intelligent etc. for increasing organizational productivity with a transitional change of the organization towards growth and development of workers and different interested groups involved with the industrial activities for greater and more perfection.

It is imperative to say that human motivation relates to moral ethics and organizational climate that infuses in mind of workers behavioural re-engineering at work place and hence, an organization has to evaluate from time to time as to how to help workers and employees to commanding height of industrial productivity along with human performance; if there exists a work culture that requires different motivational patterns for increasing human productivity, then only managerial goal dealing with the different needs of man in an organization has to be perpetuated by means of an objective analysis of work behaviour which goes to enhance such order of life to embrace the utilities of marginalizing every element of human productivity in terms of those various motivational techniques and processes. Thus, an organization, at the present changing situation of global business activities has to follow the traditional path with some sort of modification of human behaviour, according to the changing needs of the society in new dynamics of organizational behaviour. Considering the aspects of human growth and development in other developed countries in the world, Japanese culture[16] can be an explanatory example to set aside for the purpose of implementing in other developing countries like India. It is further to be dealt with a strategic approach in India, because there are different conditionalities at work place in Indian organizational environment. When it is expected to motivate people in Indian organizations, there require a re-shape of those theories and practices in unified manner, where all workers are to be empowered through real democratic wills, that they are aided by advancing work-related behavioural approaches that go to produce more and more with the benefits of all interested groups so involved and working in organizations. This is being observed one of the hurdles in Indian organization, and is therefore, to be reformulated in situational decision-making processes of industrial leadership activities.[17]

This can go a long way to establish a relationship between goal and path in human process of work behaviour, for the lack of which the socialization process is further going in backward direction rather than forward approach to a far off milestone of national development along with individual and organisational development.

Morale Building in Organisation

Morale is one of the important aspects of workers and employees attitudinal idea which enriches an organization by its impact to the all-round development of individuals working in particular organization, along with organisational goal achievement. It brings in organizations a good climate, due to which workers and employees are motivated towards the work. As to this, we can go far off to the past of the 'Platonic Theory of State'[18] where it has been observed that Plato considers the state as a spiritual institution, something basic to man's nature. Here, it is apparent to note that his philosophy is important because it takes man to the concept of soul, which is clear from the remark he made whereto he holds that human soul consists of three elements – reason, spirit and appetite. These three elements respectively lead man to wisdom, courage and hunger, thirst and love. Considering all these aspects to be present in human morale building, it goes to say that the role of morale was thus, recognized in early times in military organizations where four elements of battle efficiency were recognised: the number of men, arms, regimentation and morale. Of these four, Napoleon is said to have attached maximum weightage to morale in winning a battle. Now, coming over to Indian philosophy and psychology of human mind, we see that the ancient Indian thinkers refer to this is that of attitude which is the core of human morale-building aspect for real personality development. In this regard, Prabhu (1963) points out, " Along with knowledge and skills, education also transmits the particular system of moral, social and cultural values of the group, and thus undertakes the indoctrination of both rational and emotional elements which make up the adult individual" (p.103f). Attention may be drawn to the four famous verses in the Gita which contains the essential principle of disinterestedness (also referred in Chapter 1), " To action alone hast thou a right and never at all to its fruits. Let not be fruits of action by the motive............Abandoning attachment, do thy work with a mind even in success and failure". (II, 47-48). "He whose undertakings are free from desire, whose works are burned up in the fire of wisdom, him the wise call a man of learning. Having abandoned attachment to the fruits of works, ever content, without any kind of dependence, he does nothing, though he is ever engaged in work". (IV, 19-20).

Looking from different angles, it can be said that morale is termed as the mental condition of an individual or groups that decides their attitudes and limits the degree to which they accept leadership or responsibility. It is, therefore, very important to remember that an industrial society can be overthrown if there is destruction of the morale of its industrial population. On the other hand, a high state of morale can lead to: (i) willing co-operation; (ii) loyalty and a sense of belonging for the organization; (iii) prompt spotting and equitable adjustments of conflicts as they develop; (iv) justice and equitable distribution of rewards, i.e., promotions, logical dues, facilities, etc.; (v) provision of values, both intangible and tangible, that are desired by the collectives in adequate and proper amounts; (vi) cutting down red-tapism to the minimum, employer-employee meetings, training, education and indoctrination; and (vii) satisfactory and safe work environments. It is thus, apparent to note that the consequences of low morale are more obvious and appear to be more damaging in much the same way as a man feels much more when he loses his teeth than when he has them. These may be remarked as – (i) reduced productivity; (ii) excessive tardiness and absenteeism; (iii) excessive complaints and grievances; (iv) employee turn-over; (v) antagonism towards rules and supervision; (vi) friction between employees; and (vii) alcoholism and accidents.

We may now come to the point about the building up of

morale that an organization that plans and implements programmes to ensure better motivation would be able to create high morale of the workforce resulting in positive worker attitude, better productivity and performance. Hence, it is suggested that in an organization, morale, as a group concept can be applicable under three general conditions so that it enhances productivity and performance in effective manner. These are: (1) the extent to which the members of a group have a common goal; (2) the extent to which the goal is regarded as worthwhile; and (3) the extent to which members feel that the goal can be achieved. From the overall idea on the aspects of morale development of individual as well as group in organization, it can be predicted from the opinion of John F. Mee that "good employee morale is the mental attitude of the individual, or of the group, which enables the employee to realize that the maximum satisfaction of his drives coincides with the fulfillment of the objectives of the company. In other words, the employee identifies his objectives with those of the company, not merely subordinates his own desires to those of the company."[19] Again, Allport[20] is of the opinion that morale is an individual attitude in a group endeavour. Attitude is closely linked with approaches and hence morale has both personal and social features. Katz[21], on the other hand further, believes that morale involves two factors viz. the presence of a common goal among the group members and the acceptance of socially recognized pathways toward that goal. In short, sometimes morale can be used as a group concept though it is generally associated with individual behaviour.

From the above, we should follow that a periodic evaluation of the attitudes and approaches of the people may act as eye-openers, in accordance with which motivational programmes can be planned in organizations. It is therefore, very essential that the human side of enterprise must be the focus of all policies and strategies, so that the morale can be boosted, better job satisfaction ensured, and high labour productivity can be achieved.

Despite many other issues related to the aspects of individual and group development in organisations, it is morale which impels in all an instinctive impulse to co-operative endeavour with good human relation approach and therefore, managers are to realize that employees attitude form the basis of morale towards productivity that inculcates value in judgement to revitalize the value in work. So, the workforce in organisations are to be motivated by all means of livelihood along with job satisfaction, which reduces the job stress and increases productivity. Thus, it cultivates work culture and brings in organization an atmosphere conducive to all in organizational activities, without which productivity is happened to be wasteful element of work throughout the process of management. In this respect, morale building has a great role to play in all organisations, irrespective of the nature of production system and services rendered to society. As a means towards the attainment of an end, morale boost up inherent qualities of individual, if properly cared for all, by all means are needed for the performance in organisation, considering job elements; and thus, morale has wide connotation for upbringing real values of an organisation through individual and group motivational techniques, as we have already dealt in foregoing explanations. In specific terminology and in true sense, it has to consider all such moral aspects as are needed for all in organisations which go to make personality building an element of productivity with organizational effectiveness, along with managerial leadership role in positive manner. Keeping in mind the emotional aspects, it can be suggested that in an approach to bring good morale in organisation, there should be 'we-approach' philosophy rather than 'I-ness' when workers and employees are guided by the management. This is one of the best examples of participative management in realistic manner for boost up of employees and group morale in organisation. In short, morale building in organisation can be helpful for the overall organizational development, in so far as the human development considerations are there in management of all resources for human goal oriented nature of productivity related to life, and as such, morale in organisation can further bring in relative change of individuals to the changing developmental phase of the organisation in global perspective.

Organisational Development (OD)

In this world of changing circumstances, the only permanent thing is the 'change' itself which results in disequilibrium in organisation set-up. Therefore, Organisational Development (OD) is the planned approach in efforts of managerial decision-making process that takes into account things at hand in response to various changes, which helps managers to resist that change effectively. In this regard, it is basically to be remembered that managers get every opportunity towards their endeavour to optimize the human and non-human resources of the organisations to achieve their purpose in response to organisational needs, for which there is the necessity of a blue-print for managerial decision-making, and the OD is the process gives all those opportunities to every managerial approach with their key decision-making areas; otherwise, which becomes very difficult to cope with in the fast-changing environment to handle task at hand in quite responsible manner. Hence, OD is the management of the overall organisational culture (OC), which leads to entire phase of the deplorable conditions for the developmental needs with various means and ways, and thus, it brings forth organisational strength by measuring different weaknesses and adjusts the malady in question for the purpose of bringing a balance between structure and systems and sub-systems of the entire organisation. In the words of Raymond Miles, "The jump from planned change of the total organisation system (precursed by major shifts in managerial attitudes and behaviour) to the inclusive concept of organisation development is not a large one."[22] However, considering the present global business scenario, we are to keep in mind that OD requires a long-range effort to improve an organisation's problem-solving and renewal processes, and particularly, through a more effective and collaborative management of OC – in this matter, it requires further a special emphasis in its definition of the realistic approach for bringing adequate amount of relevant change throughout the organisational activities, in its structures and any other framework for resultant development purposes. Hence, it requires emphasizing through the management on the cultural flow of work of formal work teams with the assistance of a change agent – a catalyst, and the use of the theory and technology of applied behavioural science, including action research.[23] To be more specific, we must say that an OD programme should incorporate within the framework of its approach a wide variety of change programmes that have been developed to maximize work motivation and creativity, and reduce processes such as – isolation, self-estrangement, job dissatisfaction, and aggressive conflict in organisation.

From the above discussion, it is clear that in the characteristics of the OD programme there should be a total and comprehensive approach which means that the ultimate targets of the OD must be for the entire organisation – from top management to the lowest rank, both managers and their subordinates, both formal work teams and informal groups[24], as also individual employees. It is fact that the activities performed under this approach have a wide range of dimensions – from training to counseling, problem-solving to human resource development (HRD), redesigning of structure to reorientation of the OC, etc. It is, thus, a wide connotation for upbringing the OC towards the HRD in the overall organisational structure, and thereby, it initiates a broad-based spectrum of thinking habit along with work culture in mind of people who are engaged with the organisation. Therefore, we should be careful that managers take care of strengthening both formal and informal organisation structure towards the achievement of organisational goal, besides individual satisfaction in terms of OD perspective. Considering all the aspects of development in an organisation through OD programme for the OC dynamism, it is apparent to note that an OD programme should have the educational strategy to which McFarland observes: "OD is a set of concepts and techniques by which organisation members learn to initiate, accept and cope with change, to develop trust in each other and to function effectively as members of groups and teams".[25] Some other attributes to the characteristic features of the OD like—(i) behavioural thrust; (ii) internalized process; (iii) system outlook; (iv) culture of mutuality; among important types of naturalistic ideals that are required to be concentrated by each management in organizations, so that an OD programme can be made more and more effective towards the role of different interested groups who are included along with the managers in the participative nature of development, and thus, it fosters the real growth of individuals along with the overall growth of the organization.

Keeping a track record of the developmental perspective in organization through an OD programme, it must commensurate with the sole task of some important conditionalities like – (1) fast and unexpected change; (2) growth of the organization; (3) diversification in organization; and (4) change in managerial behaviour, among others, that systematize changes brought forth for the purposive end-result of the programme, where a consultative measure is the only means for the achievement of goal in organization – the success of which mainly depends on certain conditions that makes the entire programme quite flexible to encourage, besides all staff-members of the organization. Of the different conditions, as a matter of organizational dynamism, a few suggestive points are: (i) top management support; (ii) total change; (iii) allocation of time; (iv) internal resources; (v) open participation and communication; (vi) collaborative approach, are all inclusive in an OD programme, and therefore, it is expected that the process must identify problems in an indepth analysis of different situations, which requires a diagnostic viewpoint, for the planning of strategy or some strategies, are selected with some sort of pilot project. In this regard, it is suggested that a small pilot project, or a trail run may be undertaken, if necessity arises, to find-out the relative effectiveness of the selected strategy.[26] However, an intervention makes things happen in OD, where there are a number of tools and techniques available for the purpose of such an intervention in practice. As for individual employees – human resource development (HRD), which comprises many devices of inter-dependent nature, including performance and potential appraisal and career planning, among others, are some important aspects of development. For inter-personal relations-sensitivity training to increase skills of employees for interaction. Similarly, for team or group-team-building to diagnose and solve problems collectively; for inter-group relations – integration of attitudes, liaison group, confrontation, meetings, and the like attributes. For the organization itself as a whole – survey-feedback, and for managers – grid training, all these are important aspects of development for various interested groups and individuals in an organization who are in one way or otherwise, concerned with such OD programme in an organization. As a result of this, it is further important to note that an OD must be complemented and, it should be compiled through an evaluation technique; besides being, there should also be a feedback approach inherent with the organizational approach, for it streamlines all activities towards the organizational goal, where individual as well as group goals are assimilated in conformity for the unity in strength of the overall programme. Thus, it is the OD intervention that acquaints managers with a few select norms like –life and career planning approach, role analysis technique, role negotiation technique, T-Group or Sensitivity training[27] for the perspective development of the organization along with changing elements that strengthens the organization by bringing in it a dynamic culture for individuals' and group members' personality development.

It is, therefore, an effective OD programme by which the organization is successfully moved from an undesired current state to a desired and planned future state for all its individuals and groups in parallel way to the organization as a whole. This holistic approach brings the functioning of the organization in planned manner towards the attainment of the need in its future state which meets in earlier expectations for the universality of the chalked-out programme, and so, the transition from one state to another is achieved without unreasonable cost to the organization and its members as prescribed by Moorhead and Griffin.[28] In short, an OD programme, if properly taken care of by the management results in true industrial democracy (ID), which is the need of the hour in our country, in the context of present crisis throughout the business environment; because as a whole, the OD furnishes the viewpoint of vital developments with the relevant changing circumstances of the organizational environment, and thereby, it helps building up morale (already discussed earlier in this Chapter) for a broad-based system of the sensitive OD in reality with its ultimate reality of the achievement of goal. Thus, it enriches the organization in the spheres of results in operational areas, along with other objective basis of the organization, being the subject-matter of the concept is all-comprehensive as it results to an expected way of development of the organization and its members for the greater creativity, less hostility toward others, and greater sensitivity to social psychological influences on work behaviour, etc. It thus, inculcates a wide range of behavioural goal towards the success of the organization for bringing a balance between group members, by co-ordinating different aspects of development in harmonious manner in universally accepted principles with the norms of unifying the basic characteristics of realistic assumptions towards the needs of the organization for the sociological dynamicity, for which individuals and groups conform to the policies and practices of life in futuristic development, to enhance their perfection in dealing with the organization in socialistic perspective manner. In short, the OD is the culminating principles of the OC that strengthens the behavioural pillar of the organization for the HRD goal in broad spectrum.

Organisational Culture (OC)

Organisational culture is an attempt to give meaning to the uniqueness of a specific set of human relationships in an organisational setting. It is studied here, because by this concept it will be made clear that some set of values, which are often taken as granted can be helpful for a broad understanding over the issues which lead to different human actions in a systematic manner – the issues involved with those activities for getting the work done through, are considered to be either acceptable to some occasion from organizational point of view, or unacceptable for those which go to confront organizational decision-makers at a stake, regarding the development of organization. Hence, organizational culture or in short, OC is the value concept in managerial perspective that have to be communicated through, by each management in terms of specific stories, or also with some sort of symbolic means. In other words, an OC can also be interpreted as the psychological structure of the organization in composite manner and its sub-units, as it has a significant role to play in the overall analysis of human behaviour – values, beliefs, thoughts, ideas and so on. It is therefore, true to say that the OC brings in organization a harmonious inter-relationship between different groups who are in organizational set-up mutually interrelated while going to perform some defined objectives in common to all of them at organization level, for doing the tasks in efficient as well as effective manner.

From this, it should not be out of place to mention that the OC is the quality perspective, in so far as it deals with certain norms and values in human dealings, and thus, the subject-matter of the concept covers a wide range of areas in respect of quality management ideals and notions, where each manager has to come-up with the cultivated process of enlightening the people through specific set of goals, following which an organization is always guided by the management to strengthen the organizational environment (OE) with the help of certain principles like – (i) work culture and quality circle principles; (ii) value-based management principles; (iii) participative nature of dealing with the people and the tasks; (iv) role analysis and goal concepts from different viewpoints; (v) structural adjustments and norms of behavioural attitudes of people who are, otherwise engaged with different types of jobs. Besides, job-related issues like – pay-scales and allowances, perks of other benefits related to job, job enlargement, job satisfactional other conditionalities, non-economic elements of convergent as well as divergent issues, are some of the inter-related principalities which are contained under the OC. Again, in matter of the total quality management (TQM) perspective, truly speaking, the OC has a wide meaning in organization, as it gives meaning to the uniqueness of a specific set of human relationships in an organizational setting while the TQM concept for the OC should be emphasized on symbolic means, by which the values of the organization are so communicated. All these require that there should be a teaching process for a broad understanding of the subjective view of the OC – the basic vehicle for embedding an OC is concerned with such goal of the management, as the desired objective behaviours and activities are learned through experiences, symbols, and explicit behaviour. In concentrating to the symbolic means for the application of the OC norms in their organizations, managers are to include symbols for the organizational effectiveness like – (i) symbols, stories, myths; (ii) sagas, legends, folktales; (iii) heroes, slogans, languages; and (iv) ceremonies, rites and rituals, etc.; so that the entire process of management is guided by them all for individuals and a collective behavioural conditionalities are fulfilled. However, norms of behaviour are prescribed for – how to behave under different circumstances, how to treat different questions, and similar other issues in practice. Hence, it is undoubtedly to be noted here, that culture in organization resembles with influences how decisions are made, the style of management and relations and behaviour patterns in the organization, which is created through different happenings; besides the above points already noted. In short, the culture in organization is also influenced by the use of material objects and the look and arrangement of physical settings.

About the importance of basic values, it has to be remembered that it is to show what is rewarded and what is sanctioned in the organization, though values can arise from the organization or from individuals. To the clarity of thought some examples of business values are – (i) quality is important; (ii) cost effectiveness is important; (iii) being the market leader is important; and (iv) customer service is important, which require that the OC should further keep for individuals some provisions of individuals' values, that are – (i) the right to try and to fail is important; (ii) safety is important; (iii) team-work is important—these are among others, help all individual members in organisation for good co-operation in their work environment with all those whom they perform together with a common purpose. We may now come to the point that the existing OC is the result of implemented decisions and events that have shaped the organisation's way of thinking and operating. Every new strategic decision is therefore, an attempt to influence the culture or the organisation's way of performing to achieve the desired results. If the culture does not support the new strategies, most of the time the strategies will never get implemented. Hence, the organizational culture must be "in tune with" or attuned to the strategy. In this regard, it should be right to say – "when you have the people who share the same values, goal, and purpose, and given the opportunities and incentives to excel in a supportive environment in which they feel free (empowered) to contribute as a team, then the work scope will be productive."[29] A detailed analysis of this case may throw light on the various aspects of the dynamics of organizational behavioural pattern, and is therefore, the opinion of Filley[30] in the context of the OC is obviously true to be cited here, which can be remarked about the effectiveness in organization – that the effectiveness we are concerned on the leaders' or the group members depend on the attitudes and approaches of each other within the group in an organization, and the contribution made by each. From the overall discussion, it seems clear that the cultural part as studied in relation to an organisation has a philosophical meaning as it identifies the soul of the organization towards the making of common unity between man and man, in terms of its very significant contribution for life. In the words of Vivekananda it can be said that " often in the turmoil and struggle of our lives we seem to forget it, but suddenly some one dies – one, perhaps whom we loved, one near and dear to our hearts, is snatched away from us – and the struggle, the din and turmoil of the world around us cease for a moment and the soul asks the old question, "What after this?" "What becomes of the soul?"[31]. Similarly, in the context of the OC there we find that an organisation has its own soul and heart. If we take into account on the history of organizational entity, it goes to say that the organizational entity concept is the soul for which purpose it is established – people, is the heart, ignoring which the goal of the organisation can never fulfill individuals' demand for human perfection in lives of their destiny toward an end of life, and therefore, the philosophical concept of the cultural assimilation which is basically felt in unity can never fall under prey, if the organisation has to be studied at all, in realistic perspective. So, the OC is the immortality concept in regard to human struggle for a common destiny through different paths in organizational life in an open (free) environment, crossing all barriers of life, i.e., managerial decision-making processes for achieving the goal of unifying the concept of the culture as we are concerned in an organisation pyramid with all capabilities, awareness, and distinctive features of the individuals who are, otherwise guided by the ship or vessel of life like – organisation. Hence, OC in action complements the inherent forces of work ethics, principles of human value, and dynamicity of life through growth and development of people who are concerned with the organisation for their betterment.

Organisational Change and its Management

The success of an organization is dependent on its adaptation to the situations of changing environment to which an organisation survives, strives, goes ahead with growth and development. In doing against this situation something, it is nothing but the possibility of organisation's complacency, stagnation, inefficiency, and decline at the end. Hence, organizational change has to be accepted by all who are managing organizations for the optimum development of man-power resources through organizational activities. It is very essential therefore, that the management should be careful about the change that would have to be shouldered in pro-active manner to reduce human stress, organizational cost and increase efficiency of work. On the overall experience to which an organisation has been observed in historical perspective, it should be said that change is a universal phenomenon and, it is the duty of the management to cope with various changes for which there should be an adequate amount of planning – both in qualitative as well as quantitative aspects; otherwise, the change is very impossible to be overcome effectively by the managerial decision-making processes. Another important task in front of management regarding organizational change is the implementation of the planned ideas and blueprints in phased manner, so that management satisfies all who are deprived from the resultant change in organisation, and thus, they come across with new discoveries and inventions at different intervals of change which relate to encompass it with the cause-effect relationship of human behaviour. Thus, there should be expected level of motivation to be infused and enhanced in mind of the organizational people, who are otherwise reluctant to adjust with the change. As a matter of fact, it is very essential that there should be adequate provisions for training and counselling services to be taken at hand by managers, for, this can build-up good morale in organizational environment.

As we know that change as a whole can take place in organisation from different spheres like – technology, technical know-how, population growth, machinery, equipments and tools, methods and procedures of production work as well as administrative behavioural norms due to change in legal system, politics and government, human behavioural phases like – human skill, talent, and education, culture, philosophy, etc. Besides, there are hundreds of issues cause to change organizational structure, management style, system of managerial decision-making and many other attributes of functioning for optimizing various resource utilization, along with human resource development (HRD) in organisation, as there is always open competition in the external as well as internal environment of the organisation in which it operates. However, an important suggestion regarding change management is the organizational development (OD) perspective from multi-dimensional sides, as it is ubiquitous to have a change in continuous manner, in which an organisation gets life due to mutually inclusive and exclusive elemental adjustments in different divergent as well as convergent conditions that give birth to a resultant change in organisation. Whatever be the pattern and form of change, an effective management of the new change every time which the management faces must have to be controlled from the perspective of organizational dynamicity, behavioural explicit order of unifying the forces to be conveyed with the mutuality principles of human harmoniousness, in so far as the result of the change is concerned for the effective development of the organisation and its people. An important way of managing change is the information processing at right time, and therefore, it is advised that managers should be cautious about each important information in organisation that has relevancy to the changing phase of the organisation. For this, there should be mission-oriented tasks to be covered within the range of informations that management is required to be adopted for successfully overcoming change, so that it brings in positive manner all the benefits of change for all in the organizational set-up at present, and also, in future managerial effectiveness; for the organisational effectiveness is dependent of the management of change in such manner as it can produce maximum benefits for all in organisation, who are guided by such mission of the organisation that perpetuates optimality of the journey in relation to human perfection.

In this regard, it can be asserted that organizational dynamics provide for necessary change in the organisation charts and manuals from time to time. This is perhaps, the reason why the charts and manuals always present an approximate picture of the organisation in cohesive manner. Therefore, every change must be managed through participative management principles which guides the organisation in regard to attaining the goal from universalisation of the managerial attitudes that embraces with the tools and techniques of change management, for the purpose of unifying the principles of work in integrating manner. Because, by means of integration it produces result towards an end that establishes relationship of 'path-goal' approach – an approach always felt with the need satisfying thrust of the organisation for its people who are motivated by this technique for effectiveness in their action-oriented journey of life in organizational set-up. It is further to be remembered that resistance to change, if any, observed in organisation, which may be either positive or negative, or it is also true that it can be constructive according to circumstances – for if, it causes management to rethink the problem, re-evaluate alternatives, confer with involved personnel, and search for better solution; in which John Kotter and Leonard Schlesinger[32] has given six methods for managing resistance to change, the study of these methods will help managers for their effective implementation while coping with changing environment with an enhanced capabilities for running different activities in their organizations, and thereby management might be able to grasp at different situational analysis as prescribed aforesaid in various discussions. It is suggested that planned organizational change can effect in anticipating for the re-designment of managerial policy implications, as it involves the organisation in programmed way of dealing with problems that are encouraged for the optimal solution, which is defined by John M. Thomas and Warren G. Benins as: "the deliberate design and implementation of a structural innovation, a new policy or goal or a change in operating philosophy, climate and style.[33] Thus, a planned change is the preferred avenue for dealing with change. Kurt Lewin[34], a well-known psychologist, further developed a three stage process to be followed when introducing planned change for the effectiveness of the management to bring for organizational effectiveness.

However, it is sometimes criticized that Lewin's model is though very simple and straight to the point, it often fails to encompass some of the critical dimensions of the change situation in organisation, and hence, a change process model that expands on the Lewin model and views the process from a top management perspective, was developed by Moorhead and Griffin.[35] It suggests that in the first phase of the expanded change process model, top management scans the environment and perceives that certain trends dictate a needed change. The change problem then goes through the organisation's normal problem-solving and decision-making processes and thus, the alternate change actions are generated therefrom, and also evaluated, and consequently, an appropriate one is selected out of it. Often, early in the process, the organisation seeks the assistance of a change agent.[36]

From the above analysis, we may consider the fact that the effectiveness of an organisation is influenced by the organisation culture, which affects the way the managerial functions of planning, organizing, staffing, leading, controlling are carried out. Given the choice, most people would probably prefer to work in an organisation, in which one can participate in the decision-making process, one is evaluated on performance criteria rather than on the basis of friendship, one has open communication channels in all directions, and one has the opportunity to exercise a great deal of self-control. As it is observed that many managers emphasized the management of their organizations from different cultural implications, in their search for excellent companies, Thomas Peters and Robert Waterman, the authors of a best-selling book on management, found that the dominance of a coherent culture characterized these organizations.[37] Thus, it should be remembered that effective enterprises develop and nurture an appropriate organisation culture, for which there should be actual value system guided by human resource development programmes, and wherein, it is suggested that the success of organizations should commensurate with value-driven corporate leaders.[38] To conclude, it can be undoubtedly said to give direction to the divergent cultures, Smith[39] distributes "culture cards" that states the company's mission: "The fundamental purpose of General Motors is to provide products and services of such quality that our customers will receive superior value, our employees and business partners will share our success, and our stock holders will receive a sustained, superior return on their investment."[40] This is another good example to understand how an organisation culture has to be managed for the overall effectiveness of the organisation by the management. Hence, we should always keep in mind that management of organisation is to be guided by good cultural heritage that necessitates a clear vision of a common purpose elicits commitment for which communication must be open and diversified through different channels in the organisation.

In management of organizational change, it is another interesting sign of move to be kept in mind of leaders that the entire move is guided toward a unified operational theory of management is the way that research and analysis have tended to merge motivation and leadership theory[41]. However, the management of change in organizations can be effectively brought through an understanding that organizations may be in a state of equilibrium, with forces pushing for change on one hand, and forces resisting change by attempting to maintain the status quo on the other. This is one of the techniques for initiating change and its management for organizational effectiveness in managerial pursuit of handling tasks at hand in planned manner. For which Kurt Lewin[42] expressed this phenomenon in his field force theory, which suggests that it is maintained by driving forces and restraining that the resultant change motivates all people in organisation.

Synthesis of Thought

We have seen that the genesis of organizational thought is encompassed on the scales of human life which is based on an understanding about human creativity.[43] This creativity being differently opined by scholars, it is expected in our case, to deal with organization in systematic manner for the purpose of attaining perfection in men. As we know that philosophy of work is related to human life in societal order, therefore, it should be remembered that the systematization of the societal goal is attained through such path which provides, in every endeavour of man a relativity

– the mathematics of our relativistic assumptions are based on logical considerations. Hence, human organization is one of the best logic that enlightens human knowledge, and this knowledge being related to human life, there should be optimum development of man, for which purpose in historical perspective people are observed to be organizing in society. This is aimed at a common purpose, wherein men have been searching for their ultimate aim of life – liberation. Because of attaining this end of life, among other considerations in the midst of human grouping efforts towards any endeavour for living, human perfection is thus, guided by their liberating questions, for which we should keep in mind that management is one of the most important aspects of liberation in systematic order of life through synergistic[44] group effort. In organizing so, there should be true consciousness which tries to harmonise all those philosophical aspects of life as aimed at a unity in time and space for managerial goal of problem-solving affair. The synthesis of thought in organizational pursuit of man should therefore relate to an understanding which not only compounds and serves as complementary to the morality of human beings for the ultimate results, but also assimilates the different diversities of managerial responsibility that guides people in mission-oriented, vision-related, and an idealistic-order of life – this is being aimed at, in science and philosophy, from time immemorial periods in the history of mankind, both in the Eastern as well as the Western hemisphere, there is the necessity of an optimum order in society, which is felt through universal idealistic principles by all scholars from different subjective point of view, and hence, an organization is said to be an actual forum that guides human beings to establish in such super-structure of life. As we see that man finds himself unable to tackle many of the things he comes across, he fails to understand some of the'mysteries' of Nature. This is one of the reason that an organization is the orderliness in an instrumental manner that binds men in society for the harmony in the midst of human cultural diversity, for the purpose of attaining different ends of life that ultimately gets man in the journey of perfection for understanding the different principles related to work, and its philosophy to give exact perfection as enshrined to the aim of life. In management of human resources to the organizational pursuit of man, it has been followed that there is always disparity that produces inefficiency in work. This is due to lack of such knowledge that disinterestedness in work is the purified concept of bringing harmony[45], for which, we are here, trying at our level best on this Earth. It is therefore, my aim is to search for the ultimate unity through human organizational concept that binds man and man in society, without being binding for a bondage of life; but to seek for the liberating tendency in moral pursuit of human activities in managing other resources; so that human creativity, as explained in Chapter 1 is applied for the cosmological beauty of the truth of life through different socio-economic activities which cause to establish a good human relationship to an attitude for the development and growth of society by organizing abilities, capabilities, and effectiveness of people. This is one of the aim of unifying the principles of work for the common pursuit of development in one hand, and to reduce conflict between man and man on the other; that being the actual order of life, the ideal of organization must therefore, be guided by human ethics of providing a secured foundation and for the freedom of life[46]. Keeping in mind this principle of organizing aim of human beings, we must remember that all concepts of the philosophy regarding human religion and its nature are merely abstractions, because we nowhere come across the ideal humanity, but we are asked to believe in it, otherwise progress of man will be impossible to the society in years to come.

In course of describing management as the fundamental break-through in universal phase of human development, it is to be noted that organization by its creative process guides people for their destiny that unfolding towards managerial talents and competency regarding each work performance for the goal of harmonious life; and as such, it is better to understand the subjective notion on the basis of cosmological boundaries, so that human conflict can be minimized for increasing human skills and efficiency towards the need of satisfying the goal of liberation by attaining tasks in effective manner. Thus, the approach of human behaviour is guided for relativistically accumulating the different purposes in one common aim at the end – liberation. As we know that human nature is always prepondering to work-out the 'Infinite' from various sources which can never be described in any language, it is the organisational pursuit wherein different aspects are related for such an end, either in managerial style of leadership, or through communication processes in organizational structure, in different manner that fulfils the various conditions of life towards the destiny. Hence, each activity must be carried on, in an understanding that "There is One Unity"[47] which assimilates in diversity, and in diversifying those elements, or the forces acting and inter-acting together, each group in organization is motivated towards the competitive nature, or zeal of human performance, so that their collective effort guides them for such a common end of life that bridges the entire journey of life – from cradle to grave. In human history, it is observed that many a times people have been in conflicting situations, for which human civilizations are ruined as the prey of their unfinding destiny. It is, therefore, suggested that in organization, there should be a universal approach bringing men in unity, instead of multi-facets diversity; because, by this process each organization will be able to guide the social-being for a unified theory that man needs for the harmonious cause-effect relationship in behavioural pursuits for optimum development and growth of society, by collective development and growth of each individual in organizing different activities of their everyday efforts toward the attainment of result for crossing the barrier of life, in matchless beauty of the nature of management – to synthesize this aspect of development, both from within and without, management has been given due importance to cater this need in organization of human activities through relentless efforts in an unflinching manner.

References

1. This civilization was very simple and organized where people had their complete socio-political will in an administrative system, guided by civilized nature of living. In towns and cities, there were well-developed roads, and trade and commerce was completely organized, besides being, though the entire civilization was urban-economy based. Therefore, it is essential to note that there were highly developed art and culture, architectural design and organized agricultural trading centres prevalent in many parts of the whole civilization, as comparing the relative developments. It is thus, said in the historical perspective that Indus Valley people, as their way of life, organized the entire social administration, on the basis of articulated and civilized means of human progress as their ends of life. In short, there was good social co-operation between man and man, people to people interaction, and besides, ideal collectivism throughout the whole administration of the organized way of their living. As such, it is quite essential and right to say that many records of this civilization give an illuminating view on the overall organizational system of the society, whereby the people in such a developed civilization were found to be mutually progressing by means of communal harmony and perpetuating for life, a great deal of their socio-cultural activities. In conclusion, it may be pointed out that the basic character of the Indus civilization was secular, utilitarian and urban. This civilization centred round big cities with great amenities of city life and the people preferred utility to beauty. – Maiti, Provatansu, *Studies In Ancient India,* Shreedhar Prakashani, Calcutta, Seventh Edn., 1988, p. 20. Thus, *"the integrity of the Indus civilization stands unchallenged"*. – Wheeler, M.: *The Indus Civilization.* See also, Basham, A.L., *The Wonder That was India.* About the systematic organized way of life of the

Indus people, it can be said from the authoritative work of Pusalker that they used various types of weights and measures. A strict control was exercised to maintain proper standard of weight. The decimal system was also known to them. -Pusalker, *Vedic Age,* p.178-79. It is true that there were well-designed public bathing-place, latrines and bath-rooms, well-sketched maps of roads, among others, in the progressive mode to the life of such civilized people. Besides, it is argued by the historians that the Indus people had a brisk trade link with Western Asia which is evident from the discovery of the Indus seals in these areas. It is therefore, apparent to say that the organisational approach of human management system is a time immemorial concept of the history, where this civilization is a glaring example that furnishes a view on the cultural heritage of the life of ancient people who were, in many respects of their social life culturally concerned with the entire phase of socio-economic activities, and thereby their organisation was strategically developed for the purpose of the ends of their perfection.

2. In discussing about the *"Science of Unfreedom"*, Zygmunt Bauman (1976: Ch.1) in his famous work on "Towards A Critical Sociology: An Essay on Commonsense and Emancipation" has argued about the second nature and the commonsense as: "...........Answers to this challenge occupied the whole continuum from the outrightly manichaic solution to that which tried hard to steer clear of temptations, and which, in the end, put in question the omnipotence of the central power". As we know, he further argues...........It was accepted, again from the time of St. Augustine, that evil is a purely negative phenomenon rather than another 'substance': evil is the non-possession of grace and derives from the inability of the wan, imperfect human creature to reach the 'ought' prescribed for him in God's mind; the possibility that God may be somewhat less than

omnipotent, or - worse still - that He might be a source of evil as well as the source of God, was considered unacceptable................On the one hand, the occurrence of deviant, and by definition disruptive, acts was traced back to the technical imperfection of the many means applied by society to keep its members in check - to the society which was not quite upto the task. On the other, particularly in the Adam Smith - Max Weber tradition, departures from the 'normal' pattern sponsored by society were ascribed to the intrinsic, or residual irrationality of human action - and, in particular, to the emotional, non-intellectual layers of human personality. ....By Comte as well as by Weber, this superiority was organised along historical lines - the rational system superseding that founded upon affection - and was thereby projected as the axis of societal progress. However, it can be well said that sociologists, on the whole, side with the social practice which tends to denigrate, condemn and supress drives defined as 'biological', deriving from the human animal infrastructure and in opposition to those socially inspired and legitimized. They, therefore, posit their own formula of objectivity and truth-pursuit as the historical tendency of the human world as such.

3. Arnold Toynbee says, "...........it is already becoming clear that a chapter which has western beginning will have to have an Indian ending if it is not to end in the self-destruction of the human race ......At this supremely dangerous moment in human history, the only way of salvation for mankind is an Indian way. If India were even to fail to live upto this Indian ideal which is the finest, and therefore, the most exciting, legacy in your Indian heritage, it would be a poor look-out for mankind as a whole. So a great spiritual responsibility rests on India. However, the unified approach of the management thought which is mainly, guided by the organisational mission and

the relevant philosophy of human socio-economic activities, are all, believed to be, as one of the social thinker Revered Sri Guruji, so called by this name and style in Indian order, as said and explained in the works of Dattopant Thengadi - (Third Way: p. 306) that the world unity and human welfare can be made real only to the extent that mankind realises the ultimate, absolute Vedantic Truth that 'All is One' what he envisaged was not elimination of all distinctive features of nations and rolling them all into one uniform pattern...................It is the one real practical world-mission, if ever there was one. Many social scientists and political philosophers in India, in the reconstruction of the society as to what should be human base in organising to the society, has said on these principles of the Vedanta philosophy that management of human resources are required to be implemented in different socio-economic activities for the highest end of life, for attaining organisational goal with perfection of life through an orderly based sociological foundations, as the fundamental approach of unification through human different types of organisations.

4. Freedom, as we know, that Buddha had also given importance on it in His philosophy on the teachings of human life. He gave the highest place to fraternity as the only real safeguard against the denial of liberty or equality. Fraternity was, as propounded by Himself, the another name for brotherhood of humanity; which was again, another name for Dharma. Hence, it is true that only brotherhood can protect freedom and equality in beings. In short, this brotherhood is also called social oneness, which has to be preserved while working in organized way for living social life in universal order. Thus, it systematizes the entire fabric of the vitality of life in commonness of thinking along with diversifying the goal of life in an unending journey, to get the ultimate perfection

by human organization and, its correct philosophy that guides people with respect to their numerous social activities.

5. It is a revolution in the field of industry. However, during the period from 1400 to about 1700 modern civilization passed through its first great economic upheaval. Industrial Revolution may be said to have embraced: (1) the modernization of industry and agriculture; (2) the application of power to industry; (3) the development of the factory system; (4) a sensational speeding up of a transportation and communication; and (5) a marked increase of capitalistic control over nearly all branches of economic activity. Although the revolution began as early as 1760, it did not grow its full momentum until the nineteenth century. Many historians divided the movement into two great stages, with the year 1860 making the approximate boundary line between them – the stage from 1860 to the present is often referred to as the Second Industrial Revolution, and the former as the First Industrial Revolution. However, the first being is also called as the Commercial Revolution in historical perspective.

6. In England the number of inhabitants rose from 4,000,000 in 1600 to 6,000,000 in 1700 and to 9,000,000 by the end of the eighteenth century. The population of France grew from 17,000,000 in 1700 to 26,000,000 about a hundred years later. This is one of the good examples about the growth of population in the West, at the time of the Industrial Revolution periods. Again, the initial stage of the Industrial Revolution, from about 1760 to 1860, witnessed a phenomenal development of the application of machinery to industry. As for examples, it can be said that 'spinning jenny' by James Hargreaves in 1767, water frame by Richard Arkwright about two years later, the mule by Samuel Crompton in 1779, and power loom, which

Cartwright patented in 1785, and besides many other applications of the discoveries and inventions of modern science like – the steam engine in the field of textile and other industries, telegraph for communication purposes, and introduction of a jet of air into the molten iron in blast furnace, are all commandable tasks of industrial achievements for the present gigantic size, and commercial activities that would not be otherwise possible in so large-scale at the present situation of all its applicational patterns in global perspectives. Besides, many others like –in the field of agricultural activities and the resultant large-scale production and distribution of – (1) better breeds of livestock; (2) the introduction of new crops, such as the sugar beet; (3) the development of agricultural chemistry; and (4) food supply, medicines, etc., are all to be great achievements of modern science in the field of various industrial and commercial activities, which also helps in the growth of banking, insurance and many other sectors of businesses of modern socio-economic growth. In short, by 1929 electricity provided two-thirds of the power required by industry in Great Britain and an even larger proportion in Germany. - Heaton, Herbert: "Economic History of Europe", p. 518. Thus, we see that population of Germany which rose from about 25,000,000 in 1815 to almost 70,000,000 a hundred years later, as against in Europe as a whole which mounted from an estimated 190,000,000 in 1800 to 460,000,000 in 1914; and during the same period, the population of the United States which increased from 5,000,000 to almost 100,000,000 – these along with other efforts of scientific development bore more amazing fruit. By 1914, Russia was producing more iron than France; her coal production had more than doubled; and in textiles she ranked fourth in the world. No fewer than 3,000,000 people were engaged directly in manufacturing, while some of her industrial establishments employed as many as 10,000 workers.- Day, Clive : "Economic Development in Modern Europe", p. 388.

7. They summed up together that : (i) the concept of work is a group activity; (ii) the social world of the adult is primarily patterned about work activity; (iii) the need for recognition, security and sense of belonging is more important in determining workers' morale and productivity than the physical conditions under which they work; (iv) the workers is a person whose attitudes and effectiveness are conditioned by social demands from both inside and outside the work plant; (v) informal groups within the work plant exercise strong social controls over the work habits and attitudes of the individual worker; (vi) group collaboration does not occur by accident; it must be planned for and developed. – Miller, D.C.; and Form, W.H., *Industrial Psychology*, Harper, New York, 1951.

8. Bakke, Wight E., "Concept of the Social Organisation", in M. Haire (ed.) : *Modern Organisation Theory*, John Wiley and Sons, New York, 1959, p. 60.

9. Luthans, F.: *Organisational Behaviour*, McGraw-Hill Kogakusha (2nd edn.), International Student Edition, 1977.

10. The systems management approach gave birth to the McKinsey 7-S Framework, which identified seven interdependent organizational factors that need to be managed harmoniously. The 7-S factors are: (i) strategy, or the plans, (ii) structure, (iii) systems, (iv) staff, or the key human resource groups within an organization, (v) style, (vi) skills, or distinct abilities of the organisation's personnel, and besides, (vii) superordinate goals (shared values), or the significant meanings or guiding concepts that an organization instills in its members. See also,

Pascale, R. and Athos, A.: *The Theory and Management of Systems,* McGraw-Hill, New York, 1981.

11. William Ouchi and A. Jaeger studied Japanese and American management practices under the Theory Z Concepts about the organizational stability. According to their study, the three fundamental headings on which both these firms were classified are: (1) Type J firms which use typical Japanese management practices; (2) Type A firms which use typical American management techniques; and (3) Type Z firms which are those highly successful American firms that use many of the Japanese management practices. More about this, it can be said that they confined their studies on the basis of comparison among the management practices of Type J, A, and Z firms, which is the most striking element of Theory Z of the organizational concept in management. It is thus, assumed and worked out that the Theory Z management is its adoption of Japanese management practices when they can be made compatible with the practical demands of the American business environment. – Ouchi, W. and Jaeger, A.: "Type Z Organizational Stability in the Midst of Mobility", *Academy of Management Review,* 1978. Hence, they set, to demonstrate other examples, of the manner and similarly said, in which Type Z management incorporates......it is the task of every manager to study and adopt appropriate management practices from other cultures. – Burton, Gene and Thakur, Manab: '*Management Today* – Principles and Practice', Tata McGraw-Hill Publishing Company Limited, New Delhi, 1996, p. 58.

12. In regard to human motivation to work and moral, it can be observed that Maslow has presented 13 propositions of human motivation; Allport is of the

opinion that morale is an individual attitude in a group endeavour; and Katz, on the other hand, believes that morale involves two factors viz. – the presence of a common goal among the group members and the acceptance of socially recognized pathways toward that goal. Finally, Herzberg and others in their studies have conceptualized the aspects of job content and job context, in the context of job satisfaction.- See Maslow, A.H., A Theory of Human Motivation, *Psychological Review,* Vol. 50, 1943, pp. 370-96 (Reprinted); Allport, G.W., The Nature of Democratic Morale; in Watson (Ed.), *Civilian Morale,* Boston, Houghton, Mifflin, 1942, Ch.1; Katz D., Group Morale and Individual Motivation, Hulett Jr.and R. Stanger (Ed.), *Problems in Social Psychology,* Illinois, 1952, Ch.14; and Herzberg F., Mansuer B., *The Motivation to Work,* Wiley, New York, 1959.

13. According to Abraham H. Maslow, the basic needs of man, classified in five categories, stand in hierarchical order. These are: (1) Physiological needs, (2) Safety needs, (3) Belongingness or Social needs, (4) Esteem needs, and (5) Self-actualisation needs. See also Maslow, A.H.: *Motivation and Personality,* Harper & Row, New York, 1954, and Maslow, *'Motivation and Personality',* 2nd ed., Harper & Row, New York, 1970.

14. Davis, K.: "Human Behaviour at Work: Organizational Behavior", McGraw-Hill, New York, 1977, p.107. Thus, any manager should have leadership qualities, while all leaders need not necessarily be managers. However, if a good manager possesses leadership qualities, which can be an asset, he can be more effective in motivating his people. This requires his communication abilities, among others, which is a composite of (a) information given and received, (b) a learning experience in which certain attitudes, knowledge and skills change, carrying with them alterations of behaviour,

(c) a listening effort by all involved, (d) a systematic fresh examination of issues by the communicator himself, and (e) a sensitive interaction of points of view leading to a higher level of understanding and common intention. See Ordway Tead, The Art of Leadership, 1935.

15. As qualities of leadership may change from situation to situation, place to place, and time to time, and hence generalization may be difficult. Therefore, Kolasa's observation regarding leadership qualities though seems to be self-explanatory, yet he observes: "it seems clear that while there is no such thing as a 'general leadership trait' or any trait that seems to be necessary in all situations, there may be generality or transfer of characteristics from one situation to another. As might be expected, the more alike the situations, the more the composition of leadership remained the same". – Kolasa, Blair J.: *'Introduction to Behavioural Science in Business'*, Wiley Eastern, p.520. It is therefore essential to remember that a leader should have such qualities which go to motivate his people in positive manner to get actual guidance for perfect journey of life through organizational vision, mission and alike other elements of work to the goal of enterprising.

16. In this regard, a Japanese technique such as Quality Circle (QC) can be enthusiastically applied in Indian industries and organizations to motivate people at work place. However, the concept of the QC is small team of employees (say 8 to 12) from the same area/ unit/shop/department doing similar type of work who meet together voluntarily for about one hour a week to identify, analyse and resolve work-related problems. Thus, the themes taken up by QCs for discussion do not always relate to the problem of quality alone but any issues affecting quality, safety, productivity, cost reduction etc. Hence, in Indian organizations this can go a long way to motivate

people for enhanced productivity and organizational development along with individual as well as group goal satisfaction, and so the modified version of this technique, as like Japan had adopted in its own way taking from America long back to Japanese culture, Indians further according to the realities in management in Indian environment can prefer to equip with the need-based schemes of such preferential treatment in different organizations and industries as a measure of new motivational technique, as arising in practice from time to time in changing phase of social development and organizational role playing for the overall goal achievement in society. – See also Grapevine, Norfolk : " Virginia Naval Air Rework Facility", 1982; Cammann, Cortlamdt and David Nadler: "Fit Control Systems to Your Management Style", *Harvard Business Review,* January-February 1976.

17. In this context, it is suggested that for motivational purposes in organizations the leading which we are concerned here, means influencing the behaviour of others. It must not be thought of as a single event. Thus, leadership and management are full-time responsibilities that must be practiced every hour of every day. Similarly, it is worth-noting to remember that situational leadership is an important motivational technique, and therefore, in organization it has a great role to play as it provides a vehicle for talking performance problems in a rational way that focuses on the key issues involved. In summarizing, we can at best predict that managers have to know their people to understand what motivates them in organization; they cannot just make assumptions. Even asking employees how they feel about something does not necessarily result in accurate needs assessment, because individuals (both managers and employees) will act on the basis of their perceptions or interpretation of reality and not on the basis of reality

itself. In fact, it is one of the reasons that we study the behavioural sciences because they give us ways to get our perceptions closer and closer to reality. Peter F. Drucker suggested that one's attitude toward security is important to consider in choosing a job. – Drucker, Peter F.: "How to Be an Employee", *Psychology Today,* March 1968, a reprint from *Fortune magazine.* In short, it should not be out of place to mention here that educational settings provide us with numerous examples of situational leadership in operation. See also Blanchard, Kenneth H. and Hersey, Paul: " A Leadership Theory for Educational Administrators", *Education,* Spring 1970. Hence, it is expected that Indian organizations can adopt those principles of human motivation that inculcates cultural values, moral ethics and organisational climate in work culture to uproot individual goals and assimilate it towards the success of Indian organizations, and thus, human perception has to be correlated to the process of organisational effective communication channels, so that there exists open understanding between managers, workers and employees at all levels of organisational functional relationships. This can establish real behavioural traits for strengthening human personality aspects to grow more in diversified manner in free atmosphere at the organisational internal as well as external environment throughout operational boundaries and human resource development (HRD) at the fullest level possible by this behavioural approach of managerial communication flow towards each undertaking, to venture the goal in result-oriented manner for human performance with perfection in quiet to the antiquity of management. See also Batten, J. D.: "Beyond Management by Objectives", American Management Association, New York, 1966; Miller, Earnest C.: "Objectives and Standards Approach to Planning and Control", AMA Research Study'74, American Management

Association, New York, 1966; and Reddin, William J.: *Effective Management by Objectives : The 3-D Method of MBO,* McGraw-Hill, New York, 1971.

18. Plato was born in Athens in 428 B.C., and he died at the age of 80 years in 327 B.C. He was nicknamed Plato which means 'broad'. It is important to note that the Socratic doctrine that "virtue is knowledge" became the basis of Plato's philosophy and led to his important concept, i.e., the Rule of Philosophy. About his famous contribution to society, it is worth-while to remember that Plato in his Republic constructs an 'Ideal State' which is to serve as an ideal or a model for the states of his times as well as of future. His ideal state is described as a Utopia – a city of nowhere, a state in the world of words. At the same time, it has been appreciated as a perfect model for the actual state, an ideal political system to do away with the ills of a contemporary social order. It is in short, a city based on actual conditions; it is thus, meant to mould or to influence actual life.

19. Mee John F., *Personnel Handbook,* p. 926.

20. Allport G.W., "The Nature of Democratic Morale" in Watson (Ed.), *Civilian Morale,* Houghton Mifflin, Boston, 1942, Ch.1.

21. Katz D., "Group Morale and Individual Motivation", Hulett Jr. & R. Stagner (Ed.), *Problems in Social Psychology,* Illinois, 1952, Ch.14.

22. Miles, R.E.: *Theories of Management: Implications for Organizational Behaviour and Development,* McGraw-Hill, New York, 1975.

23. French, W.L. and Bell, C.H., Jr.: *Organization Development: Behavioral Science Interventions for Organization Improvement,* Prentice-Hall, Englewood Cliffs, New Jersy, 1978.]

24. Friendship groups, cliques or subcliques are some of informal groups by which the informal organization may be formed. According to Keith Davis, "the informal organization needs to be strong enough to be supportive, but not strong enough to dominate". – Davis, Keith: *Human Behaviour At Work,* McGraw-Hill Publishing Co., New Delhi, 1975, p. 272.

25. McFarland, D.E.: *Management: Foundations and Practices,* Macmillan, New York, 1979.

26. Deb, S.: *Contemporary Issues On Management,* Atlantic Publishers and Distributors, New Delhi, 2001, p.126.

27. T-Group or Sensitivity Training is also known as Laboratory Training, Group Dynamics Training and owes its origin to the Group Dynamics concepts developed by Kurt Lewin. The first specific sensitivity training activity took place in 1946 on the campus of the State Teachers College in New Britain, Connecticut, U.S.A. However, a more systematic start was given to the technique at the National Training Laboratory established by one of Lewin's disciples, Leland P. Bradford at Bethel (Maine) in 1947. – "The Laboratory Method" in Bradford, Gibb, Benne (eds.): *T-Group Theory and Laboratory Method,* Wiley, New York, 1964.

28. Moorhead, G. and Griffin, R.: *Organizational Behaviour,* 2nd Edn., Houghton Mifflin, Boston, 1989, p.752.

29. Mink, Oscar G., Owen, Keith Q., and Mink, Barbara P., *Developing High Performance People: The Art of Coaching* (Reading, Mass.: Addison – Wesley, 1993).

30. Filley Alan C., Robert, J.House, and Steven Kerr., *Managerial Process and Organisational Behaviour,* 2nd ed., Scott, Foresman & Co. III, 1976, pp. 219-222.

31. Swami Vivekananda, *Jnana Yoga,* Adviata Ashram, Mayavati, Almora, 1930, pp. 273-74.

32. Also see Kotter, John and Schlesinger, Leonard: "Choosing Strategies for Change", *Harvard Business Review,* March-April, 1979. The six methods given by them are: (i) education and communication; (ii) participation and involvement; (iii) facilitation and support; (iv) negotiation and agreement; (v) manipulation and cooptation; and (vi) explicit and implicit coercion.

33. Thomas, J.M. and Benins, W.G., *The Management of Change and Culture,* Penguin Books, Baltimore, 1972.

34. Lewin's three stages in the change process are: (i) unfreezing; (ii) changing; and (iii) refreezing. According to Lewin, the first step in the change by process is unfreezing, which means preparing the situation for change by creating a felt-need for it. In order to do this, the manager must establish good relationships with all the people who will be involved with the change. It is important to make sure that everyone understands that present behaviours are simply not effective. Therefore, this action will minimize expressed resistance to the change process. Whereas, during the changing phase the actual change is implemented. In the process, it is critical for management to carefully identify the new, more effective behaviours to be followed as well as the associated changes in tasks, people, culture, technology, and structure......The changing process follows good problem diagno-ses and careful consideration of appropriate alternatives. Lastly, refreezing is the final stage of the change process by which the change is stabilized by rewarding appropriate new behaviours. Here, the management's task is to create an acceptance and continuity for the new behaviour. It is further necessary that management provide the required resource support for the change......In a nutshell, performance-contingent rewards and positive reinforcement can be used to refreeze the new

behaviour so that it is noι easily forgotten or abandoned. – Lewin, Kurt: " Group Decision and Social Change", in G. Swanson, T. Newcomb, and E.Hartley, Eds. *Readings in Social Psychology* (New York: Holt, Rinehart, 1952), pp. 459-73.

35. Also see Moorhead, Gregory and Griffin, Ricky: *Organizational Behaviour,* 2nd Ed., Houghton Mifflin, Boston, 1989.

36. A change agent is a person or a group of persons that will manage the processes. However, the agent may be a member of the organisation or an external consultant.

37. Peters, Thomas J. and Waterman, Robert H., Jr., *In Search of Excellence,* Harper & Row, New York, 1982.

38. Such leaders serve as role models, set the standards for performance, motivate employees, make their organisation special, and are a symbol to the external environment. As for example, it can be said that it was Edwin Land, the founder of Polaroid, who created a favourable organizational environment for research and innovation.

39. Roger B. Smith, Chairman of General Motors, who has been attempting for long to change the company's culture. Also see, Whiteside, David E., "Roger Smith's Campaign to Change the GM Culture", *Business Week,* Apr. 7, 1986.

40. Clemens, John K., "A Lesson from 431 B.C.", *Fortune,* p.164.

41. It is quite interesting to note in this regard that a high degree of motivation can be also obtained through self-leadership. See, for example, Mary, Charles C., "Self-Leadership: Toward an Expanded Theory of Self-Influence Processes in Organizations",

Academy of Management Review (July 1986), pp. 585-600.

42. Lewin, K.: *Field Theory in Social Science: Selected Theoretical Papers,* Harper & Brothers, New York, 1951. As the OD is the relevant factor for initiating the process of change, it is expected that a discussion of the history of OD which contributes to the field will serve the purpose, which is not possible here. Also see, French, Wendell L., "The Emergence and Early History of Organization Development: With Reference to Influences upon and Interactions among Some of the Key Actors", *Group and Organization Studies* (Sept. 1983). As a suggestive measure, it can be asserted that the typical OD process for management to be balanced effectively with the change elements and its constituent forces require that there should be in organizational level recognition of each problems, the diagnosis of the organisation, feedback of information on the organisation, the development of change strategy, interventions, and measurement and at last, evaluation of the overall efforts. Thus, for unifying the goal in realistic manner there should further be a number of different OD programmes are used to improve organizational effectiveness and efficiency. Thus, Michael B. McCaskey's creative process is quite illuminating and relevant in this respect. See McCaskey, M.B., *The Executive Challenge - Managing Change and Ambiguity* (Marshfield, Mass.: Pitman Publishing, 1982), Chap. 8.

43. Creativity has been approached differently by different thinkers. Sinnot (1959) equates creativity with life itself by virtue of its organizing, pattern forming and questing quality. Whereas, Murray (1948) defines creativity in terms of the product. Rogers (1957) further sees creativity essentially as a process. Creative process, he defines, that it is the emergence in action of a novel relational product,

growing out of the uniquenesses of the individual on the one hand, and the materials, events, people or circumstances of his life on the other. Again, Rollo May (1959) considers creativity as process of bringing something new into birth. For Maslow (1962) creativity is a maximum of self-actualizing. He says that creativeness is not the sole prerogative of certain professionals like theorists, artists, scientists, inventors, writers or it cannot be confined to certain conventional areas. Rather, it is universal heritage of every human-being that is born and which co-varies with psychological health. From this short description, we can say undoubtedly that creativity is now regarded as the greatest asset of mankind. It is an ability that is most vital for shaping the future of man for which people organize themselves in society. Although it is fact that the subject-mater of creativity is viewed from some components like – (i) the act; (ii) the process; (iii) the object; (iv) the person; and (v) the environment – there is a common belief that any organization to be successful in this age of competition must give due importance on the meaning to understand creativity, because without creativity nowadays, it is quite impossible that any nation can develop its citizens. Hence, in management of human resources in organizational set-up creativity is the only yardstick to measure up the performance of individuals and groups for the purpose of attaining the goal of individual, group, and organization at a destined way of life. – Also see, Sinnot, E.W.: Scientific Creativity in *Creativity and Its Cultivation,* H.H.Anderson (ed.), Harper & Brothers Publishers, New York, 1959; Murray, H. A.: Vicissitudes of Creativity in *Creativity and Its Cultivation,* H.H. Anderson (ed.), 1959, pp. 96-118; Rogers, C.R.: *On Becoming a Person,* Houghton Mifflin, Boston, 1961; May, Rollo: "The Nature of Creativity" in *Creativity and Its Cultivation,* H.H. Anderson (ed.), 1959, pp. 58-63; and Maslow, A.H.: Self-actualizing People: A Study of Psychological

Health, in *The Self: Explorations in Personal Growth,* C.E. Moustakas (ed.), Harper, New York, 1956, pp. 325-32.

44. In competitive complex business environments, the present and future challenges in front of managers is the organizational effectiveness, which may be defined as the ability of the organization to obtain and efficiently utilize resources for the attainment of stated organizational objectives. Thus, effectiveness is a function of efficiency as it contributes to goal attainment. Hence, it is suggested that 'Systems Theory' in organization may be used by the manager to develop a more comprehensive methodology to create effectiveness in complex environments. Of special value to the manager is the concept behind systems theory that there is a special interrelatedness between the component parts of a system, which is similar to a universal system in the great 'Nature'. Hence, the system is prescribed because it may be defined as "a goal-oriented organism composed of parts that are interrelated in such a way that the total system is greater than the sum of its parts". Again, it is because of the fact that every goal-oriented system has the following characteristics: (1) its primary purpose is survival; (2) it must have identity; (3) it must have the ability to test reality; (4) it must have the ability to adapt; and (5) it must have the ability to cope. – Burton, Gene: *Exercises In Management,* Houghton Mifflin Company, Boston, 1990. It is therefore, worthnoting to remember that the essence of the systems theory is the "wholeness" of a system which makes it something different from, and something greater than, its individual parts. In short, notion behind this is that the total system is greater than the simple sum of its components and is, therefore, known as 'synergy', wherein two plus two is more than four. It means that if the manager effectively coordinates the efforts of related

subsystems, the result is greater than the sum total of similar independent efforts. To the mathematician, synergy is achieved when 2+2 is greater than four. To efficiency expert, synergy is achieved when two employees, work together on a task, can do more work than two employees working independently. Similarly, it can be defined in many ways from different subjective view to get result in objective manner in organizational way of life while dealing with people to get the things done through and with others, as explained in Chapter 1.

45. Bertrand Russell (1872-1970), one of the most eminent philosophers of the twentieth century opines that the Stoics, Greek philosophers led by Zeno (335-264 B.C.) in their periods aimed at living in harmony with nature because their doctrine on virtue of life was based on pure knowledge. Thus, it was assumed that to live harmony with reason is the good; everything else is worthless. Further, it was believed in ancient Indian Vedantic philosophy that the basic understanding of life and habituation is an integral quality of living which moulds human personality through scientific forms of learning. It is therefore, what is needed in management in the changed context of the world at present is the harmonious synthesis of what is best in each, and is to be adopted in the human resource management policy in organization for the betterment of society–being, it is agreed upon by all humankind from long past in human organizing behaviour in societal order, the suggestion can further, lead ahead to the goal of the society, once an organization implements such practices in work behaviour as a process of management for effectiveness.

46. As a matter of fact, we can suggest also that the 'Yoga' is one of the way for understanding such practice of life, as it is accepted and occupied in the cultural history of India from time immemorial an

unparalleled and distinct recognizance as the one and only practical system of physical, mental, moral and spiritual culture. It is now believed all over the world at large that 'Yoga' is an absolute sine qua none of the ultimate achievement of life – metaphysically, and of the religious endeavours – theologically. It cannot be denied that even today to positive sciences such as anatomy, physiology, biology, therapeutics, psychology, mental hygiene, psychotherapy, psychoanalysis and others and to cultural arts such as music, dancing, painting, sculpture, and even literature, yoga had and is a constant source of human inspiration. – Shri Yogendra, *Yoga – Asanas Simplified,* The Yoga Institute, Santacruz, Bombay, 1980, pp. 17-18. Also see, Havell, E.B.: *The Ideals of Indian Art,* p.32. From its rich variety, we can observe that there is also exact answer to get actual freedom of life in an organizational life through yoga practices, and hence, in organization of human resources it can bring real effectiveness to optimize our goal and need satisfying thrust about life processes in managing the self with such otherwise rich subject in practical exposition for betterment.

47. As we know that water from different sources ultimately mingles to the great ocean, so also in managing through different paths and techniques, we reach at the same goal through organizational process to the destiny of our life – 'Infinite'. This Infinite is though, very impossible to be described, yet the philosophy of management of the self is related to work, and is identified to an 'Unity with God', either in Law, or otherwise through integral process. By means of an agreement, in manner of ancient Hindu Philosophy, it can be said that the 'Common Unity' of the Universe once felt in mind, then only man is able to pass beyond the cycle of births and rebirths that he is able to attain immortality. Hence, it is true that births are guided by the karma performed by the self, by actions again

the activity of body-producing karma can be stopped. This is the notion of guiding life in an involvement to the Unity concept for which people organize themselves in society. This principle of organization is for the common good to the greater interest of all humankind in the world to be adopted in management philosophy with scientific temper of human knowledge base. In this regard, it should not be out of place to mention that Vivekananda, almost like an Advaitin says that reality is one absolute Brahman. Thus, he emphasizes the monistic character of reality to such a great extent that he says that reality is one but not a 'whole'. The concept of a 'whole' implies that there must be parts, which, when organized, give the whole. He therefore says, "The Infinite is indivisible, there cannot be parts of the Infinite. The Absolute cannot be divided". – Vivekananda, Swami: *Complete Works of Swami Vivekananda,* Vol. III, Mayavati, Almora, 1963, p.7. Also, it can be predicted from all such realistic perspectives that organization is but a different from the unity concept by which people are motivated to work for this sense of unity in the Nature in an integral way of doing things, with human consciousness of disinterestedness in work.

3

Transactional Thought

Ideational Background

Human behaviour is always guided by some motive, which has caused for the evolutionary process of growth – be it instinctively taken or not, there is already an existing entity in the process of the existance of life, and therefore, it is very essential on the part of human beings to unite with those elementary thematic ideas that have necessitated man for the uprooting of the personality aspects by each motive force behind human activities. Hence, psychologists and humanists in different spheres of their independent thinking have come-across with the transactional motive, while dealing with the behaviouralism conceptualities, and thence, it is observed that any theory of human psychology that has its own boundary for the exclamation of the highest attitude for finding out the goal of human personality development has gone above those limitations that are guided by motive force for undying the absolute truth in the history of making mankind's evolutionary process of existential growth, along with the survival need. It is here, the 'Transactional Analysis' (TA) has been given due importance which helps for the development with growth of human personality aspects in organization of human asset for the common pursuit of development in collective manner. Though it seems that Eric Berne, along with others, had dedicated long back for this approach[1] in modern times, we are here, dedicating to the same concept on the assumptions of work in organizing efforts of man to the managerial goal for effectiveness.

It is, therefore, very important to note that this (TA) has a wide role to play for the development of organization in modern context of globalisation of human socio-economic activities and in parallel to that to unify the principles of harmony in life which no society at present condition of the world finds to be unattainable. It is hoped that the TA would lead to strengthen the pillar of organizational structure, in so far as there is the necessity of peace in the world on the one hand, the requirement of growth and development of nations in equal setting, on the other. By putting due and balanced stress on such concept every individual would be developed for the adequate level of growth, by bringing thereby in organization attitude towards universalisation of the ethics of work for unifying the principles of human development in harmonious manner, keeping thus thereby, for all, an adequate provision for open atmosphere in organization culture, so that the universal goal of unification is guided towards one such unity where all human beings are given a chance to be adaptively accumulated for the infinite journey of human existence to the balancing of organizational health for cultural affinity in every business activities of men to the social set-up.

Because of human transactions, which go to make an organization success in attaining both the individual as well as group goals, there is the necessity of understanding arises on human transaction, due to lack of which there is mismanagement to all resources of the organization that are, in terms of input analysis guided by human asset to work-out the real output for the developmental purposes of men. So, it is the TA guides an individual in an organization for the understanding of such common pursuit of working that brings balanced state of individual as well as organizational growth by personality development of each individual in organizational setting. Thus, naturally question arises in mind as to how to deal with various transactions quite in scientific manner and with philosophical aspiration for the perfection of human life in organizational objectivity towards the attainment of human goal in an integral approach. Let us, therefore, analyse the concept from the very deep-rooted philosophy of work principles.[2]

TA Concept for Human Resource Development

Transactional analysis (TA) has come to be well-known in the field of human resource management (HRM) from the fundamental and primary famous work of Freudian psychology, who for the first time has immensely contributed to the understanding of human behaviour, though the credit goes to Eric Berne, as we have already seen from the previous discussion, for initiating the concept of TA. However, it is forth-coming to note that another important psychologist Thomas A. Harris[3] also deserves appreciation for popularizing it (TA) in his famous book entitled: *I'am OK – you're OK.* It is thus, immensely helpful for understanding as to how this basic approach has a role to play in organization, the aim of which is, basically the enterprising mission through different activities of men for the human resource development (HRD) in wide perspective. We should therefore, keep in mind that the TA is based on psychoanalytic theoretical approach, where various psychological theories and postulates on human balanced behaviour is analysed for the effectiveness of organizational work culture that fulfills the need of human enterprising goal of life through the process of adequate attitudinal development, in regard to enhance an effective human-face with proper value and judgement in different sociological intercourse of human activities rendered towards the best contribution of managerial entrepreneurship abilities – this results in the growth of human personality, that needs to be developed from the mental as well as emotional stature of fellow-feeling in entrepreneurial mission, dedicated for the sake of establishment of unity in organizational goal of life of people, who are otherwise, seen to be perverted in organization, especially, in the strife-torn business environment of India.

It is further important to know that the transaction which consists of stimulus and response of human behaviour, in the inter-personal relationships in organization it might be true and fact that one ego state of human conduct either matches, or conflicts with another ego state, and therefore, a balancing behaviour in human relationship, in terms of various transactions can be expected as and when there remains a steady-state norm over the dynamics of human behaviour in organizational set-up. Thus, the fundamental framework of human transactional thought must be understood by each manager in organization, who should come-up with such a strategic thinking in mind for the perspective development of the human resources in organization that binds all in one common knit. It is only possible, when the managerial communication is guided by the philosophy of self-surrendering attitude towards the making of a relativistic journey while going to deal with different inter-personal and intra-personal relationships for the attainment of tasks in effective manner. Hence, the TA approach as the basic tool for HRD can be known from the understanding of some norms of ego state, as we have mentioned earlier – parent, child, and adult ego present in all human beings as believed by the psychologist. But for the sake of understanding and entering into an indepth analysis, we should further better to make a journey to our thought from the view point of Indian Vedic Concept on human ego state that is guided by the naturalistic principles (called the gunas of Prakriti) – Sattva, Rajas, and Tamas, inherent in mind of people who are believed to be bound by these three conditionalities of 'Nature', an example has already been cited in Chapter 1 regarding analysis of work-related assumptions and consequently, development of human beings.

It should be remembered that getting the work done through and with others is not so easy task, once the managerial philosophy is not guided by the ethics of self-surrendering attitude towards the self-actualisation in the process of managing human activities effectively[4] that an organization is established for such important and the highest need of mankind in social history of human socialization principles, bound with the work for the ultimate cause of human liberation, as found to be given the most priority to the Indian Vedantic Philosophy in work and human life processes. However, we should try to explain all the states of human behavioural conditions as depicted above under the following short descriptions.

Human Ego States

Every individual may possess all the three ego states – parent, child, and adult; though one dominates over the other two. The parental deed seen by the child and the messages received from them are recorded straight in the mind in the early five years. The hostility of parents is recorded with apprehension and the love with pleasure. Many do's and don't are recorded in this set. It is thus taught concept of life. These are reflected in such words as 'exert more', 'donot be tense', 'everything will be O.K.', 'done well', 'never do this again' and such actions as outstretched arms, hugging, blessing, rebuking etc. Another observation about human being is the child ego state which is the recording of the response of 'little person' to what he observes and listens. It is done simultaneously with the recordings of external and imposed events which we have described as parent. Thus, most of the reactions of the child are 'feelings'. He is small, dependent, clumsy and so on. It is in short, the felt concept of life. It is reflected in such words: 'do not leave me', 'I shall not do so again', 'I wish', 'I want' and in such actions as tearful eyes, surprise on face, anger, pleasure, pleading for something, being playful, etc. One important aspect of human behaviour can further be seen from the adult ego state. About this state of life, it is asserted that the self-actualisation is the beginning of the adult. Hence, an important function of adult is to examine the data in parent: whether or not it is true and to examine the child to see whether or not the feelings are appropriate to the present. It is, thus, the thought concept of life. It is very important to remember that during early years adult is fragile and tentative. It cannot change or wipe out the recordings in parent and child. Therefore, the adult in human beings is reflected in such words as 'why', 'who', 'what' and such actions as 'listening', 'thinking', 'pondering' and 'reflecting', etc.

From the above, we may now note that any social intercourse may be parallel or crossed. The parent-parent, child-child, or adult-adult transactions are said to be parallel. These are complementary and can go on indefinitely (except child-child transactions are few as the child is a get stroker rather than give stroke creative). Parent-child, child-parent, parent-adult, adult-parent, etc., are the examples of crossed transactions. It is very important to remember that every behaviour of man is guided by stimulus-response concept of human behavioural psychology, be it guided by any type of the ego states of the mind as prescribed above. Hence, the main difficult in organization is a matching behaviour through particular type of transaction. However, in the process of organizational behaviour, the recurring set of transactions takes place in which a balance between the three ego states is achieved as Wagner remarks,[5] as far as possible. When a manager is able to motivate his people to foster an interest, self-confidence, and positive perception about the situation or job which can work as a morale booster, it would result in their functional effectiveness on the one hand, and the manager's effectiveness on the other. As we know that there may function various groups within the organization, particularly trade unions, and that such groups would have power structures, leadership structures, role structures, communication structures, and sociometric structures – reckoning with the respective needs, philosophies, and temperaments, the manager is expected to formulate a strategy to deal with each situation, which is a decisive job in making every transaction effective towards the attainment of the goal of management. Hence, it must be considered by all that mutually satisfying way of dealing with people in the organization is likely to lead to increase cohesiveness and commitment of the individuals concerned, resulting in better relations and bondage, and thereby better effectiveness, in so far as the TA is taken into consideration for increasing organizational health, and as the most vital tool for the organization development (OD), in regard to enhance a strong and good human inter-face to the organizational structure, its climate, and working conditions prevailing throughout for effective management in realistic manner. Thus, the TA can increase and work-out each members potentiality in organization, if properly implemented by such managerial effectiveness which is the important aspect of development, and in which manager's ability to deal with people is the basic ingradient.

In concluding the human ego states, it should be noted in mind that parallel style may influence the way these patterns are expressed, but parental style is also partly a response to the child's style. Parent behaviour and child behaviour, as the psychologists believe can influence one another in an ongoing cycle. According to one group of thinker, in psychology about human behaviour, it is stated that viewing the parent as "the cause" and the child as "the effect" would certainly be a serious mistake, just as it would be a mistake to think that every trouble child is a product of poor parenting. However, an ideal adult behaviour is accepted by most of the thinkers. The way how the individual deals with the people in the organization and how he behaves may be substantially, influenced by his very personality. At the same time, his personality development depends on various factors viz., heredity, environment, learning, and so on are the determinant variables[6], which can further be seen from different notion to be analysed at length elsewhere in this Chapter, so that human transactional analysis is being made effective in terms of knowing in better way about the self; which is the core of behavioural attribute, and is related with the aspects of human growth and development for the unification of life in realistic manner.

Philosophical Synthesis of TA

In discussing about the TA, we have seen that human behaviour is the guiding concept of this thought that has been explained so far in psychological order. Human management process is nevertheless, guided by the philosophy of human mind, which is the another attributing factor towards an understanding of the TA coglomerates and dagglomerates, and is thus, it is mainly necessitated by the process of the self-related concept[7]; considering which a manager can be successful in interpreting every aspect of human behaviour. The author of the Gita describes three different typologies about the types of human personality aspect, viz., typology based on the three gunas, the typology based on morality, and the typology based on social classification. However, the author of the Gita, like Samkhya theorist, accepts that nature, including human nature, is composed of the three elements called gunas, threads, or strands, or qualities, viz., sattva, rajas, and tamas. These three gunas are mingled in varying quantities which bring about differences in qualities. It is apparent to note that the empirical ego manifests the operation of these three gunas.

In matter of organizational effectiveness, it is paramount importance of having correct knowledge about the self, and so, the Indian philosophical order of life as Sri Aurobindo (1976) describes about these gunas of the Gita goes like:

"Three qualitative modes of nature are inextricably interwined in all cosmic existence. Tamas, the principle of inertia, is a passive and inert nescience which suffers all shocks and contacts without any effort of mastering response and by itself would lead to a disintegration of the whole action of the energy and a radial dispersion of substance. But it is driven by the Kinetic power of rajas and even in nescience of matter of met and embranced by an innate though impossessed preserving principle of harmony and balance and knowledge, the sattva" (p. 413).

He further says that "the Gita applies this generalized analysis of the universal energy to the psychological nature of man in relation to this bondage to prakriti and realization of spiritual freedom" (*ibid.,* p. 414). It seems that the man dominated by *tamasa* develops a personality which is prone to confusion and delusion. That is, he has neither the energy or zest of the man dominated by the rajasa, nor the enlightenment of one in whom sattva is predominant. This type is characterized by inattention, lack of understanding, indolence, and langour. It is, therefore, essential that such philosophy should be preserved in mind while dealing with people in organization which gets involved with the best essential characteristic feature as noted above, so to bring in TA an effective element for the purposeful attainment of the goal of the organization. And by contrast, the person in whom rajasa is predominant is given to attachment to the objects of desire, should be carefully guided for organizational end. Because, he is full of unrest. He is lustful and greedy. He is a creature of impulses and emotions. As a result of all these, the lust for action inevitably leads to grief and pain – because, either his ability or the opportunity available, may not help him to achieve what he desires to achieve, or his very success may lead him to further and endless exertion to get more and thus, it can be said philosophically that it generates in him intense hostility, which is affective to the organizational way of life, among others, with whom, or for which he works.

Again, contrary to this notion, we can observe from the philosophical thought that the man dominated by *sattva guna* is characterized by intelligence and clarity of vision. Hence, it should be inculcated and preserved in organization behaviour, as it would lead to good and harmonious interrelationships among groups and individuals in organization. The basic feature of behavioural attribute of a man with sattva character is that his desires and emotions are under his control, which is mostly needed in organization for the self-actualization of man. Besides, he is free from lust, anger, and greed. His actions in society are motivated, not by personal gain at the cost of others in society, but by *lokasamgraha* – the well-being of the whole society, which is the need of the hour at the present conditions of organizational sufferings and restlessness of man throughout the world environment. The additional advantage of such philosophy is that the man having such attribute of behavioural trait is guided by the speech of his personality which is related to truthful, pleasant, and beneficial; and gives no offence to others. He is scheming of mind, gentle, silent and full of self-control. He works and fulfils his obligations without the expectation of reward (The Gita, Ch. XVII, 15-17).

From the above analysis in brief, we should keep in mind that the philosophical synthesis is done with a view to understanding how 'Divine Nature' permeates in man for actualization of his own self towards the realization of the order of life in work, as it has been found that the work principle guided by such aspects can bring in effective result, though one has to work in disinterested way, not by surrendering the self from the action (through inactive), but by means of remaining in action – doing for the common good of all with sacrificing attitude, as we have seen in Chapter 1 also. It is therefore, apparent to know that the Bhagavad Gita does not endorse any one system of philosophy among those current in its time, but rather aims at achieving a synthesis about the behavioural processes, of the most and prominent among them, the Samkhya Yoga, and the Vedanta.[8] Though one cannot speak of any consistent metaphysical view-point underlying the Gita's teaching, the author tends toward a kind of theistic Samkhya regarding human attributes of behavioural qualities, which embraces the spirit-matter dualism of the Samkhya, and is here, important as well as relevant to the TA, which perculates the postulating norms regarding human personality and its growth with correct nature of development. It has a relevancy with the ultimate monism of the Vedanta – 'One in All' concept, and the all-powerful God of devotional religion, can be practised with the devotion of work, realized through the disciplined activity and the process is practicable through the meditation of the yoga – disinterested way of doing for the universal self and the common welfare.

It may now be treated undoubtedly that the word 'guna' literally means "strand", as the strands of a rope, but it also came to mean "quality" about human behaviour. Thus, though the gunas had both cosmic and psychological significance, the latter use predominates in the Gita. Hence, the translation "disposition" is more suggestive of this connotation regarding human transaction – it is because, the three dispositions manifest in organizational activities themselves in the highest order or directing faculty of the human mind, i.e., the intellect (buddhi), as three fundamental tendencies or drives, which are present in all of us in various proportions, and is intensively to be studied which requires a more indepth analysis of the scriptural views for exactly knowing the fact. Even when "purity", the drive toward knowledge and liberation, predominates, it binds the soul to the world of matter and therefore to karma (work) and rebirth; but once the intellect reaches the saving knowledge, the drive for knowledge and liberation, and a fortiori the other dispositions, now without purpose – as termed by the "disinterested" notion, wither away, leaving the soul, freed from specious connections to the phenomenal world, to enjoy its own immutable bliss – it is to be done through practices in work behaviour to achieve the goal of unification in all.

Dynamics of TA

Organisations are man-made social institution which help people to live in society to aspire for their needs related to life-process. In this course of living, people also find themselves secured when their needs are satisfied in the process of attaining the goal of the organization. If the organization does not take into consideration carefully the effectiveness of its work, it is not possible to think achieving the desired goal. Hence, an understanding on dynamics view as to how every transaction should be interplayed in an organization is mainly dependent on human motivational process, and consequently, it can be said that this concept is the guiding philosophy behind human resource management for the overall effectiveness of the organization. An organization achieves its objectives only when it has right men in right positions. It can be arranged in an organization by allowing people to act in free environment by the management to ensure that those willing to join the team are capable of shouldering responsibilities and have potentialities to grow with the organization.

TA as the motivational technique brings in organization scope for human creativity for its people with such an approach that go to develop necessary skills and technical qualities by providing them decision-making opportunities in real life situations. Thus, it opens the door of bargaining process which is observed to be common in all organizations, now-a-days, because every human being is born to win. Therefore, the dynamics view on TA attributes the fact that winning does not mean only acquisition of more wealth and material comforts, although this is a must upto a certain degree. It gives idea from this that a human being, however, does not live by bread alone and he will not get the feeling of fulfillment till he becomes a whole man. We know that for winners, achievement is not the most important thing. It is the effective manager who thinks than an authentic person experiences self reality by knowing, being and becoming a credible, responsive person. For this, it can be said that in organization people interact together where the TA approach has every possibility to make an effective inter-relationships.[9] It is true that effectiveness is not uni-dimensional or one-sided. To be effective in work setting people must do many things well, and they, as people, must derive some value from their efforts. As Benjamin Schneider opines: "To have an effective staffing process, then requires as a first step the explicit specification of exactly what is that people must do well and what they will be offered in reward for doing it."[10] This can be achieved in an organization when the objectives of human resource management (HRM) are derived from the basic objectives of the organization.

As every organization as a social institution has societal, organisational and individual goals, keeping this in mind, the important objectives of HRM through TA dynamism can be depicted as follows:

(i) To maintain productive human relations within the organisation.

(ii) To enable each person in the organization to make his personal contribution as a member of the working group.

(iii) To provide well-trained and motivated workforce to the organization.

(iv) To help the organization utilize human resources

efficiently and effectively.

(v) To help individual/group development within the organization by offering opportunities for achievement through training and other methods of HRM.

However, it should be suggested that sensitivity training – also called Laboratory Training, Group Dynamics Training and T-Group Training, which owes its origin to the Group Dynamics concepts developed by Kurt Lewin, the first specific activity which took place in 1946 has a wide bearing in the management of human resource to make organizational participants increasingly aware of, and sensitive to, the emotional reactions and expressions in themselves and others; this is one of the important objective view of TA study in organizational setting, among others. Hence, in work situations where people stroke each other freely just for being, people feel better about themselves and each other and are likely to put more energy into their work. Unless this is understood, the optimum results can not be achieved despite the motivational theories. As we have seen earlier that the behaviour of a person, his communication with others (transaction) and his overall reaction to his environment depend upon his life position and predominant ego state, there arises due importance of a sound organization structure which is a necessary element benefiting the management of the organization to go forward with the task of getting things effectively done through people. It is therefore, an objective analysis of each transaction taken strategically that could bring in result to the attainment of such goal of the organization, so that the people guided by the organization are helped with every possibilities of shouldering responsibility towards this need of the organization. This basic criteria furnishes the view of dynamics study in the management of change in different changing situations through analysis of human relationships in organization in an integrated approach. Thus, the TA when looked from such perspective view attempts to minimize the time to the efficient communication process, and cost factors in the total information exchange process. It helps to overcome resistance to the change management process. In this regard, Kotter and Schlesinger[11] suggested six general methods of overcoming resistance to change.

These are therefore essential for human motivation to the critical assessment about the incidental method of enquiry, because the subjects were, as we have observed, by Herzberg along with his associates[12] who made an extensive review of the earlier literature on job attitudes in his hygiene theory of motivation, as for example, for the explanation of the facts to find out the result of their opinion building regarding each aspect of motivational factors. It is now, undoubtedly predicted that in this method morale is gauged by assessing business situations like quantity and quality of output, regularity of attendance, number of accidents on the job, grievances, rejects or defective products. All these are behavioural method required to be brought into account for managerial attention that bridges the gap of human disintegration. Hence, the dynamics of the organizational study and its implications on group behaviour is provided by the TA technicalities which produces better result in organization for the overall gain of all interested groups, who are otherwise, seem to be diversified in such interest which hampers the growth of the organization on the one hand, and the personality development aspects of individuals and groups working in organization on the other, who are not properly managed by the authenticity of their goal of life. The TA approach in organization is believed to be based on the analysis of existence and being of human resources. So, its roots lie more in the realm of philosophy than that of science. As in the Freudian model human behaviour is based on emotion, in the existential model the philosophers who have propounded it have expressed the fear that scientific behavioural analysis may destroy or lose sight of the person's true nature of being. Thus, the organizational dynamics which is the pillar of human interrelationships is strengthened towards making man in an unified way of internalization for the development perspective from the viewpoint of organizational goal-orientation, human personality, and it brings in organization a healthy atmosphere towards the making of man a real social agent to transform the whole society in new dimensional order through business and economic activities to the venture of life processes.

From the above, we may now say that the dynamics study of TA appraises leadership role in organization who responds to situation, and to the quality of subordinates. Keeping in mind this view, we can also assume the fact that Fielder's contingency model is the effective leadership, and is based on the ability to react to the situation and act accordingly. Therefore, the TA approach in this connection is, as Fielder puts it forward, for human relations or lenient style and task-directed or hard-nosed style. It is because, the group performance, Fielder feels is contingent upon the appropriate matching of leadership style and the degree of favourableness of the group situation for the leader. To make the process more effective, we are to analyse the entire approach on transactions from three important dimensions that could satisfy the need of the organization. These are: (1) The leader-member relations which determine his effectiveness. It is the most critical variable. It shows acceptance of the leader by the group; (2) The degree of task-structure; and (3) The power of position-power through formal authority. As obvious from this fact that the area of freedom shared between managers and non-managers in organization by this technique calls for redefining constantly by environmental factors and the interaction between managers and non-managers. This can strengthen the human behavioural pursuit for attaining the goal in question, when each individual in organisation gets optimum opportunity through efficient management, and ample scope for the human personality development to the potentials of successful areas in making goal, and the relevant question in solving organizational problems. Attributing the basic ideas of the human resource creativity, this (transaction) analysis can be implemented for the strategic decisions of the organization by saving time and reducing cost of operations in the organization.

It is, therefore, objectively taken on the plane of the dynamics of human behaviour which shows that unity in management action is dependent on the resultant question of personality aspects, and thus, the TA embraces the goal of effective management of the HRM perspective, doing for the common unity of the people in objective manner, who are guided by the organisation in harmonious manner for the realization of the self-actualisation need, in terms of work-related behaviour. As there is every opportunity to the development of human personality through this process (TA), it is to be said that the efficient dealing of people by the management calls for the effective transactions for managerial dynamism and the overall technicalities of the enshrined goal of human resource development – for this view in regard to the effectiveness study of human resource creativity, the organizational dynamics study is here, concentrated through human behavioural conditionalities. Hence, the philosophy of TA has a wide connotation to the subjective assessment of dynamics on organizational study that needs managerial attention for the goal of effectiveness.

TA and Managerial Effectiveness

Every manager has responsibility to manage his people in organisation. While managing people, it is the duty of the manager to see that every transaction is handled with great care, because if, the manager is found to be unconscious about each transaction, there arises lots of problems in the organisation creating thereby a conflicting situation. So that the management can be made more and more effective towards the achievement of result, there should be a strategic view in mind of manager while going to get the things done through people. It is, therefore, essential that the manager must have to shoulder adequate amount of responsibility for profitably and potentially utilizing the resources of the organisation for the purpose of effectiveness of the entire management job. Hence, there should be adequate level of manager's mental development towards the enhancement of result in objective manner. It is the effective manager, who for the purpose of attaining the tasks at a responsible manner initiates the transaction in a given set of orderliness, for otherwise in an organisation tasks cannot be performed quite in an objective manner. However, in TA where various issues are concerned regarding organizational behaviour, it is to be said that there should be missionary goal for the purpose of getting the tasks done through people. It requires that an adult-adult approach with the naturalistic concept of behaviour is much helpful, which to the extent of management of change can bring forth the result as objectively taken for performance. In organization, there are different nature of people, but all have psychologically to be taken into consideration; because when we assessed the TA from ego states of human beings in this chapter to the foregoing analysis, we have seen that there are three ego states present in all human beings who are involved with the organization – parent, child, and adult ego. Each of these are further classified into three categories, viz., aggressive, natural and adaptive. However, either in individual, or group behaviour in organization, the personality of human beings judged by all these factorial components of behavioural traits has to cope with the changing nature of management, according to situational pattern of working. It has thus, been observed from empirical research findings that human behavioural bases are concerned with all these sorts of elementary and fundamental aspects of human personality development character. It is, therefore, an effective manager must have to communicate with his people in different order, howsoever he is being concerned with the task and handling of his people at the work place.

In this context, we can predict that a manager to his basic approach is one who is actually responsible for the work of the other people. However, in recent times, there is considerable shift of emphasis from 'the work of others' to 'result of the enterprise'. As a result of this, the TA from managerial perspective can be said to be effective when a manager is seem to be more responsible for the performance of the organization as a whole, while he is responsible for the work of his people also. Here, manager's job is a specific type of work for the achievement of the objectives of the organization making the best use of the people available. Manager's principal responsibility is his function to make appropriate contribution to the organizational goals and objectives for which he would be vested with powers. Thus, power can be a distinctive criteria. Similarly, a manager may have command over people which need not be the first and the foremost aspect; his performance is the basic factor. Drucker's observation is very much relevant in this context. It is asserted as: "Within the management group, there will be people whose function includes the traditional managerial function, responsibility for the work of others. There will be others who do not carry this responsibility within their specific assignment. And there will be a third group which is somewhat ambiguous and in-between, people whose job is that of team leader or task force captain, or people who combine both the function of advisor to top management and the conscience of a business in a certain area, with supervisory and administrative responsibility over a staff in a given area".[13]

As we know that accompanying organisational reality, there underlines the importance of understanding social perception, a manager from TA point of view must remember that the people he deals in organization have quite a complex and dynamic personality orientation from cultural as well as environmental viewpoint, and it should therefore, be infused in mind of managers to make his function of management more effective by giving due importance to individual differences in the perception of others, which are critical for understanding human behaviour in complex social settings, although perception of situations, events, objects, and so on are important in themselves. It is the communication process helps the manager to deal with his people more effectively. His every communication goal must commensurate with the life blood element in the organizational structure, because when communication stops, organizational activity ceases to exist. Hence, his communicational decisions are to be carried with the organizational strategicity and is relativistically with each transaction of his people and his own responsibility towards the making of the best effort regarding performance orientation goal. To be effective, managerial transactions must be re-engineered, so that diverse role of each group as well as individuals concerned thereto, seeks to be benefitted from those transactional approach. Nevertheless, the very purpose of managerial communication must have to be carried for controlling, and to cement relationships between sub-units, coordinate and to provide information; and to adapt the organization to changes in its environment so that the organization can survive and grow with the stability in managerial goal. He must put therefore, due attention while communicating from all concerned directions within the system and across the organisation's boundary with the environment. Another important area of managerial function to make his transaction effective for the effectiveness of the goal of overall management is that he should be very much careful to conflict in organization, while dealing with people, his tasks, and the relevant responsibilities concerned thereto for the specific goal.

As a whole, the concept of TA must have to be contained through reducing human stress and so, it is very important that managerial responsibility must also be commensurate with the stress management[14] problems and its consequences in organization, which is found to be the most vital aspect of development, and keeping thus aim in mind, human activity must be related to each in performance oriented manner for enhancing group cohesiveness in organizational setting. Moreover, for organizational development (OD) along with managerial effectiveness, there should be naturalistic bases of managerial approach conditioned with the relativistic assumptions and the strategicity of transactions, and to make the aim of OD successful, the practitioners will have to make adjustments in the techniques suited to a particular culture.[15] It is the work culture must be inculcated by behavioural attitude of managerial practices, so that each transaction can be made effective towards the attainment of organizational goal along with individual satisfaction by means of need satisfaction of people who are otherwise related to the organization. To the contemporary issues of management at this time of global change of the scenerio in the field of economic as well as business activities, the TA must be seen from managerial leadership perspective also. As regard this, it can be said that the effectiveness in management is concerned with managerial notions toward the true meaning of leadership which lies in its symbolic nature and in its substance, in so far as the interrelationships of diverse individual behavioural conditionalitiens are there, as found in organization work environment, and with group dynamics fundamental approaches; which is basically a universally accepted principle of human behaviour, be it related to the management of business or other social activities. The symbolic action perspective in leadership role for the transactional approach argues that the day-to-day actions and decisions of the leader are of little consequence to the leadership situation. What is significantly more important from effective and naturalistic viewpoint is the symbolic aura that the actions of the leader carry with them. Suppose a manager always tries to remember to send each subordinate a birthday card. Traditional leadership theories would consider this part of considerate behaviour and would assume it would result in employee satisfaction. The symbolic view, however, would see a more complex picture. If the cards are always on time and personally signed, for example, this would symbolically indicate caring and concern. To the extent that other behaviours are consistent with this interpretation, the manager will be respected. On the other hand, suppose the cards are often late and obviously signed by a secretary. Worse still, imagine that the subordinate's name was misspelled! This sequence of events would denote a lack of attention and concern by the manager and would likely result in resentment or disrespect. Thus, it may not be content of the decisions (i.e., the decision to send the card) but the symbolism of the act (i.e., how it is carried out) that really matters.[16] This is a good example as to how to deal in managerial decision-making process with the leadership qualities that has been furnished with the help of very simple but lively made examplification of the fact of the issues concerned with the TA procedural manner that has to contain in it the principles of effectiveness towards the understanding of managerial behaviour in work environment. The implementation of such rule in practice regarding work effectiveness will have much benefit to the organization for the attainment of its goal.

TA and Conflict Management

Conflict in human society is a universal phenomenon. In the history of human civilization, all the ups swings are seemed to occur due to individual or group conflict. Therefore, business organization which is the sub-system of the total social system is not free from conflict. Conflict is thus a reality for managers. Management can be made more and more effective when managers apply carefully the transactional norms in organization. However, in communication with persons there should be an aim in mind of managers that they bring result of their performance in regard to job by reducing conflict at organizational level (both intrapersonal and interpersonal conflicts). TA is therefore, an essential tool for managerial communication where conflict levels are seemed occurring very much higher in organization, which will impair or injure performance. Under such circumstances, a manager needs to reduce that particular type of conflict. It is here suggestible, if the excessive conflict stems from differences in goals, the manager can reduce such conflict by focusing every one's attention on a super ordinate goal, such as defending against an external threat. Again, in case of more and more complex and dynamic organizations, conflict may be reduced by enhancing coordination activities.[17]

In this context it is true to note that TA is an essential tool which attempts to reduce conflict by keeping in check the impulsive id and the conscience of the super ego of human beings in organization. As the behaviour of a person, his communication with others (transaction) and his over all reaction to his environment depend upon his life position and predominant ego state, it is essential to remember that unique talent of each person will be appreciated by the management, and is to be potentially utilized for the purposeful attainment of tasks performances in organizational behaviour, and thus it is also worth-noting that the TA approach helps improve organizational health by reducing conflict in such manner – both intrapersonal and interpersonal conflicts, along with other types of conflicts at organizational level. It is here, imperative to say that there is an illustrative reference being made by Sigmund Freud[18] which explains about the Id and the human ego that have been henceforth referred to the conflict of definite kind of an individual, for which he attempted as a solution to make managers aware of their total personality through sensitivity training. According to this study, it appears that in an organizational setting an individual may be found facing with –(i) two competing job offers; (ii) two opposing needs or goals; (iii) two different roles or task which clash with each other; and (iv) two different courses of action, of which one is alternative to the other; and so on. All these are simply explanatory and result in happening conflict in an individual. On the other hand, the works of Fred Luthans which has contributed tremendously in human relationship at organizational level can best be cited here, because he has discovered four resourceful sources of conflict within the individual, which prevent his adaptation to the work situation. These are: (i) competing needs and roles; (ii) different ways in which drives and roles can be expressed; (iii) barriers which intervene between the drive and the goal; and (iv) both positive and negative aspects attached to desired goals.[19] Thus, in seeking through mutual accommodative behavioural constraints there needs to be a managerial balance between human inner mind and outer mind which prescribes that the TA postulates are to be considerably mechanized through human talents and needs of the organization, so that the creative zeal of behavioural pursuit for organizational performance can be enhanced with a view to confine the judgement of motivational forces that inculcate an attitude towards the unifying goal of journey in life processes in an organization. However, in case of interpersonal conflict, it is found that conflict situations in organization either in group of small or big one, if inevitably crops up of at least two individuals who hold polarized points of view regarding the particular job aspect at work place. Thus, one of the experts in this line, Joe Kelly[20] has observed: "Conflict situations......are quick to jump to conclusion". It is thus, evident that in case of interpersonal conflict TA is a proactive measure to shared goals[21] which relate to either – differently not, posed in general for a chaotic condition but indirectly cumbersome who cannot attain a single goal; where as other(s) attain(s) it very easily, or with some sort of ultimatum. In regard to conflict resolution under this subjective view, it is - (i) self-disclosure and feedback approach; (ii) win or loss strategy; (iii) win-win strategy; (iv) lose-lose strategy; among others, which have wide bearing with human interrelationships to the process of human resource management (HRM) and thus, the TA concept is deliberately undertaken in organization to unify the goal of management in universal manner, because it is well-known to all that an organization is a human element and the success of an organization depends on the nature of effective management of human resources where TA implications are quite a naturalistic idea to uproot the human policy resolutions to resolve conflict of any nature under this type of problem. Thus, it seems the interpersonal conflict has under the above types of strategies some policy formulations, of which, third party role is of immense value towards the arbitration process, who is (third person or third party – who acts as the arbitrator) referred the issues in conflict. To overcome drawbacks, it is essentially important that the arbitrator should be acting otherwise than required for solution of the problems. He should be playing the entire role quite impartially to the effective management for resolution of conflict.

From the above viewpoint, it is suggested that the TA

for conflict management in the nature of interpersonal relationship should take into consideration some important methods, of which – (i) removal of differences; (ii) smoothing of the areas of conflict; (iii) better understanding of each other's functions; (iv) confrontation and use of authority; (v) conciliation or co-ordination by a liaison unit; and (vi) restructuring of the organization are a few conflict resolution measures that work as remedial application in organisation to the backgrounds of work groups, overall company policy and organizational climate[22] and so on. Further, there is an alternative approach to the preventive remedies of conflict in organisation, and it is also known as the engineering-psychological approach[23], which puts its emphasis on redesigning the job and its physical environment to fit the capabilities and limitations of the individual working in the organisation. It is, therefore, apparent to note that there should be managerial technique as the perspective of HRM which consists of love and affection in dealing with people in organisation, so that every one is responded towards the unification goal of life for perpetuating the essential qualities of human creative nature of workmanship. Hence, it is the TA which magnifies the values and ethos of life on which stands the very process of life in management of human resources. It is the human resource that binds an organisation with the qualities of competitiveness, performance orientation goal – both in the nature of individual goal as well as organizational goal towards the making of human life socially beneficial for all times to come, because individuals and groups are required to be a voluntary agent in organisation. When it is augmented by each human transaction philosophically towards the achievement of these goals in organisation, management is said to be successful. In modern context of organizational undertaking, it is the responsibility of management to provide for the essential basic necessities of human need, as we have observed earlier in Chapter 1 in the analysis of Maslaw's need theory with a reference to management for manpower development. As Blair J. Kolasa has observed that in regard to managerial goal, they (managers) have their own choice and therefore, it might be expected while applying the TA principalities – the more alike the situations, the more the composition of leadership remained the same.[24] Thus, the effectiveness of management in organisation to reduce conflict is dependent on the initiative of managers which is concerned with self-assurance and self-confidence of each manager, and thereby, organizational dynamism is balanced through adequate HRM policy that has to be contained in TA.

TA and Organisational Development

In the field of human resource development (HRD) TA has a great impact in the sense that it provides clue to an understanding on human behaviour, which is a must for the purpose of effective organizational development (OD). It is, therefore, expected that an assessment over the issues of OD and a relativistic analysis between TA and OD would lead to enhance organizational effectiveness in the changing circumstances of the world environment. It is well-known fact that the OD is the process gives all those opportunities to every managerial approach in an organisation with their key decision-making areas, without which it becomes very difficult for the management to cope with the fast-changing environment to handle tasks at hand in quite responsible manner. We further know that OD is the management of the overall organisational culture (OC) leads to entire phase of the deplorable conditions for the developmental needs with various means and ways. Consequently, it brings in organisation strength by measuring different weaknesses and adjusts the malady in given situation for purposefully bringing a balance between structure and systems and sub-systems of the entire organization. It is therefore, apparent to note that the TA with all its synthesis will bring in organization a coordinative atmosphere that every manager has to follow with their plan of activities in organizational process orientation, so that there is the team spirit development being made in mind of executives as well as others, who are otherwise related to the organizational goal. Hence, an effective utilization of TA practices and principles, if taken into consideration in proactive manner guides the management with the philosophy of work culture, which is the need of the hour in all organization world-wide, in the context of the present crisis of the world around. In regard to bringing a change in organizational set-up, it has to be remembered that the work culture that we are concerned mostly in the twenty-first century, it is expected that every human being who is either directly or indirectly connected with many types of social and business organizations must possess human value orientation that needs TA principalities for an effective development of their respective organizations. In this regard, the works of Warren Bennis[25] is quite illustrative because he gives an illuminating picture – how to structure an organization, which in a dynamically changing business situation work in realistic manner and with stability to perpetuate the process of a wholistic development.

As we have seen earlier in Chapter 2, captioned under the point: "Organisational Culture" (OC) that an OC conceptual framework relates to an understanding of human behaviour with respect to psychological boundaries regarding the structure of the organization in composite manner and its sub-units, the significant role of the TA being played in it, if problems are contained thereto—to understanding of human value conceptions, where transcendental science has a quite bearing on the issues of human self-realisation process, which is a must for OD. It is therefore, essential part of organizational redesignment in the shape of newly created environment throughout the world in the present century, as it were. Hence, the TA requires that in an organization people's behaviour should be correlated with the approach of such a unison in different dynamic activities that go to make human life embrasive in all respects of social development. Considering the views of transcendental approach, we should bring in mind that an organization is an interrelationships of various personality aspects – though diverse in order to attain the tasks in skilful manner, yet the goal being one-self-realisation process through human activities, there is the necessity of optimum dynamicity of human behavioural conditionalities that bring in organization, a happy as well as peacefully coordial relationship for all, to all times to come. It is the duty of each management functionalities that there prevails a conducive atmosphere in an organization all through, while transacting to get the things done in systematic manner with the principles of strategicity to balance with the wholistic development in an integrative manner. Thus, the notion of transcendental process in the behaviour of tasks will find the way for mankind's real development by each transaction which is conditionally to be taken into consideration in the plane of work in organization. Not only this is enough, while it is practised in reality organizations are to be viewed from global entity concept which requires that the management should think they are but a part of life of the entire humankind. From this, it emerges that the TA approach for the OD has the following principalities that requires practical application of those norms contained in the transcendental process of human activities. Firstly, there are two ways of approaching under this notion, the reality which an organization faces: the one is to consider it in its forms (structure), and the other is to look in it for the informality (behavioural aspects). Secondly, the preliminary states of transcendental consciousness like pre-cognition, direct knowledge of the past and the limit to which they can be developed – all these are essentially a part of human transactions in an enterprising goal towards the unification of human life. Thirdly, under this approach every thought in human transaction finds its own shape, so that management effectiveness is widely dispersed in the cultural set-up of the organization through all personality traits of individuals who are in different nature concerned with the tasks for individual satisfaction in one hand, and the attainment of the goal of the organizational life on the other. Fourthly, last but not least, among others, there is the time, space and casuality conditionalities in all human transactions that bring in human perfection on the plane of organizational dynamicity, and hence, the process gives new birth to a concept for the correct OD – "engineering psychology", have already been dealt in the foregoing analysis in this chapter. From the above, we can easily say that the collectivity concept is intermingled in organizational activities, which needs that the TA perspectives are to open mind of the people who are related to the organization for the attainment of organizational goal in relativistic manner. As a matter of fact, a managerial suggestion is being placed here to the clarity of our thought which go to develop every organization and its people. "It is our own mental attitude which makes the world what it is for us. Our thoughts make things beautiful, our thoughts make things ugly. The whole world is in our own minds. Learn to see things in the proper light. First, believe in this world – that there is meaning behind everything. Everything in the world is good, holy and beautiful. If you see something evil, think that you are not understanding it in the right light. Throw the burden on yourselves!......whenever we are tempted to say that the world is going to the dogs, we ought to analyse ourselves, and we shall find that we have lost the faculty of seeing things as they are".[26] In this principle, when transactions are played in an organization there comes the developmental prospects in the midst of problems whatsoever or howsoever a manager is being concerned with. Because, it gives in him managerial qualities with patience and endurance, along with real teaching and learning philosophy of the work, so that it brings peace and harmony in entire organization along with the perfection for his own realisation.

The paradox of modern man is that only as the individual joins with his fellows in groups and organizations can he hope to control the political, economic, and social forces which threaten his individual freedom. This is especially true now that massive social groupings – in nations and combinations of nations – are the order of the day. Only as the individual in society struggles to preserve his individuality in common cause with his fellows can he hope to remain an individual.[27] The leadership must design and put into action an organization that will be congruent with the new beliefs and values. Thus, the leadership in organization for the purpose of effective development must have to acknowledge resistance to the change and deal accordingly with it as a necessary stage in the process of abandoning the status quo and embracing the new vision with its beliefs and values. It is very important that the TA applicationability for dealing with resistance requires well-conceived plan of action regarding the process of developmental means, which find its place in the areas like: (i) a willingness to listen; (ii) some tolerance and patience; (iii) clarification and repetition of the need to change, among others – all these are beneficial to a transformational change in organization to set it in correct path, so that the goal attainment becomes realistic with creativity and sensitivity analysis. Hence, the leadership must re-engineer for the designment of its tasks in specific terms and conditions which govern the principles of human satisfaction to bring about a radical change with fundamental breakthrough, being necessitated by the process of humanization in exact approach towards the making of life perfect in relation to work ethics as well as goal directedness, in means and ways which cover up the principles of – (i) modeling and anchoring the required beliefs and values as enshrined upon with the aforesaid areas, in appropriate new roles and actions; (ii) implementing strategies, structures, and systems including a power network that is clearly aligned to, and supportive of, the actions that need to be accomplished in order to realize the vision and enact the new beliefs and values; (iii) replacing key staffs, or staff in key positions, who are not suited to the change; (iv) introducing education, training, and retraining in the actions required by the transformation of the organization and specifically by the new beliefs and values; and (v) implementing a reward system that will reinforce actions that are congruent with the new set of beliefs and values. Substituting all such principles, it can be well-said that the TA for a dynamic organization must be applied keeping in view the well structured organizational framework philosophy and contain in it the principles of unison that would go to make the entire organization effective for the purposeful utilization of all resources to bring forth and enhance required level of development, which is the paramount success of managerial goal for organizational process orientation and needful development for all types of human beings related to the organization.

It is thus, related to behaviour on the one hand and action on the other, and is a moving or guiding force. According to Luthans[28], "needs set up drives to accomplish goal; this is what motivation is all about". This motivating element in humanizing the goal of the organization being contained in the cultural aspects of human behavioural conditions, there is, in a systems sense three essential issues which require particular attention while motivation has to be conjoined with the work ethics – in interacting and interdependent elements of human needs, drives, and goals, which again, in Luthans view has a wide bearing to the process of individual development with the growth of the organization – it is the integrative idea to be contained in organizational mission, vision, and objectivity analysis in correct as well as perfect synthesis to the attainment of both the organizational and group goal. All these are managerial guidelines having perceptual notions and organizational spirit to uproot the human values. As such Peter F. Drucker suggests, "every organization needs performance in three major areas: (a) it needs direct results; (b) building of values and their reaffirmation; and (c) building and developing people for tomorrow. If deprived of performance in any one of these areas, it will decay and die. All three, therefore, have to be built into the contribution of every execution in an organization. But their relative importance varies greatly with the personality and the position of the executive as well as with the needs of the organization."[29] It has already been referred to the preceding chapter on the analysis of OD where it has been observed that the OD is the planned change in an organization bringing thereby radical transformation for the all-round development of the organization. Hence, the TA provisions and norms to it requires that there should be five important key areas which Moorhead and Griffin[30] have suggested in their combined work for the OD intervention management for its effectiveness. All these are to be relatively taken into consideration with their rationalistic approach, so that organization becomes fit to equip with the adaptability, applicability, and acceptability of respective changes required for the OD. OD is not restricted to business but is widely practiced in the military, which may be a surprise to those who perceive the military as an autocratic, mechanistic organization with values apparently incompatible with OD technologies[31]. The managerial grid is but one of several approaches to OD. Another one is the survey feedback method; it emphasizes the collection, organization, analysis, and feedback of data to participants. Still another technique of OD is process consultation. While the TA principles are applied in right direction, in organization it is apparent to observe that the OD programme reduces employees absenteeism and turnover. Besides, employee job satisfaction is enhanced, job is enriched, productivity is also increased, petty grievances are reduced, departmental morale is improved, and lastly, it facilitates for the better interpersonal relationships.[32] In short, OD is eclectic while TA principles and its innovative postulates are maintained in reviving the organizational culture, in the sense that it chooses from a variety of tools, methods, and techniques that facilitate the solving of particular enterprise problems. Thus, it becomes necessary tool for innovative research to inculcate human values, moral as well as work ethics, cultural transformation in new dimensional order to the changing circumstances and its phenomenal surroundings to uproot organizational values in life, so that human perfection is based on the nature of development that causes for eternal peace and harmony in mind of people for all times to come through organizational activities, and the resultant impact on the attainment of human goal in terms of organizational mission, human vision, and integrative life style for the greater unison in its systems and sub-systems, which brings in organization a universal atmosphere to all-round development.

References

1. Taking cue from the findings of Sigmund Freud regarding id, ego, and super-ego, Dr. Eric Berne developed the concept of psychotherapy which

has practical application in dealing with intra (within the person) and interpersonal conflicts and communication in industry. Thus, it is observed that making use of Freudian psychoanalytic model, transactional analysis (TA) has identified three ego states, viz. child, adult, and parent, which are identical to id, ego, and super-ego of Freud. In management of human resources for organizational effectiveness, ego state is an essential reality of human personality, and therefore, it is true to note that this concept is an attempt which helps man to keep the impulsive id and the conscience of the super-ego in check. As the behaviour of a person, his communication with others (transaction) and his overall reaction to his environment depend upon his life position and predominant ego state, it is essential to remember that unique talent of each person will be appreciated and utilized in organizational behaviour, and thus it is also worth-noting that the TA approach helps improve organizational health. So, there is an urgent necessity to identify a more positive and non-threatening method which enables managers to become sensitive to their ego states and behaviour without becoming uncomfortable. TA fills the bill in the present context of complexities of business management principles, where it has been found that organizational communication has been growing very fast to the changing environmental circumstances that could meet the demand of human personality development as well as interrelationships in various socio-economic activities for the purpose of attaining the goals of the organization in objective manner. See also, Berne, Eric, *Games People Play,* Grove Press, Inc., New York, 1964; Berne, E., *Principles of Group Treatment,* Oxford Univ. Press, New York, 1964; and Muriel, James and Dorothy, Jongeward, *Born to Win,* Addison-Wesley Pub. Co., Inc., Mass., 1971.

2. One of the aspects of human development in work is

contained in the Indian Hindu Philosophy where it is observed that the Lord (Srikrishna) says to Arjuna (Son of Kunti): " O Arjuna, take complete refuge under Him (God). By His grace you will attain Supreme Peace and His Eternal Abode." –*Gita* XVIII.62. Hence, the concept of TA can be felt from the mind of human beings as a surrendering attitude while dealing with different persons in organization. This surrendering attitude should be made by every manager through mind, speech and every action, so that it produces atmosphere of love and affection in all to the organization. This could bring a fellow-feeling atmosphere in organizational culture and to the overall climate of working conditions, to enhance universal brotherhoodship inherent with the philosophy of work dedicated towards the betterment of all interested groups that go to satisfy the need (the highest need of mankind) for realizing peace and, keeping a balanced state of organizational tranquility for transformational as well as reformational change for the great cause of humanity, to the ultimate development of life through work ethics of good behavioural traits of human personality - this is felt to be the most modern and scientific norm of behavioural attitude of managerial goal for human developmental aspects that increases better understanding regarding intra as well as interpersonal relationship, to the process of the greatest unity in mankind through organisational effectiveness.

3. *Harris, Thomas A.:* I am OK – You are OK, *Harper & Row, New York, 1961.*
4. In this regard, it should be preferred to follow from the Vedic concept that manages while guiding people with the motive of self-surrendering attitude must have to do in sacrificial manner for their self-actualisation in living with God through action-oriented principle. It calls for their performance to the path through sacrifices, charity, austerities, and

other virtuous deeds, and observe Brahmacarya – seeing everywhere the presence of God, and while rendering service to all creatures to treat them with humility and love is what may be called living with God through action. This way, they would once know automatically that the entire activity in this world is related to God for the realm of love, where no trace of shyness, pride, fear, and ceremonious politeness exists vis-à-vis the lover and the beloved. In reality, they are to be realized as the one basic feature of unity in work through action-oriented deeds for all people and creatures with unification in the great 'Nature'. In such a state of mind for the work in disinterested way is ultimately realized that the 'Divine Love' is a wonderful state of life – it provides liberation through work without having a thinking in mind for the fruits or results, but for the common unity with God by serving all in perfect manner. For further study of such conceptual ideal, the work of Jayadayal is quite interesting. – Goyandka, Jayadayal: *The Secret of Premayoga*, Govind Bhawan Karyalayạ, Gita Press, Gorakhapur, 1993. It can be suggested that this philosophy of work can provide one with the best way of solving human problems and realizing through absolute bliss solidified with the concept of truth, for making life unified with the God in human activities to the organizational way of thinking.

5. Abe, Wagner, *The Transactional Manager: How to Solve Your People Problems with TA*, Prentice – Hall Inc., Englewood Cliffs, N.J., 1981.
6. As the human personality is very complex to understand, it is expected that every transaction in organization should be handled with great care, as we do not know exactly why man behaves in particular way, and therefore, taking due attention regarding the satisfaction of various needs of human beings, so that a balanced state of affairs regarding individual growth could take place, and thereby it produces organizational health and brings in a

harmonious inter-personal relationships for the overall effectiveness of the organization – it is must that there should be a comparative study of human behaviour in organization with situational decision.

7. Goffman, Erwing: *The Presentation of Self in Everyday Life*, Doubleday, 1959, p.3.
8. Such view offers to the human quest for 'full life'. It has been here, identified with the creation of free individuality for realization of life through work.
9. In this regard, it is no wonder that V.A. Graicunas in 1933 referred to the growing problem of control with the increase of inter-relationships when the number of subordinates shoots up. – Graicunas, V.A., "Relationship in Organization", *Bulletin of the International Management Institute,* March, 1933.
10. Schneider, B. : *Staffing Organizations,* Goodyear Publishing Co. Inc., California, 1976.
11. The six suggestive measures are already prescribed in the previous chapter which are now, here, taken as organizational HRM process in the context of TA integrative process that could fulfil the needs of human potential development.
12. For further knowledge on such understanding of the conceptual view of the dynamics of TA appraisal in objective manner on human interrelationships regarding the aspects of job attitudes, see F. Herzberg, B. Mausner, R.O. Peterson, and D. Capwell, Job Attitudes: A Review of Research and Opinion, Psychological Service of Pittsburgh, PA, 1957.
13. Drucker, Peter F.: *Management-Tasks, Responsibilities, Practices*, Allied Publishers, New Delhi, 1980, p. 394.
14. In this regard, yoga has become quite popular in India and is receiving world wide attention because it brings about an organic change in breathing styles. It energises people, relaxes them and gives them mental peace. It is fact that stress is our disharmony with life. It is related to *avidhya,* the denial of truth and with our *Kleshas* of selfishness, desire, hatred and anger. Continuous quarrelling and magnifying

problems leads to psychosomatic diseases. – Sharma, R.A.: *Organisational Theory and Behaviour,* 2nd Edn., Tata McGraw-Hill Publishing Co. Ltd., New Delhi, 2000, p. 497. Substituting the same view, it can be suggested that yoga can check through meditational processes, practical yoga classes and sessions, in addition to modifying routines, diets and attitudes to work. An effective manager can be fruitfully utilizing the resourceful elements of transcendental meditation (TM), yoga and similar other practices for reducing human stress at work place and outside the work environment.

15. Woodman, Richard W., "Organizational Change and Development: New Areas for Inquiry and Action", *Journal of Management,* June 1989, pp. 205-228.
16. Moorhead, Gregory and Ricky, Griffin, *Organizational Behaviour,* 2nd Edn., Houghton Mifflin, Boston, 1989, p. 347.
17. In empirical research findings (Lawrence and Lorsch) it is found that organizations functioning in a complex environment tended to go in for a high degree of differentiation integration, compared to organizations functioning in a simple environment. Further, organizations and their situations are too dynamic to permit us to proceed with static principles and stereo-typed approaches. Thus, the coordination activities when performed by managers effectively for managing conflict, meet in conformity with balancing in complex relationships among variables can be expressed more effectively; if the management adopts a conscious and deliberate effort. It all requires therefore, an understanding about the dynamic aspects of the organistic view-point – where society is seen as an evolving thing, analogous to biological organisms – will not be discussed here – but my suggestion for coping with differences that might be occurred at any given point of time in an organization is stressed for informal coordination techniques (also called mechanisms of coordination in organizations),

so that the chaos of complexity might best be suited to fit for establishing harmoniousness in the very nature of organization. This is more true in case of human life. As Kauffman suggests: "Organisms have gotten more complex since life began", in Chorafas, D.N.: *Chaos Theory in the Financial Markets, op. cit.,* p. 51. See also Messel H. and Butler, S.T. (Eds.): *The Universe and Its Origin,* Macmillan and Co.Ltd., London, 1964, p.56. "......Organic structures were becoming more and more complicated and more and more adapted to their surroundings". This law holds good in case of human organizations in society to the adaptation with the environment for efficient, systematic and effective management of organizational conflicts, in course of operations in complex and dynamic environment.

18. Sigmund Freud has contributed immensely to the understanding of human behaviour which has a strong relevancy to the modern organizations world wide. His researches led to the development of human personality aspects both in the field of psychoanalysis and psychiatry, as we have seen earlier. However, he maintained lucidly that conflicts between the three structures of human personality, namely, the id, the ego and the super-ego give rise to prejudices. Freud (1922) tried to uncover the unconscious well-springs of crowd behaviour also. Again, Freud (1923) wrote: "The fateful question for human species seems to me to be whether and to what extent their cultural development will succeed in mastering the disturbance of their communal life by the human instinct of aggression and self-destruction".
19. Luthans, Fred: *Organizational Behaviour,* McGraw Hill Book Co., Kogokusha, Tokyo, 1989.
20. Kelly, Joe: *Organization Behaviour,* Richard D. Irwin and the Dorsey Press, 1974.
21. Shared goals may be meant to a single goal towards which two or three people may be running but, it is only one who can ultimately attain it.

22. Organisation climate (OC): The internal environment of an organisation forms its climate. It is also referred to organisation's culture, already discussed in the preceding chapter. However, in regard to management of organizations conflict, it is essential to preserve organizational climate, because a healthy and conducive climate in organisation is helpful for augmenting mutually as well as collaborating development between the line and staff, besides harmonious relationship between group and individuals (inter and intra) in operational areas of the entire organisation structure. In short, human perceptions are broadened by enthusing values, needs, attitudes, expectations and so on.
23. As Bernays puts it (Christenson and McWillams, 1962), the phrase "engineering approach" refers to "action based on thorough knowledge of the situation and on the application of scientific principles and tried practices to the task of getting people to support ideas and programmes......", cited in Kuppuswamy, B.: *Elements of Social Psychology* (6th Revised Edn.), Vikas Publishing House Pvt. Ltd., New Delhi, 1983, p. 119.
24. Kolasa, Blair J. : *Introduction to Behavioural Science in Business*, Wiley Eastern, p. 520.
25. In empirical research findings on organizational structure and the philosophy of management with a view to enhance developmental impetus to the growth of an organization, it needs mention without any doubt that nowadays, at least some thinkers on organization structure do believe that the mechanistic system of organization structure should give way for an organic system. Warren Bennis, an eminent expert in this line observes: "Organizations will become adaptive, rapidly changing temporary systems. Second, they will be organized around problems-to-be-solved. Third, these problems will be solved by relative groups of strangers who represent a diverse set of professional skills. Fourth, given the requirements of

coordinating the various projects, articulating points or 'linking pin' personnel will be necessary who can speak the diverse languages of research and who can relay and mediate between various project groups. Fifth, the groups will be conducted on organic rather than on mechanical lines – they will emerge and adapt to the problems, and leadership and influence will fall to those who seem most able to solve the problems rather than to programmed role expectations. Besides, people will be differentiated not according to rank or roles, but according to skills and training". –Bennis, W.: Organizational Development and the Fate of Bureaucracy, *Industrial Management Review,* Alfred P. Sloan School of Management, MIT, Cambridge, Spring, 1966, p. 52.

26. Mumukshananda, Swami: *The Complete Works of Swami Vivekananda,* Vol.I, Advaita Ashrama, Mayavati, Champawat, Himalayas, 1999, p. 441.
27. Krech David, Crutchfield, Richard S. and Ballachey, Egerton L.: *Individual in Society,* McGraw-Hill, New York, 1962, p. 529.
28. Luthans, Fred, *op. cit.,* p. 312.
29. Drucker, Peter F.: *The Effective Executive,* Pan Books Ltd., London, 1970, p. 57.
30. The five key areas prescribed by them are: (1) Take a wholistic view; (2) Secure top management support; (3) Encourage participation; (4) Foster open communication; and (5) Reward contributors. – Moorhead, G. and Griffin, R.: *Organizational Behaviour* (2nd Ed.), Houghton Mifflin, Boston, 1989, pp. 754-55.
31. Umstot, Denis D.: "Organizational Development Technology and the Military: A Surprising Merger?" *Academy of Management Review,* April 1980, pp.189-201.
32. Robbins, Stephen P.: *The Administrative Process,* Prentice-Hall, Englewood Cliffs, N.J., 1976, pp. 340-349.

4
Meditational Thought

Meditation – What it is ?

There are different books and volumes on human meditational process which guide people for the self realisation in ordinary course of life. As such, it is found that the subject has become quite popular in recent times world-wide. In management of human organization also, meditation has occupied its place because of its universal application to the ground realities of all-round development of the global society. However, in simplest form, meditation can be visualized as the process of self-realisation. Though there are different types of it, all are related to this self-realisation of human beings. By means of meditation, it is quite possible to concentrate on human mind for perfection in work as well as realizing the inner most self which is present in all human beings. Thus, duties are performed in perfect manner when mind concentration becomes the vital force of life within the different types of activities. In management of human resources and organization behaviour, we find that people are always feeling restlessness in mind for which many a times there seems to be organizational conflict that ultimately hinders the productivity of the organization, and thereby, the natural growth of the organization is further hampered. In this case, meditation helps the management to guide people in perfect manner by philosophizing the nature of the self which produces better result at the work place by reducing various types of organizational conflict. Also, mind concentration helps people in organization to reduce and cope with different stressors. It is, therefore, expected that meditational thought would bring in organization a balanced and harmonious interrelationships among different groups and individuals who are otherwise guided by the philosophy of their egoistic feelings, for which they forget to think that the same self is present in all beings. Once it is realized, there would become automatically a cooperative atmosphere in organizational cultural development that needs essentially for the purpose of getting things done through people to attain the goal of the organization. Through meditation, it becomes possible to think in equanimity which is a must for all in organization to achieve results, with a view to attain the goal. Over and above, meditation prescribes the rule of living by doing in disinterested way[1], instead of absorbing within the work.

Thus, the meditational application in management will lead to understand the real consciousness of being which is unconsciously believed to be otherwise. It is, therefore, meditation peeps into mind for the reality of beings, and by this the egoistic feelings of man is eradicated from the inner mind to understand the basis of his work in organizational way of living. In meditation, our general mind is converted into supermind which perceives things and receives the same phenomena in right light and at the same time, at right direction. As a result of this, man understands correctly the difference between the self as an ultimate entity and the self as the empirical ego. This case has been dealt in Upanishadic version of Indian scriptural order in which we get the idea that the empirical self is transient while the other, the superior self, is permanent. The works of Kuppuswamy[2] is quite relevant in this regard, who observes that the empirical self is associated with the bodily needs and the emotions and the task of man is to realize this two-fold nature of the self, so that the lower self is under the control of the higher self.

In management of human resources, meditation means human value orientation in organizational plans, policies, strategies and mission. In this context, Gordon MacBeath has suggested that any manpower planning in an organization must be followed with the help of two types of strategic requirements. Firstly, it (plan) should have concern regarding the detailed "planning of manpower requirements for all types of and levels of employees throughout the period of the plan", and secondly, the plan of the organization must also include with the planning process concerning the "planning of manpower supplies to provide the organization with the right types of people from all sources to meet the planned requirements".[3] Again, at about more than two decades back, Peter F. Drucker raised important philosophical questions related to business: What is our business? What will it be? and What should it be?[4] He further in his another work suggests that objectives need to set in the eight vital areas of market standing, innovation, productivity, physical and financial resources, profitability, manager performance and development, worker performance and attitude, and public responsibility.[5] In all these areas, there are different approaches being made to augment orderliness at work place by modern organizations, and yet, there seems to be corporate chaos, for which, it is expected that the meditational process will come to solve all human and other problems of modern organizations with the correct nature of strategicity, adaptability in the corporate mission, so that human qualities are strengthened to anticipate proper knowledge about the environment, information about the environment, implementation of strategies, and so on. Meditational definition while visualized would lead to a transformational change in personal policies and programmes in an organization. Besides, organizational objectivity will be understood by people in realistic manner to cope with the changes that would require modification of knowledge for the purposive development of human beings. All these issues are to be taken into psychological considerations that need much development to solve human problems at the enterprise. Meditation therefore, includes in its basic principles – (i) concentration of human mind for realization of the self in own and to integrate the same with the universal Self; (ii) it prescribes rules and regulations of human activities which guide people for the higher order of life with perfection through human consciousness; (iii) it leads to people in an understanding to realize about the common unity in organizational way of life, in the midst of corporate diversities and corporate beliefs, values, mission, human vision, value system, work ethics and culture, morale building, motivational techniques, strategic exploration of things through competitive advantages regarding corporate plans, policies and programme implementation in correct phase of corporate development, along with human growth by means of utilizing human potentials which are dormant and inherent in beings; (iv) meditational norms are useful for the engineering psychology which is the preponderance of human consciousness – being free from ego, though egoistic beliefs are observed to be prevailing in mind of enterprise people. Thus, meditation has a great role to play to differentiate the meaning of work and non-work philosophy, ethical principles, cultural transformational ideas which guide to organizational goal. It systematizes activities to enhance productivity, profitability, and the stability of the organization.

In modern world, there is the restlessness in mind of people, in which meditation as the tool of modification of human behaviour guides the entire management for the path-goal relational approach, so that the organization simplifies the human value system in complex business environment through right type of enterprise mission. Hence, the definition of meditation we are concerned here, is related to human cultural transformation, which could be efficiently utilized in organization for bringing organizational effectiveness in human behaviour as well as the attainment of enterprise goal. As it is based on mental phenomena, the tools and techniques applied under this process require managerial teaching and learning ideologies and its application at the right time, in right place, and in right manner, keeping in mind the philosophy of work and the perfection of human life through work related principles by living in organization in co-operative manner towards all such human endeavours. As a whole, it provides for the orderliness of the organized behaviour of human life with the core values of human perfection, in terms of all-round development and growth of human personalities to understand the realities of management in creative manner[6].

Thus, by means of meditation it becomes possible to control human mind which is of paramount importance in any field of human management process and organizational orderliness with the help of concentration of mind, the will power of people is strengthened and they are guided for the ultimate realization of their inner self, knowing which man becomes perfect and handles tasks and activities in organization in perfect manner and with collective responsibility. Hence, meditation opens the door of managerial responsibility by creatively utilizing the intellect and vigour of mind of organizational people, and thus, it guides people in organization at the right path, and in right light through right type of directional means and ways, so that they are understanding the philosophy of work, without being guided by the concept of bondage in life, has already been cited in Chapter 1 in dealing with the work philosophy and work ethics. Meditation is therefore, helpful for solving all human problems in an organized way of living for perfection of human life.

Why Meditation is Necessary for Management

The aim of management is getting output from input which is applied as the dose of production activities. This input is applied in different forms like - man, machines, materials, money and so on, called as the resource of the enterprise or organization that utilizes all these elements in methodical way in production function. However, the fundamental element being man-power resource behind everything in the production function of the enterprise, there is the necessity of optimum as well as perfect utilization of it, depending on which other resources are converted as the perfect output of the organization. It is here, meditation is essentially a vital part of management, because there is the consciousness in man, and also mind present in all human beings who are there to convert other resources of the organization into output. This output being produced in terms of result – there arises optimum necessity of the utilization of all other resources of the organization. In this connection, it is apparent to note that meditation, which relies on human concentration, as we have seen earlier, can play a vital role to guide people for the attainment of the result of the organization. When human being understands the reality behind work, they can reason out as to how to utilize the resources of the organization in perfect manner.

There are three things guiding all such essential qualities requiring for the perfection in management – truth, value, and commitment. While managing resources for organizational goal attainment, every management should have to turn its vision for looking into matters like human factor, at the enterprise level. It is because, when things are aimed at to be given a shape in the nature of perfection for the realities, they should possess motion which must be concentrated through human entity concept that binds all things in one busket –'relativity of activity'. In a geocentric world system, there is the regard for the dignity of man. Hence, if we want to coordinate things in relativity aspects, it is to be founded on human conduct. As the human conduct is the guiding force of everything in management of organizational resources, the principles of activity are in two ways relative to the realities of management, viz., in action, and also in reaction. Thus, to get specific as well as general results on each activity, the principles that are guided by the eternal validity in management function have to conform with the philosophical fundamental standpoint on human consciousness that brings perfect result for the attainment of organizational goal in one hand, and the individual satisfaction for their harmonious life, on the other hand. It is therefore, meditational notion which brings in practice a balance between all essential conditions for organizational success like – truth, value and commitment for the entity of its dynamicity. In meditation, there is the process for human development which prescribes rules of law for the understanding of the real nature of man –

knowing which man realizes everything for the realities of management. It seems that an emphasis upon the ties between science of work and philosophy of work is one of the best methods for giving people a clear idea of what is truth. There is, of course, one great difficulty in introducing such suggestions into various institutions of education, and also for the business and other types of organizations, either in syllabuses, or in work related rules of the conduct that human beings are concerned in organization. For all these reasons, meditational schooling or lessons are very much essential in modern educational institutions, social and business organisations that will guide people in terms of human understanding by means of imparting lessons on human consciousness. This consciousness concept being one of the most vital aspect of growth and development through naturalistic principles, it will provide in management of human resources basic guidelines which are fundamental for the development and growth of individuals, groups, and the particular type of organization, or business enterprises, and in general for the whole society.

All types of human failures, conflicts, stress, chaos, and likewise things prevailed in organization, or human social institutions are related to human ignorance, from non-discrimination between the real and unreal. Here, meditation is further helpful for discriminating between the two, and comes to solve all such human problems at the enterprise level by providing vital force at the centre of all human activities, and thus, profitably utilizing the resources of the organization, so that results are achieved in harmonious manner. Thus, meditation enhances balance between the 'path-goal' journey in an organization. When people become self conscious they concentrate on all their activities in organization, because they realize that the deeds of this day is conditioned both by yesterday and also by tomorrow. Hence, in an age of information technology the overall management functionalities are to attain the realistic goal with the practices of cybernetics. In this field again, meditation helps, as the markets, economics, and financial systems are made dynamic to the respective behavioural reasons and natures. It is therefore, expected that the meditational practices will take a leading role in management of human resources through its focal point in different interactions of human beings in organization, and of their positive effects in terms of particular value system towards the goal of management.

From behavioural perspective, it is observed that human perception is the main factor by which the concept of truth, value and organizational commitment comes in practice to underlie the principles of human action, based on the nature of performance for the realities of life. So, it is simply the perception of one's own techniques in doing things where meditational rules and regulations are guiding force behind all types of human perfection in organizational activities. It is thus, asserted by Swami Vivekananda in his work on 'The Ideal of Karma-yoga' that we may reach the same goal by different paths, and these paths, he has generalized into four, viz. those of work, love, psychology, and knowledge. When meditation is applied in management, all these four paths converge and become one. Everything that we perceive around us is struggling towards freedom, from the atom to the man, from the insentient, lifeless particle of matter to the highest existence on earth, the human soul. The whole universe is in fact the result of this struggle for freedom. Hence, meditation helps for this impulsive perception by people who are in organization guided by their motive force to implement the resources of the organization in right direction for the attainment of the result, called goal of action – this impulse being the same, the struggle towards management of human resources is aimed at this conceptual view, where meditational practices help to reduce human conflicts in organization, and thereby, human stress is also reduced. Consequently, organizational chaos is further reduced to balance the malady of human actions, which go to produce results in effective manner by relativistically employing human potentials at the work place. By meditation, human beings are taught to learn about sacrifice which is the necessary element required for the development of the organization. As a whole, meditation brings organizational culture at a harmonious flow at the forefront of management to systematize all things and organizational activities together, by personality development of beings. Hence, it is said that by meditation people learn about getting things in selfless manner by sacrificing their own self for the common good, which is the core of real human and organizational development. Thus, we can say undoubtedly that freedom is the one goal of all nature – sentient, or insentient; and consciously, or unconsciously, everything is struggling towards that goal. For this reason, the philosopher thinks the difference between bondage and freedom is only caused by knowledge and ignorance. It is, therefore, meditation suggests through its practicalities how to gain knowledge – the goal of all management activities.

In interpreting Einstein's words on the 'Rationality of Nature and Einstein's Cosmic Religion', it can be asserted that the ultimate goals grow out of life itself but they cannot have any influence on the external world if science does not give us the means to work towards these goals. 'To know the truth' means, in scientific parlance, to know how to reach our goals. Truth is the value science imbues in its workers, and truth is the basic value without which even the most lofty goal has no meaning in the world we actually live in.[7] It is thus, the science of meditation teaches us how goals and values are connected and mutually determined by each other. The most important function of meditation in the organized behaviour of man and group in the life of men seems that it consists in setting up ultimate and fundamental goals and anchoring them in the emotional life of the individual, as it were; in a healthy society they live as powerful traditions which influence the conduct and the evaluations of the individuals. If one tries to bring out the purely human aspect which has relevancy with the organisational commitment as to how things are to be carried out for the purpose of organizational goal, it requires that there should be free and responsible development of the individual in order that it can serve gladly and voluntarily the community of all men. Here, meditational practices have got the important role being superimposed on the nature of human consciousness, which is the core of human management to be objectively taken into consideration, for the relativistic assumptions of the conditionalities of the nature of human work performances. Even though you have dealings and transactions with people, you should not take interest in their useless or dirty talk, but should always set your mind in tune with the supreme truth, which is the reality for the success in management to attain goal. This can be nicely observed when meditational courses are practised in organisational way of life. Thus, managing by meditational tools and techniques will help the management to impart in acquiring some qualities like – contentment, sweetness, coolness, fortitude, humility, cheerfulness, inwardliness, straightforwardness, sobriety, tolerance, surrender to the infinite creator of universe, and purity in thought, word, and deed – these are essential qualities of good management required for the perfection of men to understand the basic values of human life.

Application of Yoga Psychological Principles in Management

We have seen that human being is the central point of all human activities. In management practices, people find themselves involved with the decision-making process with a view to attain the goal. The goal of the organization is integration with the highest need of man – common unity through self-actualisation. In this regard, 'goal' of the organization is said to be guided by the mission of the said organization and 'path' in terms of connectivity with that of route. Therefore, path leads to goal and vice-versa so to attaining quality with quantitative aspect of the missionary zeal for perfection with the dynamics of organisational behaviour[8], and here, yoga as the tool of management can be synthesized for managerial effectiveness to attain the organisational goal in terms of better communication, good coordination and cooperation between tasks and people, effective as well as efficient utilization of organisation's resources for the overall success of the management practices, and bringing thereby in organization good human relationship. From this standpoint, it requires that there should be some principles of work ethics guided by the philosophy of human managerial practices. Yoga psychology is one of the most modern and scientific tool to proceed for such journey of human life. It (Yoga) means evenness of mind. Mental peace arises only when the mind is free from restlessness. The psychological practices through yoga can provide thus, freedom from mental conflicts, which is commonly not found in all modern organization, and so, it can generate a restful state of mind, which is further an essential factor of human and organisational growth with the right path of development for the overall managerial effectiveness in the long-run. The application of yoga principles and its basic postulates promote integration of human personality. Hence, there is integration of personality when the mind is united and harmonized, when it is free from conflicts and emotional disturbances and longings. With mental conflicts, concentration on any task is impossible whatever the nature of the task may be. Restlessness and anxiety, anticipations and expectations, inhibit therefore, concentration. This is how practice in meditation promotes a peaceful state of mind required for good management of things and activities.

The above conditions are not enough. It is further required that for good management people should have to introspect, and they should also have in their mind constant and continuous awareness for their desires, motives, thoughts, and feelings – all these are essential attributes of good managerial decision-making processes that must be preserved with the work ethics and psychology of guiding people in the right path for the managerial success of communicating and dealing with people in right direction to attain the goal of the organization. Here, again, yoga psychological principles promote for effective decision-making and management of human introspection for exploration of things and activities in right way due to equanimity principles as prescribed in the Gita, has already been cited previously in this chapter. The subjective view of yoga principles further, promotes people's awareness with relativity in constant and continuous manner to understanding nicely about the notions of human desires, motives, thoughts, and feelings, so that managerial communication becomes effective to the ground realities by fundamentally breaking all types of barriers and solving human problems at enterprise level, to establish peace and harmony in work environment, which is the essential condition for the success of managerial goal. The principles of meditation helps one to overcome both impulsiveness and mental automatisms by insisting on awareness at every moment of walking life.

Deliberate conscious action is the goal and the means is freeing oneself from all unconscious as well as conscious tendencies. In this connection, it is worth-mentioning when the individual is free from emotional conflicts, which is not found in modern organizations world-wide, and is fully integrated he has at his disposal all his abilities, and energies. He is able to think clearly on the problems confronting him being free from all prejudices and predispositions. For this reason, on equanimity principle stress has been put forward by the Gita, which implies that yoga psychology, as its practices demand in organization, can be a good tool for increasing human skill in action, required for the efficient management of the organization and guiding its people; besides, steady practice of asana and pranayama, as prescribed in yoga through meditational practices, brings relaxation of the body and thus, steady practice of concentration brings relaxation to the mind. These are essentially required because, in management people are lacking freeness from mental anxieties and restlessness. Hence, the principles of yoga practices will provide organizational people to take at a stage of mental freeness from all types of anxieties and restlessness towards their work environment. It also helps one to gain mental stability and tranquility. As propounded in the Gita and various Upanishadic versions, this will further bring in person with steady wisdom that lacks much in organizational people, for which the entire system of management turns into an unsystematic process as well as procedural manner when it is expected to dealing with people to get the work done. By meditational practice in work culture people attain peace undisturbed by any external agent. Due to ego feelings in human mind, all conflicts in organization arises, where yoga psychological practices and principles further help people guiding to free from all sense of egoism (*ahamkara*), and all the sense of mineness (*mamakara*) (*Gita,* II, 70-71). Thus, people attain equanimity (*samatva*), which is undisturbed by various dualities described in the Gita, and will be a equiminded (*samadarsivah*) towards all human beings – it is one of the most vital task of management behind all types of human action in organizational way of life. It is, therefore, important to note that this principle in enthusiastic manner is conceived in mind of organizational people, for which they think no one is afraid of them, and they are also afraid of no one. As a result of this, man becomes friendly and compassionate towards all persons in organization. In short, freedom from fear and anxiety helps in the achievement of inner harmony and peace which in turn promotes harmonious social relations, and as a whole, it brings in good interpersonal as well as intrapersonal relationships within the organizational structure, system, and services.

As regards thinking, the effects of meditation are three-fold. The thinking of the ordinary man is of the confused variety. He does not differentiate between perception, memory and imagination. He relies more on what he remembers than on what he perceives. His remembrance again is confused with what he imagines. On several occasions, it may be observed when facts are shown to be different from what a person asserts, he persists in stating, "but I thought it was......" In an organization therefore, one of the important effects of the various steps in the meditation process is, it enables people to distinguish between facts, memories and their own fancies. It imparts knowledge thus, to behavioural techniques by which people become realistic and enthusiastic to uproot human values which go to attain result in effective manner. The second important effect on human thinking is the promotion of deliberate speech and action. Instead of repetition and automatic speech and action, the training in meditation promotes in people awareness at every moment. In the place of habitual thoughts, speech and action, there will arise awareness. It is essential on the part of good management because it reduces organizational conflict, and thereby work culture is strengthened by effective time management – it helps to cope with the technicalities of time wasters, and saves much of managerial time which further produces the good impact of organizational effectiveness in managing resources of all types at the organization. As a result of awareness people also become aware of what they think, what they speak and what they do. Thus, man becomes creative in his activities and thoughts. Consequently, routinization of life and its activities will be prevented that is mostly important in an organizational way of life. The third, and most important effect is the awareness of one's prejudices and predispositions and freedom from the influence of unconscious desires and emotions. Hence, management of human resource becomes more and more effective towards bringing human perfection, in so far as the reality, as it were, persists and deserves for the all-round development and growth of human personality to the ground rules of managing the HRD in perspective manner. It is therefore true to mention that when the area of awareness increases in people, the area of thoughts and motives based on latent impressions, will decrease. This is a universal condition in any nature of work and is established through the principles of 'engineering psychology' and 'business process re-inventing' notions. All these happen due to the practice of detachment through the process of yoga psychological principles in a mutually all inclusive goal of management. The outcome of detachment being responsibly absorbed in action, loosens tensions and anxiety states, as a result of non-identification of one's self with one's experiences and the desires. It helps one to realize that one is playing one's role in society. Hence, responsibility aspect of management is strengthened by such principle. As a whole, there will be an awareness of the extent to which one's thoughts and feelings are influenced by the members of the group to which one belongs. The principle of communality is infused in mind of people, and they think the organization as a greater entity of the whole society.

From the above, it can be asserted that yoga psychological principles through meditational practices promote a total transformation of the self.[9] Instead of being a person whose desires and thoughts are based on bodily needs, the present perceptions and the social norms of the limited group to which he belongs, the practitioner becomes a free individual who takes into account the limitations engendered by the bodily needs, the sense stimuli and the limited social norms, and becomes more universalistic in his outlook. New insight, as it were, generates new outlooks and in turn, the new outlook leads to new insights. Thus, the individual becomes creative in the real sense of the term and not a mere creature of needs, habits, and social norms. In concluding the fact of the principles of yoga to uproot human psychological considerations and human value, it can be said that the principle of union – unity in all, is the main foundation stone of the subjective view to bring in organization in an objective manner the relativity of the 'science of work' and the 'philosophy of work'. It thus, prescribes for the liberation principle on the basis of work culture, work ethics without being involving people in bondage, but liberation in terms of doing everything in disinterested manner for greater and more perfection of human life, by increasing effectiveness at the work environment. The principles of action and not in-action, as said earlier in Chapter 1, has a greater value when collective responsibility is enhanced at the work environment. Hence, the psychological development in human thinking is strengthened by yoga principles when people become one with the universalization process of the managerial techniques and procedures of handling tasks with greater responsibility, to develop the whole society along with the organization, and people where they are concerned. As a whole, the equanimity principle which makes the organizational people to believe the organization is but an agent of social change, brings in practice universalization of managerial communication[10] through all such meditational tools and techniques which go to increase human efficiency and effectiveness of the organization by synthesizing human beliefs, feelings, thoughts, desires, drives, motives and soon, to get the work done in systematic manner.

Meditation and Effective Management

Management, the process of getting things done through people is the key to success or failure, and this process is highly effective if it is based on righteous conducts of humans and is in consonance with the cultural tenets of the society. The universality of the discipline can therefore, be enhanced when there is efficiency and effectiveness in managing all the resources of the organization. As the human beings are primarily focussing their all types of needs in the techniques and behavioural parameters of doing different business and socio-economic activities, each social institution or human organization has a greater responsibility towards the outcome of their activities – this is being contained in the performance appraisal of individuals, groups, and the organization as a whole, there is the necessity of meditational thought in converting things in practice into effective mobilization of resource outlets by optimization of the utility concept of the economic order in social life for attaining the objectives, and this requires the minimization, at the same time, of all unnecessary costs so forth relative to the production goal. As a whole, there should further be a tendency of each manager to maximize the allocated resources of the organization in terms of better and greater effort in their tasks and activities. In this regard, it becomes imperative to note that the responsibility with responsiveness is one of the factors of human real growth and development in organizational as well as social environment. For attaining such sort of goal, there is further required that each man from organizational viewpoint must be consistently pure and perfect to understand the value of own potentials, which they do not always know exactly that human potentials are infinitely endowed with the gift of creation in naturalistic way. Along with this, the effectiveness in management behaviour calls for self sacrifice while doing the activities at organizational level. This can only be enhanced when people are meditating in their action-oriented process in organizational behaviour. From this standpoint, it seems that meditation has all the principalities for preserving organizational effectiveness, so that the managerial activities are consistent with path – goal relational approach to make the entire management process an effective one. We should therefore, keep in mind that by meditation people understand the universality concept of managing themselves in organizational way of life, as they are, by this discipline automatically imparted a lesson that an organization is an instrument of social change in positivistic reality along with human perfection – this (meditation) discipline can only preserve human values in progressive manner, in so far as the goal of matching concept in utilization of resources is concerned to the realities of management. This can be substituted by association principles between human motivation and leadership qualities. Managers, as leaders, have to establish, both by conduct and expression, the community of interest which prompts people and groups to work together for certain given ends. Leader is judged by the extent of positive motivation he creates among his group members and by the manner in which motivation is translated into performance and productivity. Thus, leadership and motivation are positively related, meaning that effective leadership leads to successfully motivating people. This can be attained in organization, when there is the exact application of the rules and principles of the concept of meditational process in work environment while managing activities and people for such an end of life – for the growth, survivality, and the stability of the organizational life and order. As we know that meditation rectifies human morale, it is important to say here, that high morale leading to positive results are consistent and corollary to the extent to which the organization is achieving them, if the effectiveness of the management has to be actually measured from employees morale in organization. Hence, in the foregoing analysis of this book, we have attempted to stress on morale-building in organization; because, it is the key note of the paramount success of any organization.

The organization is the ancient terminology, either formally, or informally taken into human consideration for the evolutionary process of human growth with development, has come to a milestone of journey in human life with all its perfection, where dedication of masses are found to be either intrinsically, or extrinsically withstanding by human behavioural principles of biology which, by the science and philosophy of notion has further led man for the obligations of the inherent nature to abide by the laws of meditation – though there is common understanding between science and philosophy in this regard, but ignorance of man has not yet understood well to optimize the inherent potentials for furtherance of the self-actualization process. Only meditation can lead to this goal of human behavioural practice by solving human life related problems, when people, in their organized undertaking visualizes the organization as the instrument of real change. Thus, the management can serve more effectively and in responsible manner to the purpose of human life while handling the tasks that is to be achieved for the performance goal leading towards the perfection of life, by integrating the matchless potentials in strategic vision. The entire gamut of things are realistically taken into consideration in historical perspective, so that human life in organizational way of thinking can be made to succeed to obtain the result of their performance through appropriate principles of doing for living in effective manner. Thus, meditation and effective management are two sides of the same coin, the space of which is intermingled with the cosmological beauty of the result of human endeavour, and people have ever been searching this without knowing exactly as to how the things are to be done in universal thinking. If the meditational techniques are followed in organization, there would be optimum development of the people throughout the world in their journey of life in organization, and thereby, people will find ultimate peace in managing themselves in a better way by action-oriented principles as propounded in Indian Vedantic Order of life. In the light of these various conceptions of organic unity available here, we may infer that according to the indications provided by the Gita, society must be regarded as a unity, in fact, as an organic unity. The parts of it are necessary to each other, as the parts of an organization are. The human organism through which the divine revealed itself was indicative of this interdependence of the members of the society. Surprisingly enough, the Marxist view of society[11] is also more or less the same in which the society has been seen as a 'self'. Again, Hartshorne also advocates the view that social unity is not empirically realizable. He says: "Nothing can be social that is without experience. The minimum of experience is 'feeling'. Therefore, the creatures are social if they feel."[12] This type of vision, which was given to Arjuna to see the organic unity, may be called, in Whitehead's language a 'prehensive unity'. The prehensive unity as Whitehead explains 'is a process of prehensive unification as working behind the atmomic individuation'.[13]

We have so far observed that effective management is concerned with the result of human performance consistent with the nature, and is unflinching with the cosmological beauty of the earth. If this has to be brought into practice, humankind must have also to be trained with the zeal of perfect leadership role in sociological upliftment. When an organization perceives things at right direction, the missionary goal of work can be strategically taken into action, which causes for every behavioural attitude of the people for the effective result–effectiveness not by the end of selfish goal attainment, but the techniques and principles of humanization should be forwarded with the psychological upliftment through mental growth and development for human value-oriented system, and it should counteract with the process of perfect journey of life for unifying the goal of managing by objectives. As the objectivity is the foundation stone behind the subjective assessment of human performance, there should be universal thinking in terms of unity in perspective way of doing things for the community of interest. Hence, the meditational techniques are to be practically contained with the job analysis, which must further be entertained with the enrichment of job, for the functions of management are conditioned with the creative process of human development along with every possibilities of individual growth potentiality. The entire economic as well as social behaviour of man is guided thus, by the motivational factors and morale-building qualities, depending which effective leaders are made for futuristic development potentials of the social goal of life in man. As man in common parlance is found, flexibally bound by the notion of work in bondage, he has to learn how to get the things without involving in such practice, and rather searching for the common unity, and to mingle with the great universe by means of his activities in an organization. Thus, it all calls for better management in terms of value-based concept, and is philosophically coined with meditation, has been attempted to seeking for human perfection inaction to the process of managing, to search for such an unfinding destination, has yet to be achieved in the world. Here, spiritualization of human action has no other alternative, but a strategic goal for making human life effective through effective management in realistic perspective. Gita has put stress for solution of such type of human management problems as found in the modern world, long back. It is the alternative concept of the four-fold purusartha, including dharma, artha, and kama –meaning thereby, the duty, economy, and action based on the principles of human sociological life. It implies therefore, that economic prosperity would flow from dharma (if every one discharges his social obligations honestly) and not vice-versa. The corollary of Marxian standpoint is that instead of positing a social force like 'dharma', as the basis of human progress, Marx retains the same economic factors, which he himself wanted to transcend. He said in his combine work, "Lacking any material basis and resting on a purely theoretical foundation, it would be a mere freak and would end in nothing more than a monastic economy".[14] However, the Gita with the idea of Dharma, artha, and kama, comes forward with a more ethical approach that is not evil but the perpetuation of Dharma, which is the moving force behind the history of human aspirations and human motivation, and is an important aspect of human management for effectiveness at the work environment. Here, we may think as to how this philosophy can be made more practical and is established in management behaviour of human beings in organization. It is simply in affirmative, can be asserted that the ideal before both the principles of communism and the Gita is to re-establish the lost unity of man with mankind and to realize his essence as 'Man' – as a species being. This is the ideal of self-realization also called by the name of self-actualization, as the need of man in Maslow's Need Theory, and is to be attained in organization by meditational practices and its correct implementations with the work principles for human perfection with the unity of management function, when things are required to be done in a nature that causes to attain this goal of life for the effectiveness of human behaviour in bringing a balanced stage of feeling in mind of the people; who are guided by this philosophy through meditational aspirations in work-related unification towards making human life for experiencing the science and philosophy behind all works of man in society, in correct perspective. According to this principle, it can be well-said that the moral worth of action is to be judged in context with this goal for managerial effectiveness. Thus, by meditation effectiveness in management can be brought in organizational process of human development with the resultant growth, where the end to be realized by both –the Marxist view and the concept of the philosophy of Gita's Anasakti (disinterestedness) yoga, is also the same, viz., self-realization. Gita names it Brahma-Nirvana and Marx called it man's returning to himself duly socialized. The words may be different but they both express the urge of a man to become one with the totality of mankind.

In concluding on meditation and effective management, we should remember that the ethical considerations are primary need of man regarding self-realization process, and hence, a good suggestion has been put forward by Ginsberg that "the ethical principle in constructing a systematic hierarchy"[15], which is the necessary precondition of the success of human management process and its real effective way of dealing with the things, while getting the tasks done in a well-managed environment at the work-related principles of human life process leading towards unification as the goal of human all behavioural approaches. It is therefore, apparent to say that meditation which relates to this principle of the concept of 'Dharma' is highly effective one, for the entire regulation of individual and social life is concerned thereto, for which people in organized process have been trying for ever in this world.

Meditation and HRD

Human resource is the core of any organization – be it business, government, non-government, or any other social institution like educational, philanthropic, religious and so on. The development of human resource (HR) in an organization is mainly dependent on the training in proper way that requires mental development, so that people feel the actual need of an organization in scientific manner. It is true that science relates to a systematic study about the facts and to find-out therefrom, the inherent meaning of each fundamental truth, based on cause-effect relationship. This is done with a view to establish a unity between facts and happenings. Because, unity is the real search behind any scientific investigations for which scientists are playing a dominant role to know every truth behind all sorts of human endeavour. It is, therefore, human resource development (HRD) which fulfils the conditions of human need in actualization process through realization of the self in man, and can be brought to the ground realities of management when the principles of meditation are applied on HR in organization to search for mental development of people, so that the organization can optimize its resource utilization capacity in objective attainment of the goal of management. Thus, meditation has tremendous role to play for the optimization of resource potentials and its objective utility by means of actualization process in different types of activities to social journey of life. By meditation, organizational culture is strengthened as it works out human creativity in a manner which guides people towards the fulfillment of life-related goal in their managerial objectivity, which finds the truth of management – the strategic analysis of things in organizational policy resolution, is aimed at obtaining organizational stability, in terms of human growth and required level of development in specific manner; which has to be seen from situational approach that has the root of effectiveness in management, as it were, in organizational policy implementations from time-to-time. Today, modern organizations are encountered with the problems of rapid change due to fast change in technology. Hence, the issue of acquiring, developing and maintaining the employees of the organization poses a challenge of formulating and adopting a right strategy and approach to human resource management (HRM).[16] In this regard, we must remember that meditation, by its underlying principles of optimization theory can uproot values in human beings in organizations, so that every managerial system and procedure is kept free from bureaucratic control of the organization for bringing in organization development potentials in every human being. Thus, meditational advantage for the HRD can be assessed when we review the transitional changes that could be served in terms of –foresightedness, vision, entrepreneuring zeal, managerial qualities of good governance, MBO, organizational mission, responsibility accounting with the responsive norms for organizational development, among others, are all human motivating factor; either directly, or indirectly related to work-environment, and can provide for human potential development by strengthening the base of mental elements like attention, emotion, impulse, interest, and many other psychological treatments on the grounds of actual experimentation of organizational policies, programmes, quality circles, team building, and as a whole, the total human quality (THQ) for the all-round and steady-state development of any modern organisation.[17] From all these, it can be well-said that meditation has in its subjective role on human element in the organisation who are otherwise, committed to the organisation by exerting knowledge and learning mission to the destiny of organizational life in regard to self-realization process, when they are guided by all the principles of meditation for optimising their own potentials in sacrificial manner. This happens in organisation with greater possibility only when people are imparted knowledge about the self and the real definition of man, has already been discussed earlier. However, it is further to be noted that meditation leads to the highest journey of life in organizational activity – self-actualisation through engineering psychology, and it can be experimented when an organisation can demonstrate by practical utility to feel for the science of consciousness in relativity of work, which is guided by the principles of value-orientation, and the universal declaration of human right (UDHR). In this context, it is apparent to note that the UDHR has four important premises which provide us human rights view of governance. The premises are: (i) individual is the bearer of rights; (ii) the state has to be both a protector and also promoter of the rights guaranteed; (iii) the rights include civil, political, economic, social and cultural aspects of human beings; and (iv) the rights are universal. Besides, meditation fulfils the conditions of good governance in public organizations by restructuring the management system in public undertaking in line with human information system and synthesizing the human policy on technology upgradation in new dimensional order that includes the communication of human skills and knowledge to the path of value system with specific norms like – productivity, profitability, and stability of the organisation, in terms of satisfying minimum common needs of each human being in the organisation for living, along with the realization principles of the self by means of people's participation in management.[18]

From the above discussion, we may now turn our view to human phase from technological viewpoint, in so far as the development of human being needs an assessment of the future prospect of the organizational life of mankind in the world. The present system of development concept is consistent with the Technological Ombudsman will become a reality in the not-too-distant future, if it goes on at a pace ignoring the human phase which is the core of human management required to be preserved with the betterment philosophy; but due to lack of adequate human policy on the principles of universal entity of business and social activities, it has made the world unconcerned for human welfare in realistic manner, but intellectually developed people for only the material gain towards the destructive element, and thereby impairing the real growth potentials of human beings. So, it is expected that meditation as a measure of HRD in real perspective will open the door of universalization of human activities on the basis of real entity concept for unifying life principles towards journey of human liberation, in terms of suggesting the views of the 'technical know-what' which can tell us what purposes are worth being achieved for human development in organizational way of living, instead of 'technical know how' –which tells us how to achieve the given purposes. Thus, meditational application in work-related behaviour of man has the peculiarity of value-related notion and distinction of our concept of Swadhinata (Self-dependence) and Swatantrya (Self-subjection) which lies in the grandeur of the connotation of the word (Swa) or 'Self'. This, being the central point of human guiding philosophy, in organisation, there is the optimum necessity of this 'Swa' –which means not only 'I-ness' thinking but also with the same there should be thinking in mind of organizational people –'we-ness' ideology, which regards all human beings as in 'one-ness'. It is therefore, true to say that the Swa is both the individual self and the Universal Self; and the two are really one. By this philosophy, in management of human resources, there exists in organisation a climate which is related to the man's range of real freedom or self-dependence as we call, and it expands in proportion as he (man) is able to realize his unity with the Universal Self. This kind of thinking as provided by the meditational goal in management of human behaviour at organizational environment would lead to the great mission – humanization vision, to replace the existing international competitions by international co-operation through fellow-feeling concept in human being, and thus, manpower creativity will be optimally utilized for the purpose of peaceful consultations and reasonable compromise through basic values of human life. As a whole, the impact of this kind of solution is that there will be minimum level possible of conflict in human organizations, as it will find a world forum of discussion for maximization of benefit of the organizational results for the people in general, by transforming an ideology of the nations of the world which shall be a concept of 'One people', living at peace with one another, which is not found in common today. Thus, meditation helps further for working together for the furtherance of the common good and the revelation of God in man.[19]

In short, it goes to say that the role of meditation, if played properly in organisation, the twenty-first century can be the 'Human Millennia' in the sense that the business world has gone for a radical change with the 'Liberalisation, Privatisation, and Globalisation' (LPG) concept, which will find its way to the global socialism by means of the Oneness principles, and not by seggregative model of human developmental notions, as it is observed now. It is therefore, very essential that there should be qualitative thinking in organization, so that the creative zeal for organizational development (OD) becomes a practice of human development (HD) in correct perspective. For if, the human base at the enterprise level can be fulfilled with the learning and training concept depending on the foregoing principles of meditation practice at work-related environment in organization, there would be necessitated such a learning concept which goes to encourage human kind with the philosophy of competence-building, impartiality, morality, and human dignity – all these are essential factors of manpower development and requires for implementation an institutional process, and is to be taken into consideration as the HRD philosophy in policy resolution of the organization. When actuated of these all basic human values with the work ethics, there would be real growth of the organization altogether with individual and group development as the norms of HRD mission at the work-related environment, in terms of human perfection and the unity of the organization for the radical as well as transformational change in universal dimensional order, the motion of which will be at the very entity between the organizational and individual life conjoined together for the effectiveness of management through goal-directed approach[20], which human population in the world have been searching otherwise – in misdirectional path to attain the goal of unity in action.[21]

Meditation and Managerial Unision

We have discussed management so far in this Chapter from philosophic viewpoint to understand scientifically as to what constitute managerial goal in organizational activities. It is, therefore, assumed that meditation will lead to this goal. But that, the goal we are concerned here, is to be understood from life position in organizational managerialism. Well, it can be attained in management of human activities, when each manager concentrates on the subjective notion from objectivity. Hence, there should be unision in managing effectively which calls for real knowledge about the self-actualisation process, that which guides people towards the goal of human liberation. From this account, it can be undoubtedly said that concentration, which is the necessary elementary job behind practising with the one-track single-minded flow of the intellect, after destroying the desire and lust for all other objects, and becoming one with the ideal objective sought after, for managing things through disinterestedness to get the work done that binds in unision, the entire flow of work in such a way where the entire organizational people are required to be united with the specific goal – it is the liberating tendency of human beings in organizational activity towards the making of life, so that the philosophic movement is happened to be in existence scientifically demonstrable for understanding as to what constitute the business of self-realisation. It is only possible when people can actualise the self with the highest order of life in organization – liberation, for it requires equanimity principle, and has already been discussed in this chapter with the foregoing analysis. Thus, it goes to say that the wisdom of a person for knowing and attaining the task of unision is contemplated with the system of management in transcendental order. Because, a transcendentally conscious person can exercise his transcendental consciousness at will through the instrument of cognitive centre (caitanya kendra) resulting in the direct perception of the subtle, intercepted and such objects which lie at a distance in point of space and time, while managing in realities through business process re-engineering and so, meditation helps manager in organization attaining the goal of life. Herein, conduct means equanimity; it is to be above the feeling of attachment and aversion, likes and dislikes. In nutshel, the system of its practice is the Preksha meditation, Preksha means to perceive. Again, to perceive means to experience the object of meditation by ridding mind of attachment and aversion. This process of perception can be called the process of development of transcendental consciousness – unision conceptualization for experiencing the relativity of work and the organizational goal through universality of managerial practice, so that it produces result for the very cause of human upliftment that is necessitated for realisation of the principal values of human life destined for the highest order of making human life in organizational system, concomitted with goal of human liberation principle.

Managerial union is an approach alternative to

organizational learning[22] having its importance in the successful operation of organizations where the meditational approach can play a dominant role for the purpose of holistic development, growth, survivality, stability and so on of the organizations, because it is observed that it helps in the fast-changing environment to organizations to adapt with the changing needs of the people, within their existing cultural values and structure. However, in view of the organizational complexity growing due to diversification strategies, mergers and acquisitions, downsizing, turnarounds, globalisation, and the like with the environment becoming more and unpredictable, it seems in management literature well-nigh impossible to have a unified theory in the study of organizations. Under all these circumstances, it is worth-noting that meditation helps people to learn how to manage, as the root of the subjective view has provided the unity in action in an integrative manner, the gravitation of organization being observed with the pulse-set of its motion in cosmological boundaries, giving thereby to the management the underlying principles of human behaviour in its code of conduct, for human experience under this approach is demonstrable to the ground realities of management in terms of cause-effect relationship, to which the unision of organizational activities are found to be balanced in such order considering the aspects of human development and growth in organisational way of life. Thus, meditation, as found in a network organization, similarly focuses on how to mutually share authority, responsibility, and control among people and units that must cooperate and communicate frequently to achieve common goals. Many different networks are designed to change as the tasks to be performed and the goals to be achieved for change. Hence, the design reflects the greatest change in corporate structure through the growth of relationships based on partnerships and alliances on business principles rather than ownership. The very nerve-centre of the organization is characterized by managerial innovation, adaptive ways, shared responsibility, common goal-setting, all-channel communication networks, many diverse information technologies, cooperative attitudinal sets, organisational culture focusing on problems of external adaptation and of internal integration, and balanced goals of individuals and departments showing concern for superordinate goals and rewards.[23] Managers therefore, in organization work with the belief that there should be unity in their action, as it broadens in their mind through meditation to visualize as the multifarious colours of their visual experience in organization are only a play of refractions of the sunlight, that is indeed at the same time sunlight, and universal play of colours; as the manifold organs and structures, tissues, cells of our body we experience them only as one body of unitary Life from inside, so there is no interior Identity without exterior multiplicity, no exterior multiplicity without interior Unity; because the Being of all multiplicity of the whole organized Life is One, and the One is the multiplicity itself in an organisational pattern of behaviour. Thus, it is fact that meditation imparts knowledge to managers for understanding organisational unity of their action and the greater unision of the nature of their over all activities in the structural as well as organic sense that there is fundamental Unity in organization where people are to be trained in logical sequence for collective responsibility for fellow-feeling and brotherhoodship, while they are guided for the common goal with the multiplicity of organisational as well as managerial approaches to reach at the destined goal of life.

From the above discussion, it is now clear that meditational implications in managerial unision in an organization provides the base of human core values as to what constitute human culture in organisational environment with the socialization of the entire process, as it involves the transmission of culture from senior to new employees providing the social knowledge and skills needed to successfully perform organisational roles and jobs. For this philosophy, in management of human conduct in a culturally flow of operative norms, the integrative notion of the cosmological order with the very system of managerial functioning along with its communication base, has there been an attempt in the entity concept of the organization, as we have observed earlier, and therefore, it is suggested here that the attainment of the goal requires, on the part of management propagation of new values at every opportunity and observe the said values in managers' own behaviour. Thus, the requirement in question of this norm is – why the existing culture has become irrelevant and new culture has to be built-up has to be explained. This requires an institutionalization of the meditational approach, so that management can be felt with the basic need of such cultural flow in an organization. Hence, this is mentioned without any doubt that it also helps to develop in people a sense of history, creating a sense of oneness, promoting a sense of membership, and increasing exchange among members[24]. In short, it can be predicted the managerial unision in the overall cultural set-up of the organization transmits the same harmonious identity in work-environment of the organization, which go to enhance liberating goal in human mind and, as a consequence, managerial pyramid is strengthened whereby a manager sees himself in all beings in an organization, and all beings in the organizational Self – he sees, joined to the yoga, all the same every where while aiming to get the work done for the common purpose. It is explained in Indian Vedantic Order as 'Sarvabhutastham atmanam, sarvabhutani chatmani – iksate yoga yuktatma sarvatra samadharshanah' *(Bhagavadgita,* VI). Thus, it can be said that every culture has its own model of human development, but that in organization when real meditational knowledge is provided to the people it would lead to managerialism by bringing a universal model of human development as in consonance with the changing needs of the society. It is therefore observed that appropriate development in human mind necessarily precedes the corresponding development in the material world with the philosophic view in mind, as even the subjective revolution in human mind invariably precedes any objective revolution in the outer world. For the purpose of implementation of the meditational norms, the managerial unification theory, apart from the approaches to effective organizational change in general, a few policy resolutions in organizational planning may be paid due attention to, for a successful cultural change required to human development in understanding the practical values of life in organizational socialization and its root cause of unision in practice.[25] The synthesis of the distinctive contributions with such fresh ideas will lead mankind towards the goal of managerial unision.

Meditational Process for Organisational Mission, Vision and Objectivity

Organisations are made for human growth and development. In competitive world environment and complexities of business activities, it has become imperative for the business to set right mission which can govern people towards the satisfaction of all types of need, and therefore, meditational process in planning, organizing, and controlling towards the activities of the organization is dependent on meditational role, as the business activities world-wide are found to be concomitted with the basic fundamental notions of organizational mission, its right vision to operationalise the activities for the objective attainment of its goal. Hence, the mission statement in organization should be broadly framed and it should act as an enduring statement of intent; it is essentially an internal working document where it is observed that meditation, by way of unification in its approach for right things spells that every mission of the business enterprise needs to be both concise and unambiguous if it is to be effective. However, it is apparent to note that the mission statement to which the overall meditational prescriptions are viewed requires, for the good qualities of a mission to be included with the fundamental postulates like: (1) a statement of beliefs and values; (2) the products or services that the firm will sell (or, better still, the needs that the firm will satisfy); (3) the markets within which the firm will trade; (4) how those markets will be reached; (5) the technologies that the firm will use; (6) attitudes to growth and financing, among others. It can therefore be stated without doubt that the organizational mission statement must be wide embrasive regarding the clarity and commitment building in mind of the people rather than as it seems in most cases, tend to provoke cynicism and confusion. In specific term, it can be based on a clear, succinct statement of direction which motivates employees.

The reason that mission statements are being discussed in this Chapter, is on the belief that from the mission statement idea comes from the processes, management of the organization has to go through in drawing one up. For, the mission statement to be scientifically addressed in organizational activities, we should take help from meditation on the context of human thinking and analysis from universality aspect of such mission that it helps to attain the goal of the organization by satisfying all interest groups who are, either directly, or indirectly involved in an organizational activity. Meditation prescribes that a business being a social institution and a bye-product of human organism, it requires first such mission which must be operational for all individuals and not merely an expression of good intentions. It is therefore, essentially taken into mind that institutionalization of meditational aspects will bring in practice to the organization and its management with the job at the top, is to create direction and vision, and standards. Where people are guided by right vision in organization, leadership qualities are enhanced in managing things and they donot become afraid of strength. What is today observed as the lacking quality in management in most of the modern organizations – managers lack of confidence, commitment, credibility, consistency, conformity to the work environment, and therefore, organizational vision is expected to lead human beings to the charisma of managing in realities, when they think properly, which can only be filled in organization by meditational practice in work environment.

The managers, unlike NPOs[26] become more of a public

person than his corporate counterpart. This vision is similar to the unity of action principle, as discussed earlier in this chapter.

It is observed, in some cases, the mission of an organization, howsoever clear, is rendered irrelevant under the changed circumstances. In such a contingency, meditation comes in the way of organization being in a position to rediscover its purpose of activity. Besides, corporate mission uproots a value system and accordingly, policies are framed to implement in practice. Hence, a pilot manager in a company can comprehensively guide people by their meditational aspects of business entity concept where personal goals and vision have a place to flowering the excellance in people by way of unified thought in mind, and in action-oriented principles that go to make life free from encumbrances, in the midst of business complexities. Thus, it all depends upon the management's intent and preference to manage with love. If management understands the energise thought of love in managing things and people, the environmental considerations also shape the corporate mission. From this overall pinpointing thought on management, it is apparent to keep with managing for effectiveness through meditational goal of life; because these days of liberalization, privatization and globalisation (LPG) organizations are to share their mission statements with departmental heads, employees, and also in most of the cases with customers and the public at large. Through meditational process it is possible to draft a well-developed and advanced mission statement that invests the corporate personnel with a sense of opportunity, direction, importance and achievement. Here, meditation plays the role of an invisible hand that directs the corporate employees to strive towards the corporate objectives. When mission statement is drafted with meditational goal of life, people are motivated enough as an instrument of change by reflecting the major policies of the company to which the organization and its people stand committed. Further, in setting objectives of the organization what is more important to see is the SWOT[27] analysis. Here also, meditation helps in a sense that alternative strategies are set in organization for people's developmental purposes along with keeping in mind to become business leader in the areas of its operations, where such strategies are treated to be a subordinate parallel to guide the corporate being through its objectives. From this, it is worth-noting that meditation is an integrative process to accommodate the varying degrees of differentiation in subsystem design of the organization, and perpetuates the coordinating force of the varied subunits with the common techniques of business process re-engineering (BPR), has already been cited in previous analysis, where corporate planning provides common goals and objectives that tend to keep everyone in organization moving in the same general direction as the naturalistic way for growth and development in harmonious manner, and bringing thereby in the organizational life cycle[28], as in nature we find, the sequential order and predictable pattern followed by most organizations as they move through a developmental process in an inherent meaning of the meditational goal of life.

The primary concern of organizational mission, its vision of totality concept, and the objectivity of its varying nature of evolutionary thought in management history is reckoned through information system in a way that it transforms a radical changing of man's nature and therewith, a renovation of his understanding both of the outer world and of his own existence......The attitudes towards each other of the Hindu teacher and the pupil bowing at his feet, as Zimmer considers, are determined by exigencies of this supreme task of transformation......[which means] not a merely intellectual understanding, but of change of heart (a transformation that shall touch the core of his existence) [when] the pupil is to pass out of bondage, beyond the limits of human perfection and ignorance, and transcend the earthly plane of being.[29]

Again, an understanding on meditational process regarding corporate mission, vision and objectivity is reflected through corporate policy which enlightens all by its all comprehensive, all embrasive, and the universality aspect of human resource development mingling towards optimum perfection beyond limits, if properly implemented it impels in mind of the people commitment building, moral values and cultural transformation from generation to generation, to which, for example, we can say that 'The Art of War' of Sun Tsu[30] is uptil date an illuminating entity in socializing the process of human business with a warfare technique, though in disinterested way as required and propounded in the Gita. Peter F. Drucker himself regards management as the life giving, dynamic organ of the institution, where he emphasizes on translating the basic purpose and mission of business into objectives as otherwise they remain insight, good intentions and brilliant epigrams which never become achievement. On the objective of management, Drucker argues that business enterprise must build team-efforts, must all pull in the same direction, contributions must fit together to produce a whole – without gaps, without friction, without unnecessary duplication of effort. Thus, business performance requires that each job be directed towards the objective of whole business. This is said to be oneness from Indian Vedantic perspective of unity concept, in so far as the meditation and its value-oriented ideals in organizations are concerned. In Chapter 1, we have assessed a synthetic view on the theory of karma (action) and consequently, it is observed that the kind of philosophic (visionary) goal as enshrined in regard to the concept of management comprehensively deals with the human organizational activities in order to set free the mission of the enterprising objective of human beings towards the subjective view of management process, and is therefore, meditational process finds its place in this chapter which is the immense characteristic feature of the organizational entity concept to realize the goal of human organic life, and as a result of this phenomenon, it leads to revitalize the process of meditation towards the framing of organizational mission, its right vision for operationalisation, and the objectivity for the greater cause of human development in bringing to organization an overall effectiveness – this notion embarks on an understanding of the organizational dynamicity in scientific way to find the unfinding out of human actualization process, leading towards the goal of life in naturalistic order. Thus, the subjective view covers a wide range of value system in organization that is required to be the need of the present business in the changing situations of the world order. This philosophy of management has ever been considered in Indian Vedantic Order of life which is otherwise, termed as the 'MBO' in management literature, and is attempted again and again to analyse with the help of system approach as well as contingency approach in an unified manner.[31]

Meditation is the Goal of Human Life

Human life is goal directed towards realization of the self which is in spirited form and order. It requires a meditative approach to actualize life in the midst of action-oriented principles. But the dynamics of human behaviour as found in organizational environment is full of illusory conception of life. It can be made more and more systematic with orderliness, when people are concerned, in dealing with their life towards the attainment of organizational goal in unified manner of behavioural traits, in their approach of dealing with people in interpersonal as well as intrapersonal, intergroup as well as intragroup relationships. This is the cultural trait of an organization can be confined to meditation, irrespective of the nature of management. In realities, there are so many meditational processes, in as much as the type of institutions are there. All these are nothing but for making human life in scientific order with the nature of environment. Organisation being one of the most important instrument of human resource development (HRD) has to re-invent with innovative approach the process of matching principle to the mismatch elements of life by means of organizational right mission, vision and goal, where human life confines to the same; for managing in realities calls for an ultimate objective to the subjective notion of the overall discipline. Hence, the very object of meditation as the goal of human life requires an institutionalization with systematic orderliness; otherwise the present climax of problems of human society will further be endangered with more and more destructive nature of human philosophy of life, and thereby dehumanization process, as observed so far in the world, will have no alternative answer. The answer for solution of all problems in organized nature of life can be felt with individual nature thundering to the vivid cause of humanity. This is the meditational approach has ever been sought to implement in practice, but not yet fully attained this goal of life with the universality of the concept on the plane of perfect thinking in scientific temper. This volume is dedicated towards the attainment of such goal of life which goes to prescribe suggestions in different chapters, as to how to attain this goal. Once there is an institutionalization of the system, it can have immense practical value in society to infuse a vibrating order that fulfills all human needs people are hankering after. The technology of its approach is the simplistic mode of operation having a simulating approach on the dynamics of human behaviour to attain the goal of the HRD mission, its right vision, and the relevant conditionalities of the issues in relativistic aspect of human nature of development.

It is undoubtedly stated that one of the most important evolving nature of meditation is the rising of man and becoming a god. This is propounded in the philosophy of Indian Order.[32] Meditation is considered to be the highest order of human life, because the pure man, as Swami Vivekananda believes the concept, who has controlled the Prana, has the power of bringing it into a certain state of vibration, which can be conveyed to others, arousing in them a similar vibration.[33] At a time, this order gets in an acceleration principle multiply and thereby causes an effectiveness on the overall organizational life of people taking into account the different measures on organizational effectiveness viewpoint. Likewise, in Aurobindo's writing we see that meditation transforms matter to spirit.[34] According to Tiruvalluvar, living beings are many in number. But at birth they are all equal. When we look at this statement in the light of the exhortations, "recognize the truth from varied information and be wise to know the truth" the Kural (423). In Tirukkural the central teachings of Indian culture is provided in scientific manner which can be utilized in modern organisations and their management process, and it requires a practical exposition of the ideals of meditative value in the life of people as well as their organization for bringing effectiveness with creativity in the mode of a value system. There is no doubt that the central teachings are no less than, and same as Agnana, - avidya – absence of wisdom, ignorance. Then, how is a man to overcome this ignorance – delusion of life and have the vision of truth? The answer is provided in this work that the path of true wisdom shows the way.[35]

This can however, be equated with Karma Yoga (dedicated action, as depicted in disinterested way of action elsewhere in this book) with meditational principles, because by this time we have grasped a lot to attain karma in this book, which seems to be a testamentory edifice as an evidence of the fact, and hence its (meditation) institutionalization is very much essential, as suggested again and again in previous analysis. This can only attain the goal of human organizational life in this world, and nothing more is required. Thus, the real philosophy of managing in realities and in antiquity for the solution of the problems of life as a measure of global order for the HRD goal in perspective notion, keeping in mind the Indian Cultural heritage of 'Vasudeva Kutumbakam' (universal order in natural system), has already been expounded in Chapter 1 in sparkling manner to anticipate the root cause of human goal of life indistinguishably in all respects of living.

Integrity, Strategicity and Unification Through Transcendental Meditation

In the field of transcendental sciences vital energy and transcendental consciousness are studied, but freedom from delusion, intellect and moral, is not brought within their purview although the latter is an internal part of the science of parapsychology. It is kept outside its purview and only the four topics of clairvoyance, telepathy, precognition and psychokinesis are dealt with in this new science. The positive implication of freedom from delusion is equanimity. In other words, equanimity is the result of liquidation of delusion, intellect and moral. Thus, with the evolution of equanimity there is simultaneous genesis of transcendental consciousness. Therefore, persons working in the field of parapsychology are busy with discovering the evolution of transcendental consciousness.

In organic nature of man, the personality aspects of a man develops in two dimensions – its external dimension and the internal dimension. For the development of human beings in civil society integrity between the external and internal characteristic features with a value system requires the right strategy where transcendental meditation occupies a significant place, as it can provide the path for attaining the goal of human welfare considerations with the purity of means. The most powerful instrument for purifying the centres of consciousness is meditation. Hence, human mind, free from attachment and aversion, concentrates on centers of consciousness (e.g., centres for bliss, purity, vitality, perception, light and knowledge); then they start gaining in purity. A long-termed practice of it becomes the basis of transcendental consciousness. It is, therefore, the development of human conduct is deeply connected with the transcendental consciousness. Herein, conduct means equanimity; it is to be above the feeling of attachment and aversion, likes and dislikes. The system of its practice is the Preksha meditation – this we have already cited elsewhere in this chapter in the foregoing analysis.

In the Vedic view therefore, matter and spirit is integrated to explain the strategic idea of things and human thinking about the Absolute. In commercial world, we can assimilate this concept when we try to analyse things in order of development in higher thoughts. It is thus, when we eliminate things of irrelevant postulates of human behavioural traits and conjugate the process of assimilation with the idea of Global Order – that everything in this universal order being made to exist for the Infinitely soluble nature of the subtlity in regard to the happening of things on the pretext and context that human strategic affairs are concerning to the optimum goal of survivality along with the adaptive nature of development. It requires equanimity of an unificatory dealings with the notion that tries to achieve the professed goals of humanitarian revelation in terms of purposes that are worth being achieved – that there should be set-up of a Technical Ombudsman comprising cultured men known for humanitarianism to control, guide and direct the work of scientists and technologists. Not merely by general moral awakening, but because of the irresistible pressure of various relevant factors – ecological, demographic, cultural, developmental, strategic, etc., the demand for Technical Ombudsman also is sure to become irresistible.

Considering the accelerating principle of the various destructive, volcanic processes on the international level, and aggravation of all the consequent maladies of the present situation, it is obvious that, sooner rather than later, constitution of such a Technological Ombudsman will become a reality in the not-too-distant future. That will be the epoch-making strategy and a turning point in the modern world history, in so far as the utility of the methodological aspects of transcendentalism affairs on the plane of human thinking and action-oriented principles of life related behavioural postulates are concerned. Hence, the integrative idea on the assimilated rules of meditation with their strategicity on human action is concerned with the belief that the real humanitarianism conceptualities are the revivalistic paths, in the sense that they try to modify the principles of life on the basis of the main weapon in their arsenal—it is the soul-force, not terror. This strategy can underlie to uproot the principles of value system in organic nature of development in persisting significance of a wider moving force in changing the societal values with the perfect orderliness. Thus, the modernization concept of the Relativity of Time and Space, the unity of the universe, a Space-Time Continuum, etc. established in ancient times by Vedic thinkers and proved in this century by Einstein has a practical relevancy to the system of strategic management of things.[36] The main point therefore to be realized is that matter, living or non-living, consists ultimately of the interactions of the so-called elementary particles and therefore, it becomes almost imperative to be aware of the Consciousness-energy or the 'Vital Force' which must be involved in even the elementary particles, nay, in all forms of matter. With this view in mind, transcendental meditation is considered to be the integrative, strategic and unification ideals in the managing principles of human resources being contained in an understanding of knowing not only what matter is in its ultimate form, but also what are their working processes in different topological structures; only then can we have a knowledge sufficiently integral for the true solution of the all-important problem of the evolution of life.

It is, therefore, essential that developing a strategic perspective, as Bowman[37] has prescribed, requires as mission statement to integrate the rules of human motivating pattern in corporate management system. It eases the management team in organization into the process of thinking strategically without them having immediately confront vital and potentially controversial issues, but rather there should be pro-active nature of human welfare and development in organization. It introduces thus, a meditative principle for which a particular structure as development in organizational environment takes into team's thinking with right perspective which invariably develops new insights regarding broad aspects of strategic management tools and techniques for the purpose of human development in integrative manner. Hence, the transcendental meditation is essential because of all these ideas, what is mostly required is the – eternal principle of welfare and development concept, where every system is found effective, if strategically contained certain principles where underlie the process of human development. As we know that there is no single theory which can confine to the effectiveness of a manageable idea, expect the eternal principle with humanistic ideals of an overall system where strategic mission should be integrated for unifying the principles of a global order in the changing situation; as the change is the universal phenomenon of evolutionary perspective of human development, there is the requirement of an unfolding nature with the assimilated culture and value system where all paths are, but means to the attainment of the ultimate end of human life in organized behaviour.

From the above discussion, it goes to say that unification on the plane of human management process has quite scientific ground of justification because all knowledge is universal – therefore, it is unrealistic to think or describe any knowledge as western or eastern. So, we are to be inter-dependent rather than independent in our way of doing things for attaining the ultimate goal of human life. Because of this reason, instead of cultural differences, we are to assimilate and accommodate certain common principles for the sake of human development in common. Thus, it is essential that there should be initiating ideal rather inflicting something – not to invade but innovate for the whole rather than to be part. If possible, every part should be accommodated with the whole, so that each cultural affinity is managed with proper care for a universal order, where all find a place to revive the spirit of the goal of life – eternal principles of humanization process for universal integrity, with right type of strategy, unravelled with the notion of natural beauty for attaining the goal of effective management of human value in right directional order; where all systems are, but a unified concept of human development in matchless gift of the intuition, for invigorating human expels the ideals of growth in natural order with systematic development – it is the methodology of any kind of meditational value to be preserved in realities of management.[38]

Re-inventing Meditation for Managerial Re-engineering Process (MRP) in Business and other Human Activities

Managerial decision-making approach and the implementation procedures, tools and techniques occupy an important place in managing the modern complex organisations for social responsibility building along with responsiveness. This requires that meditational application should be re-invented as an innovative technique to produce goods and services as expected from the standpoint of sociological need and necessity in reality, in the context of changing situation as an universal order of business philosophy. Thus, re-inventing technique in meditational field should not only be formed merely to satisfy a philosophical approach.[39] In new economic environment, it should be broad-based with a view to giving special attention to human beings who are deprived, rather than just structuring organisations in new dimensional order. What is more essential, we should better concentrate on business development and commercial operations in line with co-operative principles that require a managerial re-engineering process (MRP) in business and other human activities in all society, and at all time in strategic view. This, we can adopt with the business process of re-engineering (BPR) technique, and has already been analysed in the foregoing discussions.

Here, we would like to deal with two important tools of social control of business, viz., - (i) Programme Evaluation and Review Technique (PERT), and (ii) Critical Path Method (CPM) as a broad-based measure of meditational application in managerial decision-making approach. As a matter of fact, we have so far observed that the society can only be developed to grow with all its potentials when there is the understanding of work and its value added to society to uproot the fundamental causes of human degradational conditions through management in realistic view. This has necessitated for the great cause of meditational application in business, so that managerial decision-making approach becomes an effective tool to such order of social development through business and other economic activities of human beings as expected so far in this volume, and is dealt in an objective manner for more and more subjective effectiveness. As we know that methodical application of meditation can only solve all types of social problems;

similarly, in business and economic activities MRP has to be developed taking help from Indian Order as well as system to systematize things and activities with the relativity of social cause, and its requirement for a perfect nature of modification goal. Coming over to this situation, it can be predicted that Indian Order of MRP calls for stable mind in human decision-making process with a view to really motivate people at the work place in an open environment. Hence, ignoring all other conditionalities of life, the intellect of a worldly-minded man who has no control over his senses and mind is diverted, we are to emphasize for organizational people through meditational practice at work-indispensability of sense-control for attaining stability of mind with a view to achieve the real goal of business and other human activities. Thus, a stable-minded man can achieve for self-actualisation purpose of life, which is the highest need of man, an indiscriminating practice for the attainment of self-satisfaction as well as achieving the goal of the organization from sociological standpoint. Because, he can only discriminate about good side and ill-side of all business decisions and the effect of their right application in practice – it is by means of overcoming likes and dislikes, doing everything for the great cause of the organization on the one hand, and the society on the other, leaving everything to his point of indiscrimination in disinterested way of getting things done through all the tools and techniques of meditation, and thereby re-engineering the causes and impact of each decision approach in a broad-based pattern of human development with social growth potentialities.

In re-inventing meditation there is an advantage on business process which can be re-engineered through the business process re-engineering (BPR) as the case of the search for each of the problematic pathways towards a solution, is likely to include a close examination of the possible benefits from a greater reliance on information technology (IT), which is the central theme in most BPR writings.[40] However, this focus on IT solutions is not the essence of the analysis involved in BPR. Each business process has to be reconceptualised through meditation from basic principles. Indeed, the rethinking may need to be even more radical than that. Drucker has suggested in this regard that major productivity breakthrough in services come not from speeding up or automating the task, as is generally the case in manufacturing, but from redefining the task.[41] Thus, the BPR provides, when dealt from meditational as well as right philosophic point of view in realistic principle – an alternative perspective on ways of incorporating quality assurance procedures, particularly, of human quality rather than other factors, into business process. Hence, much attention has to be given to the fact that in BPR the critical re-examination of all existing managerial processes, allowing thereby the elimination of the unnecessary steps and procedures for business effectiveness in regard to managerial decision-making approach for real human development and, to the attainment of the organizational goal in an environment of free or open reinforcing human behavioural conditionalities, based on the principle of neutrality as well as equity. Moreover, what is essentially as well as fundamentally observed that present global order of the business will not solve human problems in society as the civic system of life without including in business concept, the absolute sacrificial order and a Czar like treatment unto death, or do or die manner of working with perfect nature; where people from all strata of the society should be served by managers and leaders in disinterested way through action-oriented principles, in which human motivation must be based on concentration of the equanimity laws, for which meditational application is a must as propounded by the re-inventing theory of meditation. It will foster the growth of the society in the right path to achieve the goal of the human resource development (HRD) through training and development in a manner of sensitivity and creativity, and is thus, social goal of business would be balanced by means of the preponderance of yogic practice in realistic order, and is guided by the philosophy of human life behind human social and business activities.

From the above discussion, it has to be said apparently

that for MRP the yoga of knowledge (as prescribed in the Upanishadic Order of life) is very much essential to be included in business practices as the measure of control of the self otherwise guided by the delusion of human nature. This can eradicate human ignorance for which human organisations are failing day-by-day, and year-after-year, and consequently, human beings are labouring in business activities under this delusion from time without beginning, and is due to this that he is moving in this whirligig for world existence. Hence, overcoming all egotism, sense of possession, attachment and desire when man at last succeeds in reaching the state understanding what is really human business of life. It is, therefore, rightly said in the Gita he who succeeds in attaining this state during his life-time is the best flower of humanity. From this perspective order of managerial dynamics of human behaviour the state of equanimity is reached by remaining in action, and not by becoming in-action, or leaving the action (also see Chapter 1). Here, human delusion has been given due importance to the re-inventing policy of meditation for managerial re-engineering purposes, so that people by doing action can attain the 'Brahmic Bliss' which is the 'Absolute Order' of human life, can be experimented in business environment with the philosophic re-draft of the organizational mission, and the demonstration by practice in business and human economic activities with the theory of relativity between science of getting things done on the one hand as the cause; and the art of human skill development in real philosophic order as the effective change in business practices. With more confidence, it is said that this method of meditational goal will come in the way of solving all business problems and human suffering in this global order of business activities.

The promises of BPR as attracted from meditational viewpoint to deal with global competition and ever higher expectations of customer in respect of service, quality and value can only commensurate in all sectors of business, and in all types of human social organisations, when it is combined with the MRP. In this insistence on rapid and radical change what is needed now, and is expected from organisations, BPR takes an extreme position through meditational application along with the spectrum of viewpoints on the appropriate pace of change in the corporate transformation process.[42] So, the re-inventing of meditation as the goal for business as an opportunity in managerial dynamics of behaviour, and from the viewpoint of socialization of business and economic activities can be more and more understood when we pay due attention to Peter F. Drucker, as for example, he has suggested that it is possible to trigger successful organizational change from any position on this spectrum, from continuous improvement through managed evolution to out-and-out innovation.[43] Thus, a fundamental change can be brought to the plane of business from the standpoint of managerial dynamics of behaviour to their decision-making approaches, from the real perspective of meditational goal in regard to human sociological development through evolutionary process of life in organizational growth potentials.

Cosmological Unision : A Managerial Perspective

Managerial capabilities and competencies have a wider implication on the HRD philosophy, its genesis of unstinted growth for the purposive development of the society, which requires a perspective visionary goal towards the successful attainment of the organizational goal, and thereby it encompasses to the cosmological order in the plane of which humanistic attitude confines an underlying principle of growth potentials with all parameters of management in the organizational culture, atmosphere, and its environment. All these constitute a fabricated structure of the organization for guiding the society to the path of human welfare. Thus, meditation has caused for its right applicational idea, as an order of human development with the management of real change in society; so that humanistic attitudes are brought to the forefront of welfare of the human society. Considering this aspect of human development, in management of human resource meditational idea has been imposed with a view to understand the cosmological vision of the management goal. Hence, we have also referred the case of yoga in different places of this volume. Here, we would like to interpret it going to the depth of yoga psychology. As a matter of fact, we are to account the present global order of development, for which it goes to say undoubtedly that in business and human economic activities also, it has wider application as the basic ground of human development is mainly related to the physiology as well as anatomy of human beings for bringing right type of mental development in right order. So, while finding it important in the world of business in an era of liberalization, privatization and globalisation (LPG), we have therefore, to search for co-ordinating the principles of business on the basis of western science and eastern philosophy which should be assimilated in a point of balanced development of both the societies at large, for all kinds of people, and in all times.

The above aim of business can be challenged strategically when we try to understand the concept of human development and social growth in right perspective. For it, there is the necessity of understanding of the yoga practices at the work place which connotes and subscribes to the successful business environment. In this regard, Indian Vedantic Order of life has been put forth for enhancing right type of sociological development with the process of humanization in social activities. For this reasonable understanding, this volume in celebrated as well as sparkling manner envisages that there are three important types of yoga propounded in Indian Order for all human activities in this universe. The yoga of action (work), has been disinterestedly discussed in the foregoing analysis of this book; the yoga of knowledge (wisdom), also referred to somewhere else for human cause of betterment; and lastly, the yoga of *bhakti* (dedication), are all the important postulates of human behaviour which guide men in the world for strategic practices of human business and economic activities in the domain of environment. Again, all these are to be balanced to supplement developmental order of life, where the *bhakti* yoga finds the priority of importance to balance the sequential order of life, as the yoga of work and the yoga of knowledge, at last, assimilates to the yoga of bhakti that guides men for perspective development. Hence, the 'Theory of Balance'[44] is given due importance in Chapter 2 on understanding Organisational Thought.

As we know that Patanjali's Yoga Sutra[45] is famous for human mental development, where there is a reference in it as to how man can serve the society with the best way of understanding the self-actualisation process by doing activities in sacrificial manner. Swami Vivekananda in this regard said that while entering into the depth of consciouslessness stage, man can realize the self, where it is observed that there is no difference between the lower self (individual self) and the Higher Self (Universal Self or the Absolute). If we bring it on a cosmological point, then only it is possible a perspective development of a global order, where all paths are, but leading to the same goal of human operation and activities in society. By going to consciouslessness stage, we donot mean in-action, but rather business practices are to be considered from sociological viewpoint of equanimity concept. It can only be possible, when people meditate to understand the innermost principle of life which is similar to all kinds of environment, which causes men for bringing to the optimum growth in the right path and direction; so that once visited people donot try to remain in delusion with a wrong notion of development. As for example, Swami Vivekananda says that Gautam Buddha, the propagator of Buddhistic philosophy, himself went for experiencing this principle on the basis of Patanjali's Yoga Sutra, and consequently, realized implications of many past lives of himself. Similarly, there are hundreds and thousands of examples in Indian Vedantic Order. All these are based on the 'Theory of Balance' principles – it means that yoga of work and yoga of knowledge have to be assimilated with the principle of the bhakti yoga. At this stage, the man becomes wise, and pain and pleasure of life becomes alike, and is not tormented by these contacts. At last man becomes eligible for immortality. Again, this brings in mind that the unreal has no existence, and the real never ceases to be. The reality of both has thus been perceived by the realized souls (the seers of truth). This has to be creatively intended from the mind, rather imitating others. Hence, meditational laws are very essential to be implemented in business practices to change the unrealistic assumption of human growth and development, and the society altogether with business principles of equanimity as depicted in the Gita.[46]

This ultimately helps in Sanskara (reformation) of human beings by means of managing in realistic order that has yet to be established in the organizational mission, as a visionary goal of human progress in societal order of life. This is, what is meant by perception by the seers of truth of the reality of both the unreal and real. It has been coined as the 'Preksha Meditation' which we have already dealt in this book. The implementation of this type of principle requires an institutional process that we once again said in this volume. If this can be properly reinvented with all innovative techniques, there would be possible co-ordination between the scientific foundations of business and the philosophical order of human life to guide the whole society in parallelism to humanization process for the overall socialization as well as welfaristic view of human development potentials. This, the theorists of all disciplines from time immemorial periods have been trying to set-in-motion, and therefore, we have also expected that such managerial vision could lead to people for guiding themselves to the path of perspective goal of human civilization, as the present situation demands all over the world. Due to lack of such philosophic mission, world business activities are not in a position to come-up successfully, instead of discovering many theories of business practices from time to time.

From the above discussion, we may now conclude that cosmological vision is the scientific notion regarding philosophic understanding of human life related concept of business activities. It has to be taken from aesthetic way for getting the things done, while managing human organisations from the viewpoint of social welfare in global perspective; otherwise any theory will remain as the theory and will provide nothing more than human catastrophic order that has been going on in this world for long. It will thus, cater to the real needs of the society in changing order of business activities, and thereby the entity concept of the business should be re-established with dynamics of business behaviour by managerial process-orientation in guiding the organization, which will go to produce peace with social welfare for the development of global mankind in an integrative as well as unified manner, so far we have observed from the antiquity of business philosophy and the strategic mission of human life in an organized way of societal living. This, we have tried at length in different chapters, and therefore, it is expected that our endeavour for such a business visionary goal will only commensurate with the institutional process of meditation that go to re-build human superstructure in scientific temper with the co-ordination of a system, where all paths are possible to lead for a common codified goal of universal integrity and business management strategically through organizational dynamics of human behaviour in a manner of relativity – which finds the unfinding out as the search of a truth in human all types of endeavours that men have been perplexed so far in a materialistic changing world. Hence, the necessity of cosmological beauty arises to establish a unified thought in the field of business as the goal of human life-oriented concept for human growth, survivality, stability, adaptability, and similar attributes of human mission in socialisation process.

References

1. Equanimity feeling in meditation comes when people know how to work in disinterested way. Under this method, every action and reaction is guided by the process of fruitlessness and becomes only goal-directed. This goal of work being related to human perfection for realizing the inner self in man, disinterested way of doing activities prescribes, as suggested in Chapter 1, for the highest need of man, i.e., self-realisation, which is attained when one thinks that there is no difference between the own self and the whole universe.

2. Kuppuswamy, B.: *Elements of Ancient Indian Psychology,* Vikas Publishing House Pvt. Ltd., 1985, p. 207. See also, Goyandka, Jayadayal: *Srimad Bhagavadgita,* Gita Press, Gorakhpur, 1993.

3. MacBeath, G.: *Organisation and Manpower Planning,* 2nd Edn., Business Books Limited, London, 1969, p.55.

4. Drucker, Peter F.: *Management – Tasks, Responsibilities, Practices,* Harper & Row, New York, 1974, pp. 77- 79.

5. Drucker, P.F.: *The Practice of Management,* Harper & Row, New York, 1954, p. 63.

6. There are two types of human creativity, viz., actual and potential creativity. The former being that potential which is already developed and functioning, the latter including the total creative potential (both developed and undeveloped) within an individual. Creative potentials of human beings are having some personality traits attribute such as –self-sufficiency, independence, openness, stability, tolerance to ambiguity, feminity in interests, and self-confidence, which are related to be the first stage of their characteristic qualities. Therefore, researchers on creativity analysis have rightly hypothesized that the creative individual tends to produce adaptive responses that are original in nature. Here, meditational practices have great advantages which modern organizations can utilize potentially as well as profitably for the purpose of HRD, and consequently, creative teaching is suggested for its proper implementation and understanding in practice. Because, it is the best and the most indispensable way for promoting creative behaviour in organizational people, and it promotes also self-activity principles by encouraging people to explore and experiment different ideas and realities of life.

It thus, requires an institutionalization of the subjective view of the conceptual ideas for effective management of, and development to the manpower resources of organization with the strategic deplorable conditions of various issues regarding the process of HRD and its relevant perspective goals. – Lytton, H.: *Creativity and Education,* Routledge and Kegan Paul, London, 1971. See also, Lownfeld, V.: *Creative and Mental Growth,* Macmillan, New York, 1957.

7. Frank, Philipp: *Relativity – A Richer Truth,* Jonathan Cape, Thirty Bedford Square, London, 1951. Also see, Frank, Philipp: *Modern Scienceand its Philosophy,* Harvard University Press, Cambridge, 1949. This book presents suggestions for a restoration of the unity between science and philosophy, and contains in the last three chapters a programme for fuller integration within the college curriculum.

8. Deb, S.: *Contemporary Issues on Management,* Atlantic Publishers and Distributors, New Delhi, 2001, p. 35. This view of management is contained in the TQM principles and practices, and is enlarged here, with a view to enhance HRD as the basic and fundamental element of organization behaviour, as it denotes – the philosophy of management, its universalisation, and common unity to the global business entity, so that universalisation of the subject becomes possible through man-power research and development for the unity of management to the goal of human perfection in right direction, and as right dimensional order in systematizing human activities to the social development for all times to come. This is the unification theory being maintained, if any at all, in science and philosophy of human work related principles in time and space with relativity aspects of human development.

9. In terms of one of the yoga institutional thought, as for example, 'Prajapita Brahma Kumaris Ishwariya Vishwa Vidyalaya', it can be said the aim of all this (Raj Yoga) teaching is to enable one to rid one's self of any attachment to the body and objects of all bodily senses, and also to all worldly relationships, and thereby to stabilize one-self in the remembrance of the soul and the father of all souls, - i.e., the Supreme Soul. - Chander, Jagadish B.K.: "One-week Course – For Attainment of Complete Purity, Peace and Prosperity", Prajapita Brahma Kumaris Ishwariya Vishwa Vidyalaya, Pandav Bhawan, Mount Abu. There are similarly, hundreds of separate yoga institutions. All those institutions are founded upon human perfection by imparting knowledge about the self. Hence, this sort of meditational practice has a great impact on HRD philosophy in organization for effective management.

10. "......the sorry state of the discipline and its complex processes, we should know something about rethinking with a well-thought-out policy. In Drucker's language, we may call communication in organizations as managerial communication with a habit of continuous improvement, for without its effectiveness everything in organizations become missionless and unproductive". – Drucker, Peter F.: "Really Reinventing Government", *Span,* December 1995. It is therefore, yoga principles the application of which brings a transformational change of people in organization, and thereby, in the life-blood of the organization itself there takes place a radical change which tends to unity with perfection.

11. Marx describes the final stage of communism, as consisting of 'socialized humanity' that is 'a classless, stateless, and generally a structureless collectivity of complete individuals, who live in harmony with themselves and with each other'. He seems to have tacitly assumed the nature of the

'ultimate', which cannot be precisely described. Marx himself writes: "Here for the first time his natural existence is his human existence and nature has become man for him. Thus, society is the complete essential unity of man with nature, the resurrection of nature, the achieved naturalism of man and the achieved humanism of nature." – Marx, K., MEGA, *Historisch-Kritische Gesamtausgabe* Ed. by D. Rjazanov, p.126. It means that for Marx, the act of world history is the self-realization of 'Man' in his collective or generic sense. It is the ascent of man from the 'Kingdom of necessity' to the 'Kingdom of freedom'. – Marx, K. and Engels, F., Selected Works, Vol.II, Progress Publishers, Moscow, 1969, pp. 140-141.

12. Hartshorne, C., *Reality as Social Process,* Free Press, Illinois, 1953, p. 34.

13. Whitehead, A.N., *Science and the Modern World,* Cambridge University Press, Cambridge, 1953, p. 81.

14. Marx, K., Engels, F., and Lenin, V.I., *On Historical Materialism,* Progress Publishers Moscow, 1970, p. 60.

15. Ginsberg, Morris: *On Justice in Society,* Heinemann, London, 1965, p. 10.

16. For an understanding over the issues of human resource management (HRM) policy, an organization, at present, requires adequate research base, so that the HRD mission of the organization is underlying certain principles that govern organizational effectiveness in contingent congruency on the phase of people's development strategy (PDS). Thus, in HRD, research is necessary to ascertain: (i) the needs of the employees, (ii) their attitudes to work, (iii) their reactions to managerial behaviour and practices, (iv) the causes of their grievances and resistance to change, if any, (v) the factors behind inter-personal and inter-group conflicts, (vi) the state of the

organization climate, among others. However, such strategy is expected to be adopted and implemented in organizations for organizational development (OD), which aims at a higher quality of work life, productivity, adaptability, and effectiveness. Ultimately, it seeks to change human beliefs, attitudes, values, strategies, structures, and practices to enable the organization people to better adapt to competitive actions, technological advances, and the fast pace of other changes in the environment. – French, Wendell L. and Cecil H. Bell, Jr., *Organization Development: Behavioral Science Interventions for Organization Improvement,* 4th Edition, Prentice-Hall, Englewood Cliffs, New Jersey, 1989. Resultantly, it can be said that the HRD mission must have to be technically and strategically contained in the organizational policy because, it has immense and far-reaching benefits like: (1) It reveals the weak spots and deficiencies of employees. It also discovers their potentialities. Both these are necessary to give them training and provide for their development in the right direction; (2) It motivates the employees, improves their morale and promotes their sense of belonging to the organization; (3) Employees are inspired to take initiative, encouraged to face challenges and enabled to be innovative and adaptive; (4) Counselling by superiors or professional consultants helps in gearing up the spirit of employees suffering from frustration and apathy to work; (5) It promotes openness, trust and collaboration among the employees in general; (6) It generates a healthy organization culture which is essential to increased productivity; (7) Along with the development of its employees, the organization also moves forward and achieves prosperity. Even an enterprise that has ordinarily reached its limit of growth can gain through adaptability to change in the environment and thus overcome stagnation. HRD in different industries and businesses ultimately contributes to development of the nation as a whole. – See also Pareek, Udai and Rao, T. Venkateswara, *Designing and Managing Human Resource System*, Oxford & IBH Publishing Co., New Delhi, 1981; Nadler, Leonard, *A Handbook of Human Resource Development*, John Wiley, New York, 1985.

17. By meditation, it is possible to bring in man the total human quality (THQ) which is characterized by sense, mind, and bodily training, and thereby the intellect, vigour, vision of man is clarified for realization of everything to the Absolute Form – called in Indian scriptural order, a God-realization technique in work-related philosophy. Thus, the steady-state development of man in organizational life is concerned with the state of stable existence in God has been referred to in the Gita. It relates to the stable condition of mind and can be attained only when man remains constantly and unshakably absorbed in God, the embodiment of Truth, Knowledge and Bliss – absolutely free from egoism, the sense of possession, attachment, yearning and desire, and altogether undisturbed by favourable or unfavourable circumstances. In organisation, this philosophy of life is important because people are merged in ignorance donot know what is Brahma (Absolute), who is God, what is the nature of this world, what is Maya, what is the relation obtaining between all these, who is he, wherefrom he has come......Overcoming all these – egoism, sense of possession, attachment, desire, etc. are possible when learning and training activities are concerned with the Yoga psychological principles, and therefore, it guides man to the highest destiny of life for self-actualization process, in the midst of doing all activities in disinterested way. This, in meditation, is realized through self consciousness philosophy, according as to the nature of managerial goal towards the attainment of tasks, and performing those organizational activities for the peace and

harmony of life. Thus, meditation helps in the total personality development of man, in so far as the concept of theory and practice is assimilated with the help of such a first-hand knowledge, the approach being felt by reality which exists in nature can be visualized through organizational activities, as it produces in man by imparting knowledge – the direct consciousness of the ultimate reality behind human management philosophy in this world. For more clarification of such idea we can refer K.C. Bhattacharya, who may be understood as constituting the Absolute concept on Alternation principles, and as for instance, he says: "In one direction their identity and difference are alike meaningless, and in another direction their identity is intelligible, but not assertable. Truth is unrelated to value, value to reality and reality to truth, while value may be truth, reality value and truth reality. The Absolute may be regarded in this sense as an alteration of truth, value and reality." - Bhattacharya, K.C.: *Studies in Philosophy*, Vol.II, Progressive Publishers, Calcutta, 1958, p.143. In short, it is meditation exemplifies how to manage and realize human life at the same time. It can be practically demonstrated in scientific investigations in OD for the HRD as its perspective goal in celebrated manner.

18. In this regard, we have observed that participative management ideologies though practiced in different forms throughout the world, depending on the nature of productivity as well as organisation cultural norms, the management of human resource under each approach has yet to achieve its real goal, which is lacking behind some expectation, and can be enhanced in practice to the organisation's system of management by applying very simple ethics of the code of conduct in human behaviour. This calls for greater and greater role of outside consultant who by the counselling services on yoga methodology can

prescribe real knowledge about co-operation, and the motive force behind the success of the co-operative principle in the entrepreneurship ability-building process. Therefore, it envisages knowledge of adequate human information system (HIS) technically guided by the philosophy of human value-based management, which will exert basic knowledge and belief to each human personality in industrial and business world. It requires therefore, for the furtherance of value human interface with that of communication and information system of the organisation. From this, it can be predicted that one of the major goals of human information and communication system in any corporate strategy is to create a competitive advantage or distinctive competency – something that the organization does with sufficient uniqueness that it serves as some sort of competitive edge over competitors in some particular aspect of the market. In view of this incredible evidence, there can be no doubt that Japan's competitive advantage is its distinctive competency in operations management. The key to the Japanese success phenomenon lies on the factory floor where employees share a "culture" based on a unique mix of worker expertise and motivation, modern technology, and operations management techniques that focus on cost control, total quality, and a unique inventory control system known as Just-in-time inventory. In fact, by meditational process the productivity, profitability and organisation's ability to produce good human relationship in business as well as non-business entity can be attained in unparalleled way when it is approached and applied in pro-active manner, so that human participation is not cumbersome with the overall techniques of production goal in an enterprise or an organisation. Now, it can be adopted in more and more progressive international firms by bringing a work culture through such participative management principle which stands on the organizational and human entity philosophy in a more broader view. – Taylor, Frederick: *The Principles of Scientific Management*, Harper, New York, 1911. See also, Likert, R., *New Patterns of Management*, McGraw-Hill, New York, 1961; Newman, William H., *Constructive Control*, Prentice-Hall Inc., Englewood Cliffs, N.J., 1975; Black, Stewart and Newton, Margulies, 'An Ideological Perspective on Participation: A Case for Integration', *Journal of Organizational Change Management*, Vol. 2, No.1, 1989; and Ketzell, R.A., and R.A. Guzzo, "Psychological Approaches to Worker Productivity", *American Psychologist*, Vol. 36, 1983, pp. 468-472.

19. The path for the meditation for realizing the self in management by objective (MBO) calls for a want for the divinity in human action. If one wanted the Divine, the Divine himself would take up the purifying of the heart and develop the sadhana and give the necessary experiences; it can and does happen in that way if one has trust and confidence in the Divine and the will to surrender. For such a taking up involves one's putting oneself in the hands of the Divine,......and this implies one's putting one's trust and confidence in the Divine and a progressive self-giving. It is the central process of yoga. - Anand, K.C. (Editor): " Swami Vivekananda and Sri Ramkrishna in Sri Aurobindo's Writings", *All India Magazine*, Sri Aurobindo Society, Pondicherry, Sept.-Oct. 1993, p. 41. Thus, the meditational thought by way of its cumulating effect of the cellular health, which affects all organs of human body including the endocrine glands, is reflected through yoga practice, on the mental perspective of organizational people and, therefore, also on the character, behaviour and human personality. It is this mental transformation from the ignoble to the noble which yoga seeks to promote, in some measure, through special physical education. This specific feature of yoga is now fully recognized by all

authorities on physical education. – Massey, F.J., *Physical Education and Healthful Living,* p. 78 and Rice, E.A. and Hutchinson, J.L., *A Brief History of Physical Education,* p. 182. In the right view both of life of yoga all life is either consciously or subconsciously a yoga. For, we mean by this term a methodized effort towards self-perfection by the expression of the potentialities latent in the being and a union of the human individual with the universal and transcendent Existence we see partially expressed in man and in the Cosmos. But all life, when we look behind its appearances, is a vast 'Yoga of Nature' attempting to realize her perfection in an ever increasing expression of her potentialities and to unite herself with her own divine reality. In man, her thinker, she for the first time upon this Earth devises self-conscious means and willed arrangements of activity by which this great purpose may be more swiftly and puissantly attained. – *op. cit.,* p. 43. In short, the effectiveness of management is brought in action-oriented principles through the inherent principles of meditation as well as yoga practices to strengthen the growth and stability of the organization, in the process of HRD as its genesis as the goal of thinking.

20. The unfinding goal of human life can be demonstrated in practice to find out the consciousness in human beings, for which meditation is the only way that keeps human mind free from attachment and aversion, and concentrates on the centres of consciousness (e.g., centres for bliss, purity, vitality, perception, light and knowledge); then human beings are directed to start for gaining purity. This process, as a whole, leads to the development of our understanding for realization of the concept of transcendental consciousness – the reality behind human knowledge and intuition, can focus over the issues of goal-directed approach towards the making of human life, based on the

discovery of such a unified concept intermingled towards organizational diversity. Hence, one should realize that a proper synthesis of spiritualism and materialism can only solve the mystery of life which is our ultimate goal. With this view in mind, meditational thought is considered here in, to be an actual way for human development as the practice of organizational mission, based on human vision to guide people in the right path for the right goal of life, as a matter of understanding the basic values of human work ethics and fundamental considerations mingling to the unified theory of management as the relativity aspect of human development principles, and bringing thereby eternal peace and harmony, conjoined with the beliefs and values of managerialism process within the parameters of human organism, which find its place to the destiny of life bound by the organizational fundamental systems and conceptualities. It thus, connotes the fact that meditation when, it is related to the HRD policy implications breaks-up all types of organizational barriers to come-across as the managerial pyramid – it means organization becomes a place of self-realization through an institutionalization of the meditational goal of human life in practical way. – See also, Bhandari, M.C.: *Para Vidya – Science of the Beyond*, Para Vidya Sansthan, Calcutta, 1985.

21. In this context, the unity in action of managing human resources stands for the unification of the principles of human behaviour confined with task for getting things through a chain of command, the postulates of which comes from the 'Infinite Nature' itself which is created for the purposiveness of human action based on the principles of moral values and work ethics, that which guides organizational people towards the matchless gift of the great Nature, where infinite potentials of human beings are required to be implemented for optimizing the goal of

human management process, so that the organization can contribute hopelessly beyond imagination for the welfare of global mankind. In this regard, an opinion of B.R. Mishra, who studied about the economic objectives of the Constitution of India is quite illuminative for understanding as to what constitute the principle of HRD. He explained that "equal right to work, equal pay for equal work and adequate means of livelihood, both to men and women, are guaranteed under the State Policy. The future State shall endeavour to make provision for full employment, old age pensions, sickness and disablement allowance in order that the haunting shadow of insecurity that darken's many lives may be abolished. It shall also be the duty of the State to give just and humane conditions of work and a living wage to agricultural and industrial workers to ensure a decent standard of living. Finally, the economic system is to so operate that wealth and means of production are not concentrated in the hands of a few for the common detriment. This implies an equitable distribution of wealth and income among the masses in order that economic power, due to disparity in distribution of wealth, may cease to influence the working of the body politic of the country". – Mishra, B.R., *Economic Aspects of the Indian Constitution*, Orient Longmans Ltd., Bombay, May 1952, pp. 10-11. This can be treated as the philosophy behind right directional order, for the unity of action in management of HR is guided by the principles of human welfare towards social upliftment of the masses, as found in Indian order of life.

22. Organisations to be successful in a competitive world have to learn and relearn. It is the second-order or double-loop learning in contrast with first-order or single-loop learning, and a sudden interest in this terminology owes itself perhaps to the fast-changing environment and to the work of Chris Argyris and his colleagues. – Argyris, Chris and Donald Schon,

Organizational Learning, Addison-Wesley, Reading, Mass., 1978; and Argyris, Chris, *Overcoming Organizational Defenses,* Allyn-Bacon, Needham Heights, Mass., 1990. Also see Senge, Peter M., *The Fifth Discipline: The Art and Practice of the Learning Organization,* Doubleday, New York, 1991, and "The Leader's New Work: Building Learning Organizations", *Sloan Management Review,* Fall 1990, pp. 7-23. It has emerged as generative learning view and as the latest widely accepted view of organisational theory. In management, this can bring in teams to explore new ideas in life-like conditions without disastrous consequences and that requires meditative approach. Sooner the organizations realize the importance of this, the better it is. – Adapted from Maira, Arun, "Know-how versus Learning", *Business India,* October 24-November 6,1994, p.133.

23. Hellriegel, Don, John W. Slocum, Jr. and Richard W. Woodman, *Organizational Behavior,* Sixth Ed., West Publishing Company, St. Paul, 1992, pp. 626-27.

24. Gross, Warren and Shula Shichman, "How to Grow on Organizational Culture", *Personnel,* September 1987, p. 52.

25. According to Dumaine, for creating a new company culture, an organization has to understand first – (i) the old culture; (ii) how to support employees with a vision; (iii) to identify the most effective sub-culture in the organization; (iv) to propagate the effective subculture as an example; (v) that it does not attack the whole culture head on; (vi) to have a vision of a new culture; (vii) to appreciate that culture change takes time; (viii) live the new culture – actions speak louder than words, among others. – Dumaine, B., "Creating a New Company Culture", *Fortune,* January 15, 1990, pp. 127-131.

26. Non-profit organizations (NPOs) are termed as America's 'third sector' by Peter F. Drucker. As NPOs don't have a bottom line, they need management more. NPOs are run very efficiently – Girls Scouts, American Red Cross, American Heart Association, American Salvation Army. The volunteers working for these NPOs are unpaid staff to Drucker. NPO's performance is related to their mission which must be operational and not merely be expressed of good intentions. Leadership of NPO's has a peculiar 'behavior' and performance. Here the most dangerous and least useful thing is charisma. It is a trap that leads to non-performance and paranoia - not results. The job at the top is to create direction and vision, and after all standards. Secondly, the leader knows 'that the buck stops here'. He doesn't blame extraneous factors. He says: 'it is my job, my responsibility'. Leaders are not afraid of strength. They in fact, want strength. NPOs deal with a great, a great number of constituencies and that makes additional demands on the leaders of NPOs. It is therefore, rightly said that managers working in NPOs are more of a public person than his corporate counter-part. Hence, NPOs must have crystal clear missions to inspire the volunteers. Thus, NPOs have to stick to its mission and avoid taking on problems in the names of compassion it cannot handle.

27. 'SWOT' is the catchword which means for strengths, weaknesses, opportunities and threats. The prestigious joint venture of IBM of the US and the Tatas – Tata Information Systems Ltd. (TISL) was started formally in January, 1992. TISL had undertaken its SWOT analysis.

28. Organisations typically develop from small to large units by moving through stages of a life cycle. It is the sequential or predictable pattern reflected in practice due to adaptive nature, stability principle, and continuity with growth and development through

HRD perspective. Hence, each organization moves through the life cycle at its own pace and in its own manner, but the total process takes the organization through for distinct stages like: (1) birth stage, (2) youth stage, (3) midlife stage, and (4) maturity stage. – Quinn, Robert and Kim Cameron, "Organizational Life Cycles and Some Shifting Criteria of Effectiveness: Some Preliminary Evidence", *Management Science,* 29, 1983, pp. 31-51.

29. Zimmer, Heinrich, *Philosophies of India,* Meridian Books, New York, 1956.

30. More than 2000 years ago, the Chinese philosopher, Sun Tsu wrote *The Art of War* which can surely be applied in today's world of global business competition. Admittedly, Griffin has considered this as an exemplary evidence of the ancient roots of management thought, and therefore, our purpose of this subjective analysis can be served with its practical implications when we meditate to adopt corporate policy and implement the same in reality. – Also see, Griffin, Samuel (Translated), *Sun Tsu: The Art of War,* Oxford University Press, London, 1963.

31. The unified theory we are concerned herein, is something more of the nature of the universality of management practice in realistic attitude on the cosmological plane of beauty where all life represent an illuminating view, for which meditational aspect is quite relative to the mission statement of the organization – it is the philosophy of relativity theory in managing by objectivity.

32. Bhagwan Shree Rajneesh in his darshan diary 'Far Beyond the Stars' conforms this notion when he speaks with Paramhansa, His esoteric name being given to his disciple. He regards the opinion which is also in conformity with the Jaina and Buddhistic

concept of life. He says who descend this order they evolve and evolve and at the ultimate peak of evolution one becomes a god. According to him, there are millions of gods taking into consideration of this aspect of human life. See also, Maneesha, Ma Prem (Editing and Commentary), Bhagwan Shree Rajneesh Far Beyond the Stars – A Darshan Diary, Rajneesh Foundation Limited, Poona, 21st Series, July 1st through July 31st, 1977.

33. Mumukshananda, Swami: *The Complete Works of Swami Vivekananda,* Vol. I, p. 155.

34. *Ibid.,* p. 41. Also see, Paramahamsa, Swami Muktananda: Awaken the Kundalini. He is a renowned personality had initiated a worldwide meditation revolution for bringing an experience of the inner Self to hundreds of thousands of people all over the world. Prof. Ugo Dettore in his work 'Approaching the Reality' (p.17) has given an illuminating picture on such topic. Also see, his other works 'Laltro Regno' (The Other Kingdom), Encyclopaedia of Metapsychics, Parapsychology and Spiritualism, the first one in Italy. Thus, the viewpoint on meditation is clear to conform that it is the highest order of life, for man is guided by a philosophy in whatsoever way he or she is being concerned with the life.

35. Krishnamoorti, N.: *Saint Tiruvalluvar and His Message of Life as Dharma,* Vivekananda Kendra Prakashan Trust, Chennai, May 2000 (First Edn.).

36. According to Einstein's theory of relativity, matter is equivalent to energy, given by the famous relation, $E=mc^2$, where E is the energy, m the mass, and c the speed of light. Moreover, the energy E may contain the consciousness – energy as well, in addition to the material energy with which the scientists are well familiar. It is becoming even doubtful whether the

acts and creations of this 'Complex Energy' (Material energy plus the Consciousness-energy) itself are explicable except as interactions of the so-called elementary particles amongst themselves. –Bhandari, M.C. (Ed.) : *Para Vidya –Science of the Beyond*, Para Vidya Sansthan, New Delhi, 1985, p. 7.

37. There is little doubt that a well-drawn up mission statement is available component in the effective strategic management of an organization. – See also, Bowman, Cliff: *The Essence of Strategic Management*, Prentice-Hall of India Pvt. Ltd., New Delhi, 1998.

38. Some degree of consistency must be maintained by the management between the demands of the various organizational sub-systems. It can be accomplished through systems integration. Thus, in order to lead an organization effectively, a manager needs to know exactly how an organization behaves. Here, meditational value has a great role to play, for managerial dimensions are dynamically adapted with the changing nature of development on the plane of realities. – See also, Burton, G. and Thakur, M.: *Management Today – Principles and Practice,* Tata McGraw-Hill Publishing Company Limited, New Delhi, 1995.

39. Subramanian, M.: "Liberalisation and Co-operative Movement in India", *The Indian Journal of Public Administration,* Vol. XLIV, No.1, Indian Institute of Public Administration, New Delhi, Jan.-March 1998.

40. Champy, J.: "Management: New Mandate," *Information Week,* February 6, 1995, pp.57-58. Also see Devenport, T.H.A. and Short, J.E., "The New Industrial Engineering: Information Technology and Business Process Redesign," *Sloan Management Review,* Vol. 4, 1990, pp. 11-27; Halachmi, A.: "Reengineering and Public Management: Some Issues and Considerations," *International Review of*

Administrative Sciences, Vol. 16, 1995, pp. 329-34; Hammer, M. and Champy, J., *op.cit.;* and Hyde, A., *op.cit.*

41. Drucker, P.F.: "The Emerging Theory of Manufacturing," *Harvard Business Review,* May-June 1990, pp. 104-20.

42. Bovaird, T. and Hughes, R., "Re-engineering Public Sector Organisations: A Case Study of Radical Change in a British Local Authority," *International Review of Administrative Sciences,* Vol. 16, 1995, pp. 355-72.

43. Drucker, P.F., *op.cit.*

44. This theory we have analysed on the basis of equanimity principles from philosophic perspective and scientific relativity in a notion to develop human society through business activities. Again, the application of meditation in business is sought for equipoised mind that gives birth to a globalistic order for human development with the visionary goal of management.

45. According to Patanjali, a man can memorise about the past life of the self with the help of a special kind of meditational practice. – See *Yoga Sutra,* Chapter 3, Sutra 18. This can be demonstrated in life experience when we pay attention to yoga practices and is therefore, envisaged with a view to attain the real goal of business in human life through meditational technique.

46. "For one who has conquered the mind, the Super soul (Higher Self or the Absolute) is already reached, for he has attained tranquility." (*Bhagavad Gita* 6.7). This material world has been likened to a great forest fire. As in the forest, fire may automatically take place, so in this material world, although we may try to live

peacefully, there is always a great conflagration. It is therefore, not possible to live in peace anywhere in the material world. But for one who is transcendentally situated – either by the meditational yoga system or by the empirical philosophical method, or by bhakti-yoga – peace is possible. Hence, it is true to note that all forms of yoga are meant for transcendental life – the highest order of life. So, we have applied the concept of cosmological unity in managerial perspective of the vision for organisational life with a view to attain cosmological beauty by human achievement of the goal of life related to scientific reality through business philosophy, in terms of leading man to enter into the path of supreme abode by making life experience, in dealing with different human business activities in an equanimity principle with the help of equipoised character of human mind – while attempting creatively for getting the tasks done in co-operative endeavour, and by means of such otherwise strategic approach.

5

Creativity Thought

What it is

Creativity is a universal subject. It is related to all human beings. Persons who are having creative talent is the asset of the nation. If the human beings are treated from creative point of view, the national development is possible; because, it helps in the development of human resource. It is therefore, essential for a nation to develop the creative potentials of human beings. The nations who learn best how to identify, encourage, and develop the creative potentials in their people may find themselves in very advantageous position. Hence, it can be said undoubtedly that creative acts affect enormously not only scientific and technological progress even in this age of competition, but society at large is helped by the process of human creative endeavour in all respects of life. Although creativity has been a topic of some interest throughout man's history, but it is only very recently when efforts were made to study it scientifically.

In psychological researches, there is generally a common agreement on the belief that all persons have some creative potential, though there are wide individual differences in degree. According to Lownfeld[1], there is a difference between actual creativity and potential creativity – the former being that potential which is already developed and functioning, the latter including the total creative potential (both developed and undeveloped) within an individual. Again, Swami Vivekananda said long ago that education is the manifestation of the divinity already in man. For this reason probably, educators along with psychologists also started doing systematic research on creativity since 1950 onwards, to find out the new discoveries on the one hand, and add to the national development through the efficient use of multi-faceted talent on the other. In management of human resources, generally attention is required to be paid to the growth and development of the creative potentials of human beings. For understanding human creativity Maslow[2] said therefore rightly that the highest level at which people function, there are the self-actualizers who have growth motive in them. So, they rise above the general run of the people who have an integrated and wholesome personality, ultimately realize the purpose of life.

From the above, we may say that creativity is regarded the greatest asset of mankind. It is the ability that is most vital for shaping the future of man. Hence, there is the need for further studying on systematic and well-planned studies on creativity, especially with regard to the identification and development of creativity. Thus, it is true to say that creativity has been approached differently by different thinkers. For our purpose, we would like to deal with the topic from managerial viewpoint, so that it helps the management process for systematization of things and human activities endeavoured towards the welfare of the society and the national development altogether, in this age of competition over the world at large.

Nature of Creativity

Effective management of human activities requires a creative talent. When human mind is set-in-motion, there is said to be a balance – an equipoised order, which produces the best result in terms of an action-oriented concept of life, that is mainly intented for human welfare and social development. Hence, the philosophy behind managing the human resource is for the potential development of human beings, where the practice of silence philosophically confines to the mind of freshness which evolves a creative genius. It being the right notion regarding the nature of human creativity, there has been many attempts from various discipline to understand the creative nature of human mind. For our purpose, we already have analysed the yoga psychology as the best methodological approach in the previous chapter, where it is observed that it helps people to actualize the self for realizing the actual meaning of life by doing in silence and with creativity. However, it is true that creativity has been approached differently by different thinkers. To understand the nature of creativity, we have therefore tried to assess some of the opinions as reproduced below.

Philosophically, creative thinking is not a peculiar type of thinking that has different non-publicly observable features from other types of thinking. For a philosopher, a creative thinker is one whose thinking leads to a result which conforms to criteria of a value in one domain or another. An example can be cited in this connection. Plato, a great philosopher in the world once made a distinction between artificial art and true art. He opined that artists deal only with physical appearances and not with the reality itself. They are creative in the sense that they enlarge human consciousness. Again, if we turn to scientific notion on the nature of creative thinking as well as creative act, it goes to say that scientifically creativeness involves an imaginative leap to a new perspective. For this reason, the scientists search for a hypothesis which is most likely to fit the facts of his observation he is concerned with. In this sense, the nature of creativity in scientific order relates to surprise, which Pioncare[3] has also accepted, because most of the scientific discoveries are done in this way. Here, it is assumed that scientist observes phenomenon which many others before him have been without getting puzzled. It is because, a scientist has the capacity to surprise. So anything obvious for others, is a problem to him. His mind starts working on the problem and thus, it becomes the beginning of his discovery. However, social scientist further approaches creativity from the interpersonal relationships which is important also for effective management of human organisations for the purpose of social development in right perspective. For him, creativity is a social invention whose product is not an object but persons – creativity in human relationships. Such a person is characterized by the attributes of intelligent and possession of sharp perceptions, subtle sensitivities, respect for the individual person, and besides, boldness to explain one's point of view and to stand for one's convictions.

Psychologists and psychoanalysts have also approached the creativity but they too differ in their views. Some have equated it with mental health, some have related it to the personality development; while others have restricted it to an interplay of runconscious and conscious. In knowing human creativity we know actually life processes. Thus, Sinnot[4] equates creativity with life itself by virtue of its organizing, pattern forming and questing quality. It is only with the imagination which is quality of mind, makes possible the creativeness in a man. However, in psychology creativity is also treated to be a process. As Rogers[5] defines creative process as the emergence in action of a novel rational product, growing out of the uniqueness of the individual on the one hand, and the materials, events, people or circumstances of his life on the other. By uniqueness of the individual, he refers to man's tendency to actualize himself, to become his potentialities. Again, another famous psychologist, Rollo May also accepts this view while he agrees with the point that it (creativity) as the process helps to bring something new into birth. For Maslow, creativity is a maximum of self-actualizing.

From the above discussion, it holds good to note that Maslow's opinion on the creativity is subject to openness. Because, he considers that creativity is not the sole prerogative of certain professionals like –theorists, artists, scientists, inventors, writers, or it cannot be confined to certain conventional areas, rather it is the universal heritage of every human-being that is born and which co-varies with psychological health. According to him, self-actualizing creativeness is emitted like radioactivity like a cheerful person who emits cheerfulness without purpose, design, or even consciousness. The hidden nature of creativity speaks us that it is an optimum growth in social interaction that cannot be forced or coerced, it can only be facilitated or restricted in each and every individual as it is found in every living cell.

Creativity and Human Performance

Human creativity is considered as the manifestation of creative force inherent in life, in organic matter and it is this force that continuously brings forth new productions as are often unique and unprecedented. However, on creative performance, nowadays more and more emphasis has been laid, because it can foster social development through well-planned techniques and methods. There are, for this reason theories on creativity which count on human effective performance to bring in organization atmosphere that could guide people towards the attainment of organizational goal, by inspiring people to work for the common unity as well as integrity. In the divine inspiration theory of creativity, some philosophers hold the view that creativity is a divine inspiration. Plato considers the creative writer as an agent of some higher power. Thus, it is the higher power which makes man capable of producing anything creative. Pioncare discovered his fuchsion functions after struggling for days with the problem of the functions – though he could not reach any conclusion, on might after taking black coffee and being unable to sleep, ideas rose in his mind. He remarks himself therefore, in crowds, colliding sometimes interlocking, and finally making some stable combinations from which he discovered the existence of the fuchsion functions.[6] Another good example can be cited to understand the inspirational concept on human creativity. Otto Loewi's proof of the chemical meditation of nerve impulses is an illuminating evidence. This came to him vividly in a dream and the next day he performed the critical experiment in his laboratory that proved the truth of the solution given to him. These are but instances, there are hundreds of such explanations which go to predict that human creativity is either inspiration, or accidental, or otherwise; and depending on such mysterious notions theories have developed from time to time.

The ideational approach of creativity is necessary on our expounding truth, in the sense that organisations are agent of the social transformational change where people come from multi-cultural facets of life. It is therefore, apparent that performance of workers in managing the organization is dependent on adequate care of each individual member who must have creative potential. If their dormant potential can be worked out more and more in perfect nature, it can be expected that the particular organization can serve the society in the best way for solving all types of social problems of human beings in the process of humanization with their socialization activities. Hence, it is the duty of the management to create an environment which mostly suit for finding the creative potentials out from people. An adequate system in an organization can bring out the creative products, for which love and affection, fellow-feeling conditions at work environment are responsible, so that the insight of human personality is strengthened to flash the creative process; otherwise it might never have been able to get started. Unless the organizational people are intensely interested and motivated in the creative process, it is impossible for any creation from realistic viewpoint. So, there should be sustained hard-work on the part of the management to match the creative potentials for social development purposes. It is essential to note that creative behaviour endures in human personality aspect, and it brings ultimately, organizational effectiveness from all counts where organisations benefit, individuals and various groups working in organisations benefit, and at last, more importantly, the result goes to the social transformation in new dimensional order to the cause of human welfare from universalistic way of development and growth of social mankind, irrespective of any caste, creed, colour, religion and other attributes of people.

It is creative performance can be socially transformed from generation to generation in acceptable channels. Freud owes its origin to conflicts probably for this reason, within the unconscious mind of man. Though some believe that conflicts are harmful, but yet psychologists have come to know that some type of conflicts are source of wondering – of the development of strength for human personality. As for example, again, we can say that music as mostly catharic experience which is in fact, a process of sublimation. But still, it is creative in the sense that it produces something valuable to the society and helps to enlarge human inner personality aspect for individual growth – it is because, the self is reinforced in musical rhythm which confines to the pondering of the productive potentials in men. Thus, the psychological barrier in human mind is strengthened when creative potentials are utilized in nurturing way in an organization.

From the above, we may now turn to the compensatory theory on creative performance. It is believed in this theory that human creative potentials have endowed with learning in the field of scientific investigations, which tremendously helped the society. Besides, artistic skills developed through creative potentials bridge the gap of social crisis in times of need. Thus, by creative performance originality is brought to the limelight of certain happening whereby managing human activities come to the way of social cultural transformation. In this regard, we may quote Jung[7], who viewed creativity at two levels : (i) the psychological mode, and (ii) the visionary mode. In the psychological mode human consciousness is the main domain – in relation to family, environment, society, and other social institutions; but the release of creativity does not transcend the limits of psychological intelligibility. The visionary mode is not based on life experiences, but from the timeless depths which Jung called the "Collective Unconscious". Again, coming over to the motivational theory, it is observed that some motivation theorists have emphasized that creativity is effected by innate orientation, drive or urge such as, drive of self-actualization. As Maslow has said that goals of man are prerequisites to self-actualization because a person must first satisfy his lower-order needs before he strives for the development of his individuality or the realization of his potentials. Thus, creativity for Maslow is a maximum of self-actualizing. It is true that self-actualizing people are highly motivated as they are relatively unfrightened by the unknown, the mysterious, and the puzzling. The overall impact of creative performance in an organization can be felt from the value system it enhances to substantiate a new product that has unidimensional quality for individual growth and organizational goal attainment. Besides, it enlarges and strengthens group attitude towards the making of organizational culture, which ultimately fulfils the social mission of welfare by means of its productive value.

It is, in a nutshell, concluded that creative performance helps in effective group decision-making process, and strengthens group behaviour, as group cohesiveness is brought in organization for attaining tasks in effective manner; and thus, it fosters the rationalization process in productive environment, for which industrial democracy is illuminated for all-round development of organization in an aim to manage things in objective manner. For this reason, it should not be out of place to mention here that a creative group can be said to be a potential think-tank which is highly essential for organization development (OD) process.[8]

Creativity and Organisational Planning

The establishment of organizational goal is the first stage of the overall planning process, and the second stage is the planning itself. Goals tell management where the organization should be going, and planning tells management how the organization will get there. Management consists, to a great deal, the making of decisions – it is a choice made from available alternatives. It is rather only one element of the entire process of decision-making. There are at least four decision-making activities.[9] All these include creative approach, so that organisation's planning activities can be performed effectively. As we know that planning is defined as the management function of developing a futuristic frame of reference from which to identify opportunities and threats that lie in the future and to take action now to exploit the opportunities and to defend against the threats. Thus, an effective planning requires and involves a creative forecasting system for predicting the future which is quite uncertain. It is therefore, creative approach in making organizational plans, which helps people (the management) to determine organizational goals and the means of achieving them most efficiently and effectively. From such constructive as well as realistic notion planning demands creative decision-making in order to maximize the selection of appropriate courses of corporate action.

It is, thus, apparent to note that strategic plans can be developed by organisations for the attainment of strategic goals when things are creatively dealt in course of doing organizational activities at the top level of management, and besides, all functional areas are to be developed by the management, so that the stated goal helps to utilize the resources of the organization and its activities in order to achieve the ultimate goal in the long-run. Hence, strategic planning activities of the organization itself, in creative manner tend to proceed at a continuous pace. As the managers working on the strategic plans are engaged in a high state of uncertainty, and are required to make many assumptions about the threats and opportunities of the future; here, creativity at organizational level serves the purpose of managerial decision-making in uncertainties[10]. Again, in case of tactical plans which define the actions of major departments and other sub-units that are required in the execution of a strategic plan, creative approach also helps the middle level management in studying the overall strategic plan and to develop the particular tactical actions that are necessary – it thus usually focuses on internal data that is probably generated by accounting systems. In this way, it is observed that an overall system theory on the part of management requires for the situational analysis, an approach which is realistic as well as creative to deal with various problems of management in an organization, and resultantly, operational plans are developed by the lower level of management. It is, in order to establish actions that are necessary for the development of operational goals and also, for the support of tactical plans in the organizational environment, its structure, culture, and like other relevant attributes of functioning, for the purpose of attaining the actual or ultimate goal of the organization. In a nutshell, creativity is an adequate system takes into account for the consideration of decision situations of the management function of the organizational planning. Thus, it embraces the path-goal theory in relativity for the universality of the fundamental rules of managing, for matching with the uncertainties. According to Schermerhorn[11], tactical operational plans as : (i) production plans; (ii) financial plans; (iii) facilities plans; (iv) marketing plans; and besides, (v) personnel plans, among others are forthcoming to the realization of the overall goal of the organization, as these address in multi-level facets for the first-line managers in integrating aspects of organisation's operations within short-run phenomena for accomplishing individual tasks. Thus, creative budgets for departments or projects can be specified for efficient utilization of the organisation's resources as prescribed in operational activities.

From the above discussion, it is clear that the planning function of the management has a challenging but realistic view. It is so because, if goals are to motivate employee performance, they must not be too easily reached. Performance goals should be established that will challenge the employee, raise his aspirations, and foster individual growth and development. At the same time, if the goal is unreachable, the individual may give up without an effort or become discouraged by the frustration of chasing the impossible dream. Thus, goals should be both challenging enough to motivate improved performance and attainable so that person may enjoy a sense of accomplishment. Hence, it is rightly observed and can be said in this regard that creativity, if properly enhanced in an organizational atmosphere has a wide relevancy to serve the levels of management for the great cause of the organization, which is a social instrument or an agent in the transformational process in connection with the changing environment, so that human welfare activities can be done in continuity, and thereby, there is an inherent role being played for responding in each social activities with responsibility building in the mind of people. Besides, such planning function in enlarging attitude of people towards the organization can feel the gap of social deficiency in creative manner, by producing for the common cause of the humanization process in socializing the managerial pyramid with effective communication process and an adequate information system, which is dealt in scientific manner for philosophizing the real nature of management in relativity as well as in antiquity – this is an integrated unified approach of management, where all paths are leading to the process of human welfare but with creative nature of development, to understand the equanimity principle of organizational goal of life in society.

Creative Decision-making for Managerial Effectiveness

At a time when decision-making is so important, many corporate executives do not know how to make a good choice among alternatives. They may rely on computer analysis or personal intuition without realizing that their own cognitive biases affect their judgement. It is here, creative decision-making comes in the way of bringing managerial effectiveness at the work place in organizational environment, whereby the complexities of modern corporate life make good judgement more critical than ever. It is generally observed that many errors in judgement originate in the human mind's limited capacity and in the natural biases most executives display during decision-making. It is, therefore, essential that people must understand their own deficiencies to make the best decisions. Here, again, we may remember that creativity in decision-making processes could be enhanced by concentrating on six important biases which managers are in the prey while thinking creatively. The biases are : (1) Ignoring the laws of randomness – it means that the outcome of one event has nothing to do with the outcome of another. For example, even though retail sales should be expected to fluctuate each month, a business person decides that a slight sales dip is the beginning of a downward trend and takes significant action, such as increasing the advertising budget; (2) Hindsight bias-means that people tend to overestimate the degree to which they could have predicted an event after its occurrence. This is sometimes called the "I-knew-it-all-along effect". Research on hindsight demonstrates that people are not very good at recalling or reconstructing how an uncertain situation appeared beforehand; (3) Giving too much weight to readily available information – it means decisions are often based on information that is easily available to certain executives, which precludes their digging for additional information that may provide a more balanced view. For example, geologists at a major oil company were asked to estimate the potential yield at several drilling sites. To do so, they relied on geological features similar to those of existing oil fields. The results were probably flawed because the geologists failed to consider unproductive fields that had features similar to those of the new sites; (4) Seeing only one dimension of uncertainty in trying to estimate outcome probabilities, executives typically evaluate one dimension of uncertainty at a time and fail to consider their combined effects; (5) Misconception of change – when a series of similar events occur, managers may incorrectly gauge the probability of their future recurrence; and (6) Overconfidence – one of the interesting research findings on decision-making biases is that most people over estimate their ability to predict uncertain outcomes.[12]

The above points are illuminating on the understanding of creative decision-making processes in all fields of human activities. If these are skillfully cared off, there would have been the possibility of undertaking each decision variable in realistic manner, so that the approach of managerial decision-making process creatively takes issues at hand for effective choice among alternatives, which go to make organizational activities and managerial functioning in realistic view that has ever been coined as scientific thinking in the areas of problem solving affairs for global humankind. Thus, the creativity in decision-making approach requires that all managers should utilize a rational model of decision-making, which consists of six fundamental steps as identified in the points like : (i) recognizing and defining the decision situation; (ii) identifying appropriate alternatives; (iii) evaluating each alternative; (iv) selecting the best alternative; (v) implementing the alternative; and (vi) evaluating the end-results and follow-up action. This, according to Griffin[13] has a rational base and could be unbiased, if creativity aspects are well-considered for managerial effectiveness in course of doing particular act, for decision-making under such consideration will reduce risk management and save much of organisation's time and cost of the decisional resources. One recent study of American corporations found that good decision-making practices were followed less than 20 per cent of the time[14]. As the decision-making process is found to be distorted by a variety of behavioural influences having relevancy in organizational tasks, especially political forces and coalitions, intuition and escalation of commitment, there should be an alternative approach, i.e., managerial alertness in functional parameters to the decision barriers, so that the given amount of creativity as expected for effectiveness would not lose sight off the managerial attention. It thus, helps against group-think, as it (group-think) tends to cause the following defects in group decision-making : (i) group discussion limitations; (ii) group process that does not include the re-examination of the course of action; (iii) individual member's negligence causing unsatisfactory situation for the group majority; (iv) individual member's inattention to obtain information from experts; (v) selective bias creating group reaction to factual information and relevant judgments from experts, outside critics, and the mass media; and (vi) individual members spend little time deliberating the ways in which the chosen policy might be hindered by bureaucratic inertia, sabotaged by opponents, or temporarily delayed by unforeseen events. Thus, no contingency plans are formulated.[15] In a nutshell, a creative decision-making approach therefore brings consensus mapping technique used by a task group after it has developed and evaluated a list of ideas regarding a specific issue or problem. Again, for creativity in decision variables has role to play in joining together the unrelated elements, the synectic technique is also helpful as it uses those parametric issues that go to break existing patterns of thinking. Hence, it provides to the participants of synectics group an encouragement to generate verbal and visual analogies with apparently irrelevant things, in order to open new insights and new ways of thinking about old problems. Thus, the synectics technique has proved to be a highly effective tool for the unleashing of group and individual creativity.

From the above discussion, it is worth-noting that despite all the available decision-making techniques and the supporting qualitative tools, managers still make many bad decisions and constantly seek ways to improve their decision-making effectiveness. Hence, a creative approach is necessary in organizational decision-making process wherein, it is suggested that it should have the role of a dialectic inquiry – where groups of participants are assigned the role of challenging the basic values and assumptions that support the definition of the problem to be resolved. It can challenge prevailing organizational thinking by creating new problem perspectives, challenging assumptions, and searching for better alternative courses of action, so that managerial effectiveness is brought to the attainment of organizational goal in missionary way of dealing with the problems, for human welfaristic considerations in the changing environment where the organization operates.

Creative Leadership for Managerial Effectiveness

Management alone will not bring organizational success. Organisations of all types are discovering that something more is needed—leadership. Though, it is true that management is not leadership and leadership is not management – it is because, managers use the formal position, power of their jobs to influence subordinates; whereas leaders use social processes. It is still believed that creative leadership can bring managerial effectiveness, as it is observed that most of the time management functions in different situations at the organizational level from leadership trait approaches. However, it should not be out of place to mention that a successful leader in organization must have the potentials to utilize for the purpose of guiding subordinates, who as a manager works like a leader to the adaptive situations unlike required in social environment. His function therefore, as a managerial trait must ensure that he should be like social leader having some traits characteristic of successful leaders. These are : (i) his alertness to the social environment; (ii) he should be self-ambitious and also mentally achievement-oriented; (iii) he must have assertive, co-operative, decisive, dependable, and dominant (the desire to influence others) characteristics in his personality structure. Besides, he must possess some other attributes in his personality trait like – energetic (high activity level), persistent, self-confident, tolerant of stress, willingness to assume responsibility, among others. These all together will function like objectivity in the managerial goal of guiding people in an environment of open organizational culture. Again, effectiveness of managerial performance in an organization commensurates with the managerial skill characteristic attributes that go to play dominant role in successful attainment of tasks, while guiding people in the work environment in organization. Among important skills, mention can be made to – clever (intelligent) factor, conceptual skills, creativeness, diplomatic relationship and tactfulness in dealing with people, fluency in speaking and communicating with subordinates, knowledgeable about the group task, organized (administrative ability) characteristic personality, persuasiveness, and also socially skilled quality which go to enhance work performance for the betterment of his people and the organization as a whole.

However, management of people and tasks in an organization is consistent with interpersonal orientative nature of managerial characteristics which are more or less observed to be similar to leadership personality structure.

In this regard, Kotter[16] has conducted in-depth studies of successful general managers which he divided into four fundamental categories. It is apparently true to note that this behavioural trait approach of leadership qualities in managerial performance is highly reflected to determine those behaviours that were associated with successful leadership. Thus, the research conclusion on successful leadership was associated with three fundamental leadership behaviours : (1) task performance; (2) group maintenance behaviours; and (3) employee participation in decision-making.[17] A creative task performance behavioural attribute confines to the things, managers as leaders perform to ensure that the group reaches its real objectives. It is concerned mainly with production, directive leadership, initiating structure, or closeness of supervision which were found to be confined with : (1) fast work speed; (2) good quality/high accuracy; (3) high quality; and (4) observation of the rules. Again, the group maintenance behaviours, if creatively handled, it concerns for organizational people supportive leadership or consideration. Thus, it embraces with the managerial quality of : (1) feelings; (2) comfort; (3) stress reduction; and (4) appreciation; which are highly essential for organization effectiveness. Lastly, participative decision-making according to Tannenbaum and Schmidt study[18], is a creative decision participation factor manifests itself in the form of a leadership continuum. It ranges from a boss-centred approach to a subordinate-centred approach based on a widerange of situational factors that delimit the amount of subordinate participation. Hence, the leadership style when creatively and appropriately selected, it considers situational forces, such as time pressures, the nature of the work, the nature of the group, the organisation's culture and leadership style, and besides, environmental factors. Depending on such aspects of managerial qualities required at the work environment, there are different studies[19] made from time to time on leadership style, and therefore, it can be suggested that creative approach on organizational dynamics has a relevancy to that of managerial effectiveness that necessitates a productive environment all-through, where organizational people find ample scope to actualize the self for the purpose of optimum development, instead of work-related inconveniences. As a whole, the creative leadership in organization results in effective group performance, where job-centred as well as employee-centred behavioural rationalities are fundamentally confined to human performance, and thus, bringing efficiency in completion of job in organization on the one hand; and on the other hand, employee-centred leader behaviour developing a cohesive work-group, and also it is ensured that subordinates are fundamentally satisfied with their job.

From the above analysis, it can be asserted undoubtedly that effective management is the result of creative leadership, where the true notion of leadership as management perspective in regard to organizational goal lies in its symbolic nature, and is in conformity with situational conditionalities that go to foster the work-motivation in organizational people, in terms of productive work-environment in a cultural transformational change; and thus, organizational vision—having a clear sense of direction, and communicating this vision to others so that they become dedicated to accomplishing shared dreams, are creatively endowed with empowerment to establish and maintain a developmental orientation toward subordinates. It removes at last, performance barriers by sharing responsibilities, and delegating assignments in realistic manner that are genuinely challenging and self-actualising. Hence, a creative approach, if taken care off, for enlarging group participation goes beyond normal expectations, by inspiring new ways of thinking, stimulating learning experiences, and transmitting a sense of mission throughout entire organizational cultural attribution in theory as well as in practice. Thus, managerial effectiveness is strengthened in the sense that once leader has identified the source/cause of the subordinates behaviour, the leader can select an effective response.[20]

Creativity in Education

We have so far seen creativity from its nature, and also its content in managing human organization. In this regard, it goes to say that effectiveness in managerial approach is bound by the process of education. In a country which employs creative techniques in the field of educational practices, it produces well-trained students for prospective development in future activities. As we know that management is the essential goal of the social development, a system approach in educational institution can undertake practices of human behaviour in artistic play of things on the one hand, and the scientific display of social orientation for guiding people in infinite nature. Thus, it can have a leadership orientation in students who ultimately run the wheel of the state machinery by becoming future perfect citizen. This could bring therefore, in education, a fundamental innovative technique where both divergent as well as convergent thinking find place with the traditional and, also in new methods of discoveries and inventions to enhance social development for the whole of mankind. Thus, creativity in education opens the door of systematic managerial notion in which human knowledge confines not only to the traditional approaches; but also the biological evolutionary processes have got it to be exploited in human cultural evolution. The path of cultural evolution led people to the greatest intellectual excellence and thus, man was able to solve some technical problems but still he is faced with many serious social, educational and economic problems. The solutions here, therefore, largely depend upon the minds of men. Whether they have been trained to think creatively or not rests with education.

From this end in view, we have come-across in this volume to estimate for an understanding how far managerial approaches can be unified to the goal of social development for the present masses in one hand, and for regenerating the forces of social development for future path which actually guides people in the attainment of the ultimate goal of self-actualisation in the process of social development in perspective manner. Van Dyk is quite illustrative in this respect, because he remarks that if we accept that the development of a child is a process by which the highest order of involvement of the world is attained, then creativity should be the educationist's primary concern, because this kind of experience (involvement) is creative in nature. There are some other thinkers in this line of social orientation processes who further accept this view.[21] Thus, application of creativity in educational field requires that students need to be an active participant in the teaching learning process, by which managerial tallent should come up in the way of developing the self. The role of the teacher in this aspect of human development should be only to stimulate, to guide, to provide a conducive climate, and the necessary equipment, whereas the students have not to be a passive learner, rather they should discover themselves what they learn in environment – this could cultivate the inner self which is mostly required in managing social activities for growth and development, so that this regenerating force can equip with the changing nature of the environment in the process of managing through objectivity. It is therefore, creative teaching can promote creative behaviour in man in order to come up with a large number of solutions to the problems of life. In this process a creative teacher provides for self-initiated learning on the part of students.[22] This type of learning helps them in becoming self-starters. It requires the attribution of some essential elements in the educational processes, such as: (i) setting up of permissive learning environments; (ii) stimulating creative thought processes among students; (iii) stimulating intellectual fluency and flexibility among students; (iv) imbibing self-discipline among students; (v) promoting sensitivity to problems among students; (vi) fostering curiosity among students; (vii) assisting students to become active participants; (viii) encouraging self-evaluation on the part of students; and (ix) assisting students to become adventurous.

From the above discussion, it is suggested that creativity in education can manifest itself to the thinking process of human beings for which people are able to contribute significantly to the society and thus, it comes true in the face of managerial tallent that the learning process which manifests the inner self and actualizes for the outer intellectual capacities in social, emotional, perceptual and psychological factors help in human development, where we observe that intelligence does not involve all the thinking abilities that are necessary to the survival of mankind. It is creativity for which students should be able to discover new things in order to search for varied answers leading to their life problems than to become a passive learner.[23] Lastly, creative education will bring a relationship between an individual and his environment – such a relationship in management of things is considered as a basic component of a creative art activity. To develop the sensitivity to problems is a basic ability involved in a creative art activity. Thus, originality is brought forth for managing human resources by exploiting human potentials in right perspective. In unidimensional order of dealing with the resources of the organization, education has a great role to play, where creative thinking confines to the knowledge and wisdom of the people in which they find themselves adaptive to the changing environment. It thus, helps in establishment of the relationship between individual and societal goal of life, for it is very much essential in integrating the whole of human beings with the outer world – this is the correct notion of educative value for manifestation of the optimum potentials of human resources.[24]

Creative Approach in Strategic Management

Managing modern organisations in complex business environment to fulfil needs and aspirations of the people requires a strategic view, where creative decision-making, as we have seen earlier, plays a dominant role in attaining the goals of those organisations, for whatever purposes these are being established. It should not be mistakably taken that organisations are now, at this complex business situations aloof from each other. Every organization, either small or big, either engaged in productive activities or providing services has to be responsively managed for sustainable development purposes. Hence, strategic conditions and issues confronting the organisations can be overcome by creative approach in managing through an objective manner. It is therefore, creativity which utilizes the potential resources of human asset in an organization for common benefit of the masses in the society. In this regard, a groupthink approach in organization should take into consideration human social problems for the ultimate development and upliftment of the people in realistic sense; otherwise the organization and its management have to be responsible to give accountability to the society for any kind of deficiency in playing roles to the human development process. As the present situation of the world demands that human development is an aspect of core managing issues to the fundamental change of the society, especially in the areas of basic necessities of the masses for civilized living and survival of pillars of the society to interface with human superstructure, therefore, it is imperative to remember that creative approach should undertake in its genesis and working philosophy the process of common human development in potential areas for the masses, besides giving the society actual basic services, irrespective of technological innovations.

As a matter of fact, it is suggested that in every organization – be it commercial, political, religious, charitable, philanthrophic, or otherwise, brainstorming[25] situation has to be created for effectiveness and in maintaining the efficiency factors, while managing resources of the organization in potential exploitation for the benefit of common people. By this technique, it will be possible to attack from all possible angles of the human problems at the enterprise side to generate a large number of ideas, in order to arrive at the best solution. In the strategic solution of human problems, we are to concentrate first, on how the decisions are to be made, where corporate planning must commensurate with solving problems which are fundamentally essential for the human development aspects in socialization goal of the management process of planning, organizing and controlling things with an approach that is mostly viable, projectionable, and also achievable to the ground rules of the reality that an organization is established for, and is a demand of the society – it is the responsiveness in doing business and social activities based on creative approach of dealing with the machineries of managing different types of resources deployed in an organization for the common benefit of the masses, who contribute for social development altogether. Hence, the creative approach in both the short-run as well as long-run requires rationality based on human value system, and its due consideration from the societal viewpoint of the development purposes. Today, it is the crying need of the hour in organizational effectiveness that the masses who remain behind the scope of the fruits or results of development, an organization should fulfil social backwardness by providing services at the gross in grass-root level, by creatively and responsively taking in its own shoulder the responsibility of giving adequate services to the otherwise socially degraded people, without being transferring the role of social development to any other agency or social institution – there is no other agency remaining at the global level unaccountable to play the dominant role in social upliftment process, because the agency which is, in whatsoever form, taken into view in this regard is nothing but an instrument of social change in complexities of the global business environment.

As a factor of human economic growth along with mental development (which requires spiritual order of life), it can be safely and undoubtedly predicted that creative approach must have fundamental notion of the belief in managing organizational resources that the people should be made first nationalistic, conscious of the backwardness, and anxious to progress – they willingly bear great hardships and tolerate many mistakes and they throw themselves with enthusiasm into the job of regenerating their country. Thus, there is a popular enthusiasm which crops up with the problem of management – lubricating oil of planning and the petrol of economic development, a force that almost makes all things possible. Hence, the aim of creativity in managing the human potentials and organizational resources demands that the economics people are concerned would be not to create a huge engine of production, whether of the competitive or the cooperative kind, but to give to men – not only to some but to all men, each in his highest possible measure – the job of work according to their own nature and free leisure to grow inwardly as well as a simple, rich and beautiful life for all[26]. As Solzhnitsyn has stated in his essay " Men Have Forgotten God", in unequivocal terms that the goal of economics should be 'quest for spiritual growth' rather than the pursuit of material growth. It holds good in the present circumstances of the world economy, and the role of strategic management with creative approach to solve actual human problems in the global business environment in this connection is quite commendable.

In short, it is predicted from the above discussion that Indian Vedantic approach so far we have seen in the foregoing chapters, should come in place of realistic rationality in creative order of human development, where treasure-house of knowledge and wisdom have been lying still unutilized from centuries past from perspective of social goal and organizational effective development. And if, organisations can findout the root-cause of social degradation all thorough therefrom, it is possible to rectify the global order in right dimension. Hence, a strategic managerial view essential for this purpose, should be turned to the resources of such concept which can guide people for the effectiveness of the organization for managerial success at the work environment for the whole of global mankind; without discriminating any individual, or any enterprise, or any of the nations in the world. Its institutionalization in correct sense requires meditational practices, which we have already referred in Chapter 4. Without such an order as prescribed, no system in managing human activities becomes effective in real sense of the term, and things for getting done of the goal of management become vague as well as redundant in the present circumstances of the imbalanced global order of development. For such specific objective implementation of the human development concept, we have tried at our level best, to give to a fundamental theory in new order which is found to be unified in approach, and hence, the entire volume envisages for redrafting and reformulating organizational policies in the context of liberalized business practices all over the world to spiritualise human activities.

References

1. Lownfeld, V.: *Creative and Mental Growth,* Macmillan, New York, 1957. Also see, "Current Research on Creativity", *National Education Association Journal,* 47, 1958, pp. 538-540.

2. In theory of the 'Hierarchy of Needs', Maslow explained the person in terms of the condition of self-actualization. He has suggested this view with reference to his theory of personality. The fundamental conception on which Maslow developed his theory is the hierarchy of needs by which people live. Hence, the application of this theory is universal. In managing business organisations for developing human beings, it has wider applications. – Also see, Maslow, A.H.: *Motivation and Personality,* Harper, New York, 1954; and "Self-actualizing People: A Study of Psychological Health", in the *Self : Explorations in Personal Growth,* C.E. Moustakas (Ed.), Harper, New York, 1956, pp. 325-332.

3. Pioncare, H. : *Mathematical Creation in the Foundations of Science,* Science Press, New York, 1913, pp. 393-394.

4. Sinnot, E.W.: "Scientific Creativity" in *Creativity and Its Cultivation,* H.H. Anderson (Ed.), Harper and Brothers Publishers, New York, 1959.

5. Rogers, C.R. : *On Becoming a Person,* Houghton Mifflin, Boston, 1961.

6. *Op. cit.,* p. 394.

7. According to him, the visionary mode in creativity is not subject to the conscious control of the individual. Sometimes, such a person experiences an 'alien will' beyond his comprehension. It might be for this reason that the great work of art transcends the life experiences, personal factors, and historical periods in which such an individual happens to live. – Jung, C.G.: *Psychological Types,* Harcourt, Brace, New York, 1946.

8. According to Jenkins, industrial democracy is the power of employees working in industrial organisations for their decision-making processes, and utilizing therefrom the various resources efficiently for effective development of manpower potentials with a view to attaining organisational goals. Thus, by creative performance a change intervention can be considered effectively managed when : (1) the organisation is successfully moved from an undesired current state to a desired and planned future state; (2) the functioning of the planned organisation in its future state meets earlier expectations; and (3) the transition from one state to another is achieved without unreasonable cost of the organisation and its members as prescribed by Moorhead and Griffin. – Moorhead, G. and Griffin, R.: Organisational Behaviour (2nd Ed.), Houghton Mifflin, Boston, 1989, p.752. Thus, creative performance brings in organisation a cognitive structure which, in social psychology is considered to be the process by which the relevant perceptions and interpretations are organised in a meaningful and integrated way. In brief, it can be rightly asserted that in decision-making techniques intellectual potentials of people are mathematically utilized, where in philosophical understanding on human potential it is treated to be infinite, under the conditions and circumstances of modern industrial life. – See also McGregor, D., *The Human Side of Enterprise,* McGraw-Hill Book

Company, Inc., New York, 1960. It has thus wide connotation to participative management goal, as in the process of creative performance there is a relation between path and goal in organizational mission, its visionary way of managing things for universality of the overall things.

9. The four decision-making activities are –(i) the manager identifies the existence of a problem or an opportunity to improve a situation; (ii) the manager generates a set of alternative courses of action; (iii) the manager selects one of the alternatives; and (iv) the manager implements the selected course of action. - See also Huber, George: *Managerial Decision Making,* Scott, Foresman, Glenview, Illinois, 1980.

10. Most significant decisions made in today's complex environment are formulated under a state of uncertainty, where there is an unawareness of all the alternatives and so also the outcomes – even for the known alternatives. Such decisions demand creativity and the willingness to take a chance in the face of such uncertainties. In such situations, managers do not even have enough information to calculate degrees of risk. So statistical analysis is of no use. In the face of such uncertainty, managers need to make certain assumptions about the situation in order to provide a reasonable framework for decision-making and planning the corporate activities. If the assumptions are incorrect or inappropriate, failure is almost a certainty. For all these reasons, it is said that creativity has importance in organizational planning function of the management.

11. He is expert in operational plans and predicts that every management process should be guided by productivity approach, where in such plans are essentially to be taken very carefully as it counts on other plans of the organization – strategic and tactical

planning function of the management. – Schermerhorn, John : *Management for Productivity,* John Wiley & Sons, New York, 1989, p.11.

12. Bazerman, Max: *Judgment in Managerial Decision Making,* Wiley & Sons, New York, 1986; Hogarth, Robin: *Judgment and Choice : The Psychology of Decision,* Wiley & Sons, New York, 1981; and Daft, Richard : *Management,* The Dryden Press, Chicago, 1988.

13. Griffin, Ricky : *Management,* 3rd Ed., Houghton Mifflin Company, Boston, 1990.

14. *Newsweek :* "The Wisdom of Solomon", August 17, 1987, pp. 62-63.

15. For above stated reasons groupthink is said to be a common dysfunctional result when a powerful group develops a sense of cohesion that is so strong that members begin to think as one. Hence, the conditions have been found to foster the mindset of groupthink are : (1) Invulnerability generating excessive optimism and risk-taking; (2) Rationalising affect for which both real and potential problems are discounted; (3) Unquestioning belief in the morality of the group and its goals, causing thereby ethical and moral considerations to be ignored; (4) Nurturing of stereotyped thinking about opposing groups as weak, stupid, and/or evil; (5) Pressure on members who express dissent to be more loyal to the group and its goals; (6) Self-censorship for which doubts about the apparent group position are suppressed by the members; (7) Shared illusion where everyone agrees totally with the majority view; and (8) Emergence of mindguards which keep information that might shatter the group's shared complacency from reaching the members. – See also, Janis, Irving: *Groupthink,* Houghton Mifflin Company, Boston, 1982.

16. According to John Kotter, general managers in corporate sector have the helpful personality characteristics and categorically these are : (1) needs/motives, (2) temparament, (3) cognitive orientation, and (4) interpersonal orientation. With these, he also added two more attributes of managerial personality for successfulness at work environment are: knowledge and relationship traits. All these together constitute creative element of managerial effectiveness, in so far as the organizational complexity and human task relationship in group dynamics behavioural trait is concerned with that of competitive business environment. – Kotter, John: *The General Managers*, Free Press, New York, 1982.

17. Misumi, J. and Peterson, W.: "The Performance-Maintenance (PM) Theory of Leadership : Review of a Japanese Research Program", *Administrative Science Quarterly,* June 1985.

18. Tennenbaum and Schmidt also determined that subordinate characteristics influence leadership style. They found that a leader can allow greater participation when : (1) subordinates have a strong desire for independence and freedom of action; (2) subordinates desire decision-making responsibility; (3) subordinates relate to and identify with the organisation's goals; (4) subordinates are sufficiently knowledgeable and experienced to deal with the problem efficiently and effectively; and (5) subordinates have prior experience with previous managers that leads them to expect participative treatment. – Tennenbaum, Robert and Schmidt, Warren: "How to Choose a Leadership Pattern," *Harvard Business Review,* May-June 1973. All these are effectively bringing results in objective attainment of organizational goals by bringing members attitude towards the authoritative responsibility at the work environment, which go to

enhance ultimately, managerial effectiveness in realistic manner, so that organizational path-goal continuum is maintained.

19. Some of the important studies undertaken in this area are – (i) Michigan Leadership Studies; (ii) The Ohio State Studies; (iii) Fiedler Contingency Theory; (iv) Path-Goal Theory; (v) The Vroom-Yetton-Jago Model; (vi) Vertical- Dyad Linkage Model; (vii) Life Cycle Theory; (viii) Attribution Perspective; (ix) Leadership Substitutes; (x) Transformational Theory; (xi) Charismatic Leadership; (xii) Leadership as Symbolic Action; etc. These are all argumentative with response to behavioural conditionalities which are peculiar to organizational situations and the relevant work environment.

20. Green, Steven and Terence Mitchell: "Attributional Processes of Leaders in Leader-Member Interactions", Organizational Behaviour and Human Performance, June 1979.

21. Jackson and Getzels too admit that our educational structure is hampering the development of creativity. –Getzels, J.W. and Jackson, P.W.: *Creativity and Intelligence*, John Wiley and Sons, New York, 1962. Anderson and others again, say "that the problem is that we have not trained ourselves to cope with the creativity." – Anderson, H.H.(ed.): *Creativity and Its Cultivation*, Harper, New York, 1959.

22. The teacher needs to consider at least, three factors while stimulating creative thinking among students. Firstly, his own personality – as to what extent he is creative, sensitive and flexible. Secondly, his own ability to put himself into the place of others. Thirdly, his understanding and knowledge of the needs of those whom he is teaching.

23. It is here, the environmental needs and goals are of

prime importance, which in scientific temper involves situations concerning the solutions of mechanical and social problems and thus, creativity in scientific order from managerial standpoint is also termed as objective creativity, which is judged by the appropriateness – whether the product fulfils the demands of the situation. In short, its application in education prepares man by adapting nature to adjust in situations for bringing value in life in actual practice.

24. A restructuring of the overall curriculum should take place for its realization.

25. It is a popular method of group thinking. Alex Osborn established the 'Creative Education Foundation' at the University of Buffalo in 1957. It is here, he developed the method of brainstorming. This method is widely used by businessmen, scientists and others to tap the tremendous source of creative power. See Also, Osborn, A.F.: *Your Creative Behaviour*, Scribner, New York, 1948.

26. It is like the specific gravity of substance of matter as referred to in the beginning of Chapter 1, and is analysed in differed places of this volume in sparkling as well as celebrated manner for an understanding on the scientific temper of human thinking process on the one hand, and the artistic fulfillment of the creative endeavour in managing human organisations to philosophizing the nature of work in relativity concept, to the process of human economic activities with a view to socialization and humanization of the supreme goal of reformation.

Bibliography

Arber, A. : *The Mind and the Eye,* Cambridge University Press, London, 1954.

Aurobindo, S.: *Essays on the Gita,* Sri Aurobindo Ashram, Pondicherry, 1972.

Ansoff, H.: *Implanting Strategic Management,* Prentice-Hall, Englewood Cliffs, New Jersey, 1984.

Abe, Wagner: *The Transactional Manager: How to Solve Your People Problems with TA,* Prentice-Hall Inc., Englewood Cliffs, N.J., 1981.

Anand, K.C. (Editor) : *Swami Vivekananda and Sri Ramkrishna in Sri Aurobindo's Writings,* All India Magazine, Sri Aurobindo Society, Pondicherry, Sept.-Oct. 1993.

Argyris, C. and Donald, S.: *Organizational Learning, Addison–Wesley,* Reading, Mass., 1978.

Argyris, C. : *Overcoming Organizational Defenses, Allyn–Bacon,* Needham Heights, Mass., 1990.

Anderson, H.H. (Ed.) : *Creativity and Its Cultivation,* Harper, New York, 1959.

Athos, A.G. and Coffey, R.E. : *Behaviour in Organization: A Multidimensional View,* Prentice-Hall, Englewood Cliffs, N.J., 1968.

Aaker, David : *How to Select a Business Strategy,* California Management Review, 26, Spring 1984.

lgie, Jimmy and Foster, William : *How to Pick Priorities – A*

New Approach to Problems can Solve Disputes for Business Benefit, Management Today, March 1985.

Argyris, C.: *Personality and Organisation,* McGraw-Hill, New York, 1957.

Atkinson, J.W.: *An Introduction to Motivation,* Van Nostrand, Princeton, N.J., 1964.

Ahitav, Niv and Seev Neumann: *Principles of Information Systems for Management,* Wm. C. Brown Company, Dubuque, Iowa, 1982.

Anderson, Carl R. and Frank, T. Taine: *Managerial Perceptions and Strategic Behaviour,* Academy of Management Journal, Dec. 1975.

Albers, Henry H.: *Principles of Management,* 4th Ed., John Wiley & Sons, Inc., New York, 1974.

Abraham, K. Korman: *Organizational Behaviour,* Prentice-Hall of India, New Delhi, 1978.

Anatol, K.W.E., Kochhr, J.W. and Applbann, R.L.: *Organizational Communication:* Behavioral Perspectives, Holt, Rinehart and Winston, New York, 1976.

Allen, L.A.: *Management and Organization,* McGraw Hill Book Co., Inc., New York, 1958.

Argyris, C.: *Organization and Innovation,* Irwin, Homewood, Ill., 1965.

Argyris, C.: *Understanding Organizational Behaviour,* Tavistock, 1964.

Argyris, C.: *Integrating the Individual and the Organisation,* Tavistock, 1964.

Akhilesh, K.B. and Nagaraj, D.R.: *A Study of Stress Among Personnel Executives,* Personnel Today, NIPM, Vol.7, No.1, 1986.

Anil, K. Khandelwal: *Role and Identity of Human Resources Manager,* Personnel Today, NIPM, Vol.7, No.1, 1986.

Asch, S.E.: *Social Psychology,* Prentice-Hall, Englewood Cliffs, N.J., 1952.

Arrow, K.: *Social Choice and Individual Values,* John Wiley & Sons, New York, 1951.

Argenti, J.: *Corporate Planning – A Practical Guide,* Allen & Unwin Limited, London, 1969.

Alan, C.F.; House, R.J. and Kerr, S.: *Managerial Process and Organization Behaviour,* Scott, Foresman, Glenview, Ill., 1976.

Amitai, Etzioni: *A Comparative Analysis of Complex Organizations on Power Involvement and their Correlates,* Free Press, New York, 1961.

Arlyn, M.J.: *Structure and Process of Organisations: A Systems Approach,* Prentice-Hall, Englewood Cliffs, New Jersey, 1976.

Atchison, Thomas J. and Hill, Winston W.: *Management Today – Managing Work in Organizations,* Harcourt Brace Jovanovich, Inc., Atlantd, 1978.

Allport, Gordon W.: *Attitudes,* Clark University Press, Woreester, Mass., 1935.

Allport, F.H.: *Towards a Science of Public Opinion,* Public Opinion Quarterly, Vol.I, 1937.

Adizes, Khak: *How to Solve the Management Crisis,* Dow Jones Irwin, London, 1979.

Agrawal, R.S.: *Human Resource Accounting, The Management Accountant,* The ICWAI, NDL, Calcutta, Vol.16, No.11, November 1981.

Allport, F.H.: *Social Psychology,* Houghton Mifflin, Boston, 1924.

Arnold, H.J. and Feldman, D.C.: *Organizational Behaviour,* McGraw-Hill, New York, 1986.

Andrew, D.S. Jr. and Mare, J.W. Jr. : *Organizational Behaviour and Performance,* Goodyear Publishing Company, Santa Monica, California, 1980.

Burton, Gene and Thakur, Manab: *Management Today – Principles and Practice,* Tata McGraw-Hill Publishing Company Limited, New Delhi, 1996.

Batten, J.D.: *Beyond Management by Objectives,* American Management Association, New York, 1966.

Berne, Eric: *Games People Play,* Grove Press, Inc., New York, 1964.

erne, E.: *Principles of Group Treatment,* Oxford University Press, New York, 1964.

Bennis, W.: *Organizational Development and the Fate of Bureaucracy,* Industrial Management Review, Alfred P.Sloan School of Management, MIT, Cambridge, Spring, 1966.

Bhattacharya, K.C.: *Studies in Philosophy,* Vol. II, Progressive Publishers, Calcutta, 1958.

Black, Stewart and Newton, Margulies: *An Ideological Perspective on Participation:* A Case for Integration, Journal of Organizational Change Management, Vol.2, No.1, 1989.

Bhandari, M. C.: Para Vidya – *Science of the Beyond,* Para Vidya Sansthan, Calcutta, 1985.

Bowman, Cliff: *The Essence of Strategic Management,* Prentice-Hall of India Private Limited, New Delhi, 1998.

Bovaird, T. and Hughes, R.: *Re-engineering Public Sector Organisations: A Case Study of Radical Change in a British Local Authority,* International Review of Administrative

Sciences, Vol. 16, 1995.

Bazerman, Max: *Judgment in Managerial Decision Making,* Wiley & Sons, New York, 1981.

Barash, D.P.: *Sociobiology and Behaviour,* Elsevier, New York, 1977.

Bass, B. and Vanghan, J.: *Training in Industry: The Management of Learning,* Wadsworth Publishing Company, California, Belmont, 1967.

Bennis, W.G.: *Changing Organizations,* McGraw-Hill, New York, 1966.

Berelson, B. and Steiner, G.A.: *Human Behavior: An Inventory of Scientific Findings,* Harcourt, Brace and World, New York, 1964.

Beckhard, R.: *Strategies for Large System Change,* Sloan Management Review, Winter 1975.

Blake, R. and Mouton, J.: *The Managerial Grid,* Gulf Publishing Company, Texas, 1964.

Beach, D.S.: Personnel – *The Management of People at Work* (2nd Ed.), The Macmillan Company, New York, 1970.

Bennis, W.G.; Schein, E.H.; Beriew, D.E. and Steele, F.I.: *Interpersonal Dynamics: Essays and Readings on Human Interaction,* The Dorsey Press, Homewood, III., 1964.

Blair, J.K.: *Introduction to Behavioural Science for Business,* Wiley Eastern, New Delhi, 1970.

Bass, B.M.: *Organizational Psychology,* Allyn & Bacon, Boston, 1965.

Basu, K.S.: Motivation, *Malayan Management Review,* Vol. 6, No. 1, April 1971.

Beckhard, R. and Harris, R.T.: *Organizational Transactions: Managing Complex Change* (Reading Addison), Wesley

Publishing Company, Mass., 1977.

Behling, Orlando and Mitchell, B.S.: *Motivation Theory: Source of Solution or Part of the Problem,* Business Horizons, February 1974.

Boyd, B.B. and Jensen, J.J.: *Perceptions of the First Line Supervisor's Authority: A Study on Superior-Subordinate Communication,* Academy of Management Journal, Vol.15, No.3, Sept. 1972.

Bower, J.L.; Bartlett, C.A.; Christensen, C.R.; Pearson, A.E. and Andrews, K.R.: *Business Policy –Text and Cases* (7th Ed.), Homewood, III., Irwin, 1991.

Burns, T. and Stalker, G.M.: *The Management of Innovation,* Tavistock Publications, London, 1961.

Birdwell, L.G. and Wahba, M.A.: *Maslow Reconsidered: A Review of Research on the Need Hierarchy Theory,* Proceedings of the Thirty-third Annual Meeting of the Academy of Management, 1973.

Beer, M. and Walton, A.E.: *Organisation Change and Development,* Annual Review of Psychology, Vol.38, Palo Alto, C.A., 1987.

Baum, H.M.: *White-collar Quality Comes of Age,* Journal of Business Strategy, March-April 1990.

Band, W. : *Quality is King for Marketers,* Sales and Marketing Management in Canada, March 1989.

Buzzell, R.D. and Gale, B.T.: *The PIMS Principles: Linking Strategy to Performance,* The Free Press, New York, 1987.

Benjamin, Lewis: *Gene,* Wiley Eastern Limited, New Delhi, 1985.

Beek, William S.: *Modern Science and the Nature of Life,* Harcourt, Brace and Company, New York, 1957.

Berry, R.G.: Genetics, 2nd Edn., St. Paul's House, Warwick

Lane, London, 1972.

Bennet, Dudley: *TA and the Manager,* A Division of IMA, New York, 1976.

Benners, W. (et al.): *The Planning of change, Readings in the Applied Behavioural Services,* Holt, Rinehart and Winston, N.Y., 1965.

Bennet, D.: *Successful Team Building Through TA,* AMACOM, N.Y., 1980.

Blacky, Calow P.: *Evolutionary Principles,* Chapman and Hall, N.Y., U.S.A., 1981.

Beatty, R. and Schneier, C.: *Personnel Administration: An Experimental Skill Building Approach,* 2nd Ed., Addison-Wesley, Reading, Mass., 1981.

Blake, R. and Jane, Mouton: The *Managerial Grid III: The Key to Leadership Excellence,* Gulf Publishing Co., Houston, 1985.

Brenner, S. and Earl, M.: *Is the Ethics of Business Changing ?* Harvard Business Review, Jan.-Feb. 1977.

Braham, J.: *Cultivating Tomorrow's Executives,* Industry Week, July 1987.

Bennett, A.: *Ethics Codes Spread Despite Criticism,* Wall Street Journal, July 1988.

Beckhard, R.: *Optimizing Team-building Efforts,* Journal of Contemporary Business, Summer, 1972.

Beckhard, R.: *Organization Development: Strategies and Models,* Addison-Wesley, Reading, M.A., 1969.

Beer,M.: *Organization Change and Development: A Systems View,* Goodyear, Santa Monica, C.A., 1980.

Burton, G.: *Communicating for Results,* Security Management, February 1979.

Christensen, C.R.; Andrews, K.R.; Bower, J.L.; Hamermesh, *R.G. and Porter, M.E.: Business Policy – Text and Cases,* 5th Edn., Richard D. Irwin, Homewood, III., 1982.

Conant, J.B.: *On Understanding Science,* Oxford University Press, London, 1947.

Cassirer, E.: *Essay on Man,* Yale University Press, New Haven, 1945.

Cammann, Cortlamdt and David, Nadler: *Fit Control Systems to Your Management Style,* Harvard Business Review, January-February 1976.

Champy, J.: Management: *New Mandate,* Information Week, February 6, 1995.

Coleman, James C.: *Psychology and Effective Behavior,* Scott, Foresman & Co., Glenview, Ill., 1969.

Child, J.: *Predicting and Understanding Organization Structure,* Administrative Science Quarterly, June 1973.

Clande, George S.(Jr.): *Management in Industry,* Prentice-Hall of India Pvt. Ltd., New Delhi, 1967.

Cumming, L.L. and Scott, W.E.: *Readings in Organizational Behaviour and Human Performance,* Richard D. Irwin Inc., Homewood, Illinois, 1973.

Cherns, A.B.: *Can Behavioral Scientists Help Managers Improve their Organisation ?* Organizational Dynamics, Winter 1973.

Channon, D.F.: *Corporate Strategy and Organization Structure in British Industry,* Journal of Business Policy, Vol.3, No.1, 1972.

Crosby, P.: *Quality is Free,* McGraw-Hill, New York, 1979.

Cummings, Larry and Donald, Schwab: *Performance in Organizations:* Determinants and Appraisal, Scott, Foresman, Glenview, III., 1973.

Campbell, J.P.; Dunnette, M.D.; Lawler III, E.E. and Weick, K.E.: *Managerial Behaviour: Performance and Effectiveness*, McGraw-Hill, New York, 1970.

Costello, T.W. and Zalkind, S.S.: *Psychology in Administration*, Prentice-Hall, Englewood Cliffs, N.J., 1963.

Chave, E.J. and Thrustone, L.L.: *The Measurement of Attitude*, University of Chicago Press, Chicago, 1929.

Cruchfield, R.S. and Krech, D.: *Theory and Practice of Social Psychology*, McGraw-Hill, New York, 1948.

Conklin, Edwin G.: *Heredity and Environment in the Development of Men*, Princeton University Press, Princeton, 1919.

Deb, S.: Contemporary Issues on Management, *Atlantic Publishers and Distributors*, New Delhi, 2001.

Davis, K.: Human Behaviour at Work: *Organization Behaviour*, Tata McGraw-Hill, New Delhi, 1978.

Desai, M.: *The Gospel of Selfless Action*, Navajivan Publishing House, Ahmedabad, 1946.

Durkheim, Emile: *Sociology and Philosophy*, Cohen and West, London, 1965.

Drucker, Peter F.: *The Practice of Management*, Harper & Bros., New York, 1954.

Drucker, P.F.: *Management—Tasks, Responsibilities, Practices*, Allied Publishers, New Delhi, 1980.

Drucker, P.F.: *The Effective Executive*, Pan Books Limited, London, 1970.

Drucker, P.F.: *Really Reinventing Government*, Span, December 1995.

Dumaine, B.: *Creating a New Company Culture*, Fortune, January 15, 1990.

Devenport, T.H.A. and Short, J.E.: *The New Industrial Engineering: Information Technology and Business Process Redesign,* Sloan Management Review, Vol.4, 1990.

Drucker, P.F.: *The Emerging Theory of Manufacturing,* Harvard Business Review, May-June 1990.

Daft, R.: Management, *The Dryden Press,* Chicago, 1988.

Dobzhansky, T.: *The Biology of Ultimate Concern,* The New American Library, Inc., New York, 1967.

Davis, J.; Laughlin, P. and Komorita, S.: *The Social Psychology of Small Groups: Cooperation and Mixed-Motive Interaction,* Annual Review Psychology, 1976.

Davis, Ralph: *Fundamentals of Top Management,* Harper & Row, New York, 1951.

Deming, Edwards W.: *Transformation of Today's Management, Executive Excellence,* December 1987.

Daft, Richard and Steers, R.: *Organizations: A Micro/Macro Approach,* Glenview, Ill., 1986.

Dale, Ernest: *Organization, American Management Association,* New York, 1976.

Daniels, J. and Radebaugh, L.: *International Business Environments and Operations,* 4th Ed., Addison-Wesley, Reading, Mass., 1986.

Dunn, L.G.; Sinnott, E.W. and Dobzhansky, T.: *Principles of Genetics,* 5th Edn., McGraw-Hill Book Co., Inc., New York, 1958.

deVries, Lammert: *A Presentation to the Strategic Management Society,* The Netherlands, Amsterdam, October 19, 1988.

Dickson, G.W. and Simmons, J.: *The Behavioural Side of MIS,* Business Horizons, August 1970.

Dumaine, B.: *How Managers Can Succeed through Speed,*

Fortune, February 13, 1989.

Duncan, J.W.: *Management, Random House,* New York, 1983.

Dyer,W.; Daines, R. and Gaiuque, W.: *The Challenge of Management,* Harcourt Brace Jovanovich Publishers, San Diego, 1990.

Deci, E.L.: *Intrinsic Motivation, Plenum Press,* New York, 1975.

Dermer, J. and Siegal, J.: *The Role of Behavioural Measures in Accounting for Human Resources, Accounting Review,* Jan 1974.

Drucker, Peter F.: *Preparing Tomorrow's Business Leaders Today,* D.B. Taraporewala Sons & Co. Pvt. Ltd., Bombay, 1977.

Dalton, M.: *Men Who Manage,* Wiley, New York, 1959.

Duncan, J.W.: *Transferring Management Theory to Practice,* Academy of Management Journal, December 1974.

Davis, S.M.: *Comparative Management,* Prentice-Hall, Englewood Cliffs, N.J., 1971.

Dorothy, J.: *Everybody Wins: Transactional Approach Applied to Organizations,* Addison-Wesley Publishing Co., Massachusetts, 1974.

Dubin, R.: *Human Relations in Administration,* Prentice-Hall, Englewood Cliffs, N.J., 1974.

Dale, E.: *Management: Theory and Practice,* 3rd Ed., McGraw-Hill, Kogakusha Ltd., Tokyo, 1967.

Drucker, P.F.: *The Concept of the Corporation,* The New American Library, New York, May 1964.

Denny, W.A.: *Ten Rules for Managing by Objectives,* Business Horizons, October 1974.

Dillon, C.R.: MBO: *Setting Objectives, Supervisory Management,*

April 1976.

Dutt, V.L.: *Corporate Planning—The Indian Scenario, Economic Trends,* Vol.XII, No.7, April 1983.

Eden, C. and Harris, J.: *Management Decision and Decision Analysis,* Wiley, New York, 1975.

Elwin, Verrier: *The Tribal World of Verrier Elwin,* Oxford University Press, Bombay, 1964.

Elwin, V.: *A Philosophy for NEFA,* North East Frontier Agency, Shillong, 1955.

Evans, M.: *The Effects of Supervisory Behaviour on the Path-Goal Relationship,* Organizational Behaviour and Human Performance, May 1970.

Edgar, H.S.: *Organizational Psychology,* Prentice-Hall, Englewood Cliffs, N.J., 1980.

Erez, M.; Earley, C. and Hulin, C.L.: *The Impact of Participation on Goal Acceptance and Performance: A Two-Step Model,* Academy of Management Journal, March 1985.

Edward, H.: *Technology and Structure of Organizations,* American Sociological Review, April 1968.

Edward, E.L. and Suttle, J.L.: *A Camal Correlation of the Need-Heirarchy Concept, Organization Behaviour and Human Performance,* Vol. 7, No.2, April 1972.

Emery, F.E. and Trist, E.L.: *The Casual Texture of Organizational Environments,* Human Relations, February 1965.

Etzioni, A.: Modern Organizations, *Prentice-Hall, Englewood Cliffs,* N.J., 1964.

Eugene, E.J.: *The Anatomy of Leadership,* Management of Personnel Quarterly, Vol.1, No.1, 1961.

Ellis, A.: *Executive Leadership: A Rational Approach,* Citadel

Press, Secaucus, N.J., 1972.

Freud, S.: *New Introductory Lectures on Psychoanalysis,* New York, Norton, 1933.

Frederick, Pollock: *History of the Science of Politics,* Akashdeep Publishing House, Delhi, 1990.

French,W.L. and Bell, C.H.Jr.: *Organization Development : Behavioral Science Interventions for Organization Improvement,* Prentice-Hall, Englewood Cliffs, New Jersey, 1978.

Filley, Alan C.; Robert, J.House and Steven, Kerr: *Managerial Process and Organizational Behaviour,* 2nd Ed., Foresman & Co. III, Scott, 1976.

Frank, Philipp: *Relativity – A Richer Truth,* Jonathan Cape, Thirty Bedford Square, London, 1951.

Fulmer, R.M.: *Practical Human Relations,* Richard D. Irwin, Inc., III., 1977.

Fox, A.: *The Sociology of Work in Industry,* Macmillan, Collar, 1971.

Feldman, D.: *The Development and Enforcement of Group Norms,* Academy of Management Review, January 1984.

Fielder, Fred: *The Effects of Leadership Training and Experience: A Contingency Model Interpretation,* Administrative Science Quarterly, December 1972.

French, J. and Bertram, R.: *The Base of Social Power, University of Michigan Press,* Ann. Arbor, 1959.

Fritz, Roger: *Rate Your Executive Potential, John Wiley & Sons,* New York, 1988.

Feidler, F.E. and Chemers, M.M.: *Leadership and Effective Management,* Scott, Foresman and Glenview, Illinois, 1974.

Fuler, R.M.: *The New Management,* Macmillan Publishing Co., Inc., New York, 1974.

Fiedler, M.M.: Chemers, S.; and Mohan, L.: *Improving Leadership Effectiveness:* The Leader Match Concept, John Wiley & Sons, Inc., New York, 1976.

Francis, K.: *Changing Social Attitudes among the Work-force Mean Management Must Change Too,* Management Today, BIM, April 1986.

Faunce, W.: *Social Problems of an Industrial Civilization, McGraw-Hill,* New York, 1968.

Flippo, E.B. and Garry, M.M.: *Management, Allyn and Bacon,* Inc., Boston, 1975.

Fenn, M.: *Making It In Management: A Behavioural Approach for Women Executives,* Prentice-Hall, Inc., Englewood Cliffs, 1978.

Fred, Luthans: *Organizational Behaviour,* McGraw-Hill Kogakusha Limited, Tokyo, 1977.

Farris, G.: *Organizational Factors and Individual Performance: A Longitudinal Study,* Journal of Applied Psychology, Vol.54, 1969.

Fromm, E.: *The Art of Loving, Harper & Row,* New York, 1956.

Friedlander, F. and Brown, L.D.: Organization Development, *Annual Review of Psychology,* Vol. 25, 1975.

Getty, J. Paul: The Fine Art of Being the Boss, *Playboy,* June 1972.

Glueck, W.F. and Jauch, L.R.: *Business Policy and Strategic Management,* 4th Edn., McGraw-Hill, New York, 1984.

Gay, P.: *The Rise of Modern Paganism,* Wildwood House, London, 1970.

Goyandka, Jayadayal: *The Secret of Premayoga, Govind Bhawan*

Karyalaya, Gita Press, Gorakhapur, 1993.

Graicunas, V.A.: *Relationship in Organization, Bulletin of the International Management Institute,* March, 1933.

Ginsbery, Morris: *On Justice in Society,* Heinemann, London, 1965.

Gross, Warren and Shula, Shichman: *How to Grow on Organizational Culture,* Personnel, September, 1987.

Griffin, Samuel (Translated): Sun Tsu: *The Art of War,* Oxford University Press, London, 1963.

Griffin, R.: Management, 3rd Edn., *Houghton Mifflin Company,* Boston, 1990.

Green, S. and Terenee, M.: *Attributional Processes of Leaders in Leader-Member Interactions,* Organizational Behaviour and Human Performance, June 1979.

Getzels, J.W. and Jackson, P.W.: *Creativity and Intelligence,* John Wiley & Sons, New York, 1962.

Gurnee, H.: *Elements of Social Psychology,* Farran and Rinehart, New York, 1936.

Galbraith, J.K.: *The Affluent Society,* Penguin Books Ltd., London, 1974.

Glasu, E.M.: *Productivity Claims Through Work Life Improvement,* Personnel, Vol. 57, No. 1, January 1980.

George, C.S.: *The History of Management Thought,* Prentice-Hall, Englewood Cliffs, N.J., 1968.

Gibson, C.: *Managing Organisational Behaviour: Achieving Results through Understanding and Action,* Richard D. Irwin, Homewood, Ill., 1980.

Graham, H.T.: *Human Resource Management,* McDonald & Evans, Playmouth, 1980.

Gray, D.H.: *Manpower of Planning, Institute of Personnel Management,* U.K., 1966.

Guion, R.M.: *A Note on Organizational Climate,* Organizational Behaviour and Human Performance, Vol.9, 1973.

Guttman, L.: *The Third Component of Scalable Attitudes,* International Journal of Opinion and Attitude Research, Vol. 4, 1950.

Galbraith, J. and Kazanjian, R.: *Strategy Implementation: Structure, Systems and Process,* 2nd Ed., West Publishing Co., St. Paul, Minn, 1986.

Ghiselli, E.: *Explorations in Management Talent,* Goodyear Publishing Co., Pacific Palisades, California, 1971.

Gibson, Ivancevich and Donnelly, P.: *Organization: Behaviour, Structure, Processes, Business Publications,* Inc., Dallas, Texas, 1976.

Gupta, R.K.: HRD: Concerns, *Concepts and Framework,* Oxford & IBH Publishing Co., New Delhi, 1983.

Green, G.; Alvares, K. and Others: *Contingency Model of Leadership Effectiveness: Antecedent and Evidential Results,* Psychological Bulletin, Vol. 74, 1970.

Georgopoulos, B.S.; Mahoney, G. and Jones, N.W.: *A Path-Goal Approach to Productivity,* Journal of Applied Psychology, Vol. 41, 1957.

Ghiselli, E.E.: Managerial Talent, *American Psychologist,* Vol. 16, No.10, October 1963.

Greene, C.N.: *The Reciprocal Nature of Influence between Leader and Subordinate,* Journal of Applied Psychology, Vol. 60, 1975.

Hallmann, R. and Ulrich, M.F.: *Participative and Flexible Decision Making,* Journal of Small Business Management, Vol. 21, No. 1, January 1983.

Herzberg, F.: *Work and the Nature of Man,* World Publishing, Cleveland, 1966.

Hull, C.L.: *Principles of Behaviour,* Appleton-Century Crofts, New York, 1943.

Holton, G.: *The Thematic Origins of Scientific Thought,* Harvard University Press, 1973.

Habermas, J.: *Theory and Practice,* Heinemann, London, 1974.

Hersey, P.; Blanchard, H.K. and Johnson, E.D.: *Management of Organizational Behavior: Utilizing Human Resources,* Prentice Hall of India Pvt.Ltd., New Delhi, 1998.

Herzberg, H.; Mausner, B.; Peterson, R.O. and Capwell, D.: Job Attitudes: *A Review of Research and Opinion,* Psychological Service of Pittsburgh, PA, 1957.

Hellriegel, Don; John, W. Slocum, Jr. and Richard, W. Woodman: *Organizational Behavior,* 6th Edn., West Publishing Company, St. Paul, 1992.

Halachmi, A.: Reengineering and Public Management: Some Issues and Considerations, International Review of Administrative Sciences, Vol. 16, 1995.

Huber, George: *Managerial Decision Making,* Scott, Foresman, Glenview, Illinois, 1980.

Hogarth, Robin: *Judgment and Choice: The Psychology of Decision,* Wiley & Sons, New York, 1981.

Henry, N.: *Bureaucracy, Technology and Knowledge Management,* Public Administration Review, November-December 1975.

Herbert, T.T.: *Dimensions of Organisational Behaviour,* Macmillan Publishing Company, Inc., New York, 1976.

Heilbroner, R.: *The Making of Economic Society,* Prentice-Hall, Englewood Cliffs, N.J., 1962.

Herzberg, F.: *One More Time: How Do You Motivate Employees,* Harvard Business Review, January-February 1968.

Higgins, J. and Vineze, J.: *Strategic Management and Organizational Policy,* 3rd Ed., The Dryden Press, Hinsdale, III, 1986.

Hofstede, G. : *The Interaction between National and Organizational Value Systems,* Journal of Management Studies, Vol. 22, 1985.

Hofstede, G. : *Culture's Consequences,* Sage Publications, Beverly Hills, CA., 1984.

Hofer, C. : *Strategy Formulation,* West Publishing Co., St. Paul, Minn., 1986.

Heyel, C. : *The Encyclopaedia of Management,* Rinehold Publishing Corporation, New York, 1978.

Havelock, R.G. : *Planning for Innovation,* Michigan University Press, Crusk, 1969.

Hemphill, J.K. : *Situational Factors in Leadership,* The Ohio State University, Columbus, Ohio, 1949.

Hodgetts, R.M. : *Management Theory,* Process and Practice, 2nd Edn., W.B. Saunders Co., Philadelphia, 1979.

Insko, C. : *Theories of Attitude Change,* Appleton-Century Crofts, N.Y., 1967.

John, E. Stinson and Thomas, W. Johnson : *The Path-Goal Theory of Leadership : A Partial Test and Suggested Refinement,* Academy of Management Journal, Vol. 18, No.2, June 1975.

Jung, C.G. : *Psychological Types,* Harcourt, Brace, New York, 1946.

Janis, Irving : *Groupthink,* Houghton Mifflin Company, Boston, 1982.

John, M. : *Managing Change in Future,* Indian Management, March 1987.

James, M. and Jongeward, D. : *Born to Win : Transactional Analysis with Gestalt Experiments,* Addison-Wesley, Reading, Mass., 1971.

Jhonson, D. and Johnson, F. : *Joining Together : Group Theory and Group Skills,* 3rd Ed., Prentice-Hall, Englewood Cliffs, N.J., 1987.

Johnson, R.A.; Kast, F.A. and Rosenzweig, J.E. : *The Theory and Management of Systems,* McGraw-Hill, New York, 1963.

Juran, J.M. : *Strategies for World Class Quality,* Quality Process, March 1991.

Krech, D. and Crutchfield, R.S.: *Theory and Practice of Social Psychology,* McGraw-Hill, New York, 1948.

Kotter, John and Schlesinger, Leonard : *Choosing Strategies for Change,* Harvard Business Review, March-April, 1979.

Krech, David; Crutchfield, Richard S. and Ballachey, Egerton L. : *Individual in Society,* McGraw-Hill, New York, 1962.

Kuppuswamy, B. : *Elements of Social Psychology* (6th Revised Edn.), Vikas Publishing House Pvt. Ltd., New Delhi, 1983.

Ketzell, R.A. and Guzzo, R.A. : *Psychological Approaches to Worker Productivity,* American Psychologist, Vol. 36, 1983.

Krishnamoorti, N. : *Saint Tiruvalluvar and His Message of Life as Dharma,* Vivekananda Kendra Prakashan Trust, Chennai, May 2000.

Kotter, John : *The General Managers,* Free Press, New York, 1982.

Katz, D. and Kahn, R.L. : *The Social Psychology of Organizations,* Wiley, New York, 1955.

Kupfer, A. : *How to be a Global Manager,* Fortune, March 14, 1988.

Koontz, H.; Cyrill, *O'Donnell and Weihrich,* H. : Management, McGraw-Hill, Singapore, 1984.

Kelly, J. : *Organization Behaviour,* Richard D. Irwin & The Dorsey Press, 1974.

Koehler, J.W. & Others : *Organizational Communication : Behavioural Perspectives,* Holt, Rinehart and Winston, N.Y., 1976.

Koontz, O'Donnell : *Principles of Management : An Analysis of Managerial Functions,* McGraw-Hill Book Co., Inc., New York, 1968.

Knapp, M. : *Nonverbal Communication in Human Interaction,* Wm. C. Brown, Dubuque, Iowa, 1986.

Kiechel, H. III : *How to Pick Talent,* Fortune, December 8, 1986.

Kelley, H.H. : *Attribution in Social Interaction,* General Learning Press, Morrison, N.J., 1971.

Keller, R. : *Predictors of the Performance of Project Groups in R & D Organizations,* Academy of Management Journal, December 1986.

Katz, R. : *Skills of an Effective Administrator,* Harvard Business Review, September-October 1974.

Kathawala, Y. : *A Comparative Analysis of Selected Approaches to Quality,* International Journal of Quality and Reliability Management, Vol. 6, Issue 5, 1989.

Kearns, D.T. : *Leadership through Quality,* Academy of Management Executive, Vol. 4, No. 2, 1990.

Kantu, R.M. : *Managing the Human Side of Change,* Management Review, April 1985.

Kahn, R.L. & Others : *Organizational Stress : Studies in Role Conflict and Ambiguity,* Wiley, New York, 1964.

Kendler, H. : *Basic Psychology* (2nd Edn.), Appleton-Century-Crofts, Inc., New York, 1968.

Kossen, S. : *The Human Side of Organisations,* Harper & Row Publishers, Inc., N.Y., 1975.

Luthans, F. : *Organizational Behaviour,* McGraw-Hill, Singapore, 1989.

Lal, B.K. : *Contemporary Indian Philosophy,* Motilal Banarsidass, Delhi, 1995.

Lewin, K. : *Field Theory in Social Science : Selected Theoretical Papers,* Harper & Brothers, New York, 1951.

Lytton, H. : *Creativity and Education,* Routeledge and Kogan Paul, London, 1971.

Lownfeld, V. : *Creative and Mental Growth,* Macmillan, New York, 1957.

Likert, R. : *New Patterns of Management,* McGraw-Hill, New York, 1961.

Lewin, K. : *Group Decision and Social Change,* Holt, Rinehart, N.Y., 1952.

Locke, E.A. : *Personnel Attitude and Motivation,* Annual Review of Psychology, Vol.26, 1975.

Likert, R. : *The Human Organisation,* McGraw-Hill Book Company, Inc., New York, 1967.

Leavitt, H.J. : *The Yesterday, Today, and Tomorrow of Organizations,* European Business, Vol. 29, 1971.

Lines, J. : *The Role of the Chief Executive,* Business Books, London, 1978.

Muriron, C. (Ed.) : *Handbook of Social Psychology,* Clark University, Worcester, Mass., 1935.

Mark, J. Knoll and Charles, D. Pringle : *Path-Goal Theory and the Task Design Literature : A Tenuous Linkage,* Akron Business and Economic Review, 17, No.4, Winter 1986.

McGregor, D. : *The Human Side of Enterprise,* McGraw-Hill Book Company, Inc., New York, 1960.

Mitchell, R. : *Managing by Values,* Business Week, August 1, 1994.

Mehta, M.L. : *Jaina Psychology,* Sohanlal Jain Dharma Pracharak Samiti, Amritsar, 1955.

Muller, M. : *Six Systems of Indian Philosophy,* Longmans Green, London, 1903.

Maslow, A.H. : *Motivation and Personality,* Harper, New York, 1954.

Majumder, R.K. and Srivastav, A.N. : *Historiography* (Method of History), SBD Publishers' Distributors, Delhi, 1994.

Maslow, A.H. : *A Theory of Human Motivation,* Psychological Review, Vol. 50, 1943.

Maiti, Provatansu : *Studies In Ancient India,* Shreedhar Prakashani, Calcutta, 7th Edn., 1988.

Miller, Earnest C. : *Objectives and Standards Approach to Planning and Control,* AMA Research Study'74, American Management Association, New York, 1966.

Miles, R.E. : *Theories of Management : Implications for Organizational Behaviour and Development,* McGraw-Hill, New York, 1975.

McFarland, D.E. : *Management: Foundations and Practices,* Macmillan, New York, 1979.

Index